MW01128505

SAS ZERO HOUR

SAS ZERO HOUR

The Secret Origins of the Special Air Service

Tim Jones

Foreword by Sir Ranulph Fiennes

NAVAL INSTITUTE PRESS
Annapolis, Maryland

SAS Zero Hour
The Secret Origins of the Special Air Service
First published 2006 by Greenhill Books/Lionel Leventhal Ltd
Park House, 1 Russell Gardens, London NW11 9NN
and
Published and distributed in the United States of America and Canada by the
Naval Institute Press, 291 Wood Road, Annapolis, Maryland 21402-5043

ISBN 1-59114-805-7

Library of Congress Catalog Card No. 2005931111

For an illustrated catalog please contact:
Naval Institute Press, 291 Wood Road Annapolis, MD 21402-5043,
Toll-free telephone: 800-233-8764, Fax: 410-295-1084,
Web address: www.usni.org

Edited by Donald Sommerville

Printed and bound by
Creative Print and Design (Wales), Ebbw Vale

Dedicated to
Ray, Joy, Janet, Bessie, Louisa Mary and Vi

Contents

Illustrations

Foreword

Like his previous books on the SAS, Tim Jones's *SAS Zero Hour* deals with an area of the regiment's history that has been much neglected. Indeed, he looks primarily at the SAS's pre-history – the events leading up to its creation in mid-1941 by David Stirling. The book raises important questions about how Stirling came up with his idea for a strategic small unit behind the lines raiding force, asking exactly what factors influenced his thinking? Was he at all influenced by recent military operations, or those of the past, or both? What role did his fellow officers and men and others involved in Middle East special operations play?

SAS Zero Hour presents for the first time as complete a picture as we are likely to get. It introduces a host of overlooked characters who played a part by shaping the ideas and actions of Stirling and those who assisted him create the SAS. It pieces together evidence from neglected sources that reveals that there is far more to the story of the founding of the SAS than has been presumed. *SAS Zero Hour* argues that important factors include the Stirling clan's military pedigree of raising unorthodox military units; his interest in desert warfare; his schooling in Commando methods in 1940–41; Layforce's mainly still-born raiding programme of the spring of 1941; concurrent paratroop operations in the Mediterranean on both the Axis and Allied sides; and the deception activities of Dudley Clarke, the co-founder of the Commandos. *SAS Zero Hour* presents a compelling case that he and his immediate superior, Wavell, were the driving force behind a Middle East paratroop experiment that led to Stirling's own SAS raiders.

The roles of Auchinleck and Ritchie, and the factors making them favourably disposed to Stirling, are recounted as never before, including family connections and shared experience of paratroops and special forces. The role of Stirling's own brothers, and colleagues like Laycock, Lewes, Lovat, Courtney and Ran Churchill, is also assessed, especially regarding certain individuals' knowledge of precedents provided by Robert Rogers and T. E. Lawrence. Likewise, the impact of Admiral Keyes, General Allenby, Winston Churchill and Orde Wingate, as well as Stirling's contemporaries, such as Peter Fleming of the SOE and Ralph Bagnold of the LRDG, is weighed.

SAS Zero Hour offers the most comprehensive and enlightening version of these seminal events yet and, as such, is of interest to anyone wishing to know how the world's number one elite military unit came into being.

Ranulph Fiennes

Preface

SAS: The Untold Story

The Special Air Service Regiment (SAS) has been stamped into the popular psyche as the world's leading military special force – and rightly so. On the big screen, thriller writer Tom Clancy depicted the SAS in *Patriot Games* calmly wiping out a terrorist training camp in northern Africa, with neither mercy nor loss, many years before SAS soldiers entered the Registan region of Afghanistan in search of Al Qaeda militants in November 2001. The computer game heroine, Lara Croft – aka *Tomb Raider*, played by Angelina Jolie – also dared and won in that debut movie with a helping hand from the regiment. This blockbuster even implied that Lara was a female holder of the coveted, legendary winged dagger. Never has the SAS been so sexy! The list goes on and on, and it is the same story when it comes to books about the SAS's exploits, especially as they prove themselves time and again to be the most effective elite military force in the world, as in Iraq in 2003 (although accusations of an extra-judicial killing by a member of the SAS were strenuously denied in spring 2005, and an undercover operation sparked riots in September), and in their role in the raids carried out during the investigation of the London bombings of July 2005.

The spate of published first-hand accounts from former members of the Herefordshire-based outfit has continued unabated too, despite official distaste for the revelatory nature of many of the works that became best sellers (including fictional 'reminiscences' such as Paul Bruce's *The Nemesis File* and Tom Carew's *Jihad!*). The thirst for SAS historical treatises is equally unquenchable, with new histories of the regiment appearing every year, along with a host of other works about related special or elite forces, such as the Commandos, Special Boat Squadron (SBS) and the rest. Indeed, most people who have become acquainted with the SAS's history will be at least cursorily familiar with its origins in the North African deserts of Egypt and Libya during the Second World War – not least thanks to specialist military videos and TV documentary series. In addition, the SAS's operational history during the last world war has been documented by authors such as Tony Kemp, who have outlined the course of its development during those seminal, formative years.

Much of the post-war era has been dealt with by writers including Kenneth Connor, Adrian Weale and other ex-soldiers with past service in, or links to, the SAS, besides a whole caravan of populist literary camp-followers. However, certain aspects of the SAS's career have been less clearly outlined, especially where the Thirty Year Rule regarding the disclosure of British public records applies – notably to campaigns that occurred after 1970, such as those in Oman/Dhofar, Northern Ireland, Bosnia, Albania, Sierra Leone, Afghanistan and Iraq. In time, more information should emerge about these and other ventures. But because of the secret nature of much SAS activity, details about many of its operations, both in terms of their planning and execution, will only surface after seventy-five or more years, if at all. Nonetheless, some gaps in its history have been plugged by drawing on sources already in the public domain that, for one reason or another, have been ignored or overlooked by military historians and commentators. A case in point is the interregnum of 1945–51, about which all pre-millennial histories of the SAS simply stated that, with the war's end, there was no perceived need among the powers-that-be for such a special force, and, therefore, the SAS was disbanded. Only in 1950, when a new counter-insurgency special force was deemed necessary in the fight against Communist terrorists in the Federation of Malaya, was it resurrected – at least according to the version outlined by exponents of the historiographical consensus.[1]

In fact, as I showed in *Postwar Counterinsurgency and the SAS, 1945–52 – A Special Type of Warfare* (London, 2001) and elaborated in *SAS: The First Secret Wars* (London, 2005) some elements of the SAS survived the disbandment of the bulk of the regiment, and they continued successfully to press the case to retain a post-war special force, however small.[2] Through the post-war actions of SAS and ex-SAS personnel in Palestine and Greece, as well as in the crucial Whitehall corridors of power, the SAS fought and won its case to maintain a special forces capability in order to fight both conventional (mobile and positional) warfare and counter-insurgency against terrorist and guerilla opponents. Other historians were quite unaware of the SAS's vital covert operational and bureaucratic battles during this critical early post-war period, which is unsurprising given that few written records survived the bureaucratic weeding process that was conducted after the activities in question were wound down, while successive British governments have maintained a strict policy of keeping such clandestine undertakings concealed from the British press and public alike.

Indeed, I have found from my own experience of researching into the subject for more than a decade that, when it comes to the version of events offered by historians of the SAS (including those enjoying its official sanction) about some of the key periods in its history, one should be prepared to question whether there is more to the story presented to the public than at first meets the eye. Consequently, after producing my two previous books, I determined to address a nagging doubt that I had about the very origins of the SAS Regiment itself. In just about every text that I had ever read about it, the version of events surrounding its genesis outlined by historians was, in a nutshell, that the SAS came into being as the inspiration of one man – the founding father of the regiment, Sir Archibald David Stirling (known then and now simply as David Stirling).

This view gained almost universal acceptance both in the literature on the subject and in the wider world, with the general public's perception that the SAS was, as it were, one man's baby. This was reinforced in video histories of the SAS and UK TV programmes broadcast in the early years of the new millennium, including one written by the renowned military historian (not least of the Commandos) and former Army officer, Charles Messenger. Indeed, the most widely-read daily newspaper in the UK, *The Sun*, previewed a TV series about Commandos on 12 January 2002 with an article about the origins of the SAS. Its two-page spread asserted that, 'the SAS was set up by fearless Scot David Stirling in spring 1941', the subaltern reportedly having had an 'ambitious vision of an elite desert force ... designed to get behind enemy lines and destroy valuable installations, aircraft, arms dumps and water supplies'. This plain and simple official take on events was also recounted in the *Daily Telegraph* in October 2001 (and repeated in its Australian namesake, as the Australian SAS geared up for its own deployment to Afghanistan to track down Al Qaeda and Taliban irregulars).

A similar summary can be found – to take but one literary example – in a widely-read, highly-regarded and often-quoted layman's guide to military affairs, *The Oxford Companion to Military History*. It is edited by a historian familiar to millions thanks to his celebrated TV documentary series, Professor Richard Holmes. (Incidentally, he was a 'talking head' on TV's *Gladiators of World War 2* episode about the SAS, and he wrote the foreword to BBC TV counter-terrorism commentator Hugh McManner's 2003 *Ultimate Special Forces*, which repeated the legend.)

Holmes' *Companion* avers in a straightforward entry about the SAS that, it 'was founded by Lt. (later Lt.-Col.) David Stirling in July 1941 at Kabrit', in Egypt. The regiment's wartime and subsequent exploits are related by another of the esteemed military historians who contributed to the tome, Peter Harclerode (himself a former member of the SAS and the author of, among other works, *Para!* and *Fighting Dirty*.) Yet no attempt is made in the *Companion* to address the underlying issue of exactly *how* the force came to be conceived in the first place, by identifying the factors that gave rise to it. Although it notes in broad terms how Allied and Axis 'special forces' arose during the Second World War – albeit without delving into much of the pre-war history of such units – the solitary role played by Stirling in founding the SAS is never questioned.[3]

Another commentator has asserted that Stirling had 'an idea for a revolutionary type of fighting unit', but 'what sparked the idea we will probably never know.' He hypothesised that the Spanish Civil War of 1936–9, Major Orde Wingate's contemporary Special Night Squads (SNS) of counter-guerilla troops operating in Palestine against Arab rebels, and Colonel T. E. Lawrence's unorthodox military campaign alongside the Arabs during World War 1 (all of which are explored in due course) may have influenced Stirling.[4] However, while it is true that 'Lawrence's ghost must have haunted the Middle East at the time' of the creation of the SAS in that theatre,[5] this book aims not just to speculate about the regiment's origins, but to address the central issue

16

by identifying the main factors that played a part in shaping the SAS concept, and assessing what particular influence these factors had on its originators.

Robin Hunter notes in *True Stories of the SBS* that, 'One of the more curious facts about an innovation or invention is that an idea is rarely confined to one man.' He continues that it is usually the case that, 'Several people are thinking along the same lines and it is therefore hard to decide exactly where a story begins . . . or who should be credited.' Be that as it may, an attempt at accreditation needs to be made. Indeed, in the last few years, the true extent of the contribution made in the founding of the SAS by Stirling's comrade, Lieutenant John 'Jock' Lewes, has been highlighted in a book by his nephew, and briefly outlined in some other accounts.

Additionally, in November 2001, a half-hour BBC Radio programme, presented by military historian Julian Putkowski and researched by SAS writer David List, hinted at the role played by other SAS 'originals', as well as personnel from other Army units based in North Africa during the early war years. By this stage, I had already spent a considerable time uncovering more information about how and why the SAS came into being than any other writer, and this book will identify many more pieces of the SAS jigsaw, the scope of which the BBC's *Of One Company* barely hinted at.[6]

As a result, the origins of the SAS can be presented here for the first time in as near complete a fashion as possible from extant public records (though some of the participants in the events outlined may well be able to fill in the remaining gaps). While the importance of Stirling as the key figure in the establishment of the regiment is essentially undiminished – indeed, his pivotal role in its inception and development are reaffirmed – the crucial part played by his colleagues and other parties, some of whom have been completely ignored by historians of the SAS, are delineated here for the first time.

Equally importantly, as well as new characters entering the stage upon which the establishment of the regiment was played out, the ideas from which it stemmed in the first place are recounted. How and when they came to be, and how they were collated, affirmed and presented to those in authority as the cornerstone upon which a novel special force could be built, are detailed as never before.

Stirling's Child

The accepted story repeated *ad infinitum* about how the SAS originated is that presented in its first official history, written by the journalist and military historian, Philip Warner. His acclaimed *The Special Air Service*, first published in 1971 (and several times since) was proclaimed at the time to be 'the full story of Britain's toughest and most secret regiment'. As will be seen, this was a bold but sweeping claim. Yet the gist of Warner's historical treatise was essentially repeated in the few other books that have gained the approbation of the regiment, namely Major-General John Strawson's 1984 *A History of the SAS Regiment* and the 1992 authorised biography *David Stirling*, penned by ex-SAS officer Alan Hoe.[7]

Although the events surrounding the foundation of the regiment are related in subsequent chapters, it should be borne in mind throughout that it is Stirling who was purportedly the one blessed with the inspired idea of establishing a new type of special force comprising small units operating behind enemy lines who would be delivered covertly to their targets, notably by parachute. It is reiterated time and again by numerous authors that the idea came to him when he had time on his hands while recuperating in an Egyptian hospital bed after an experimental parachute jump over the Western Desert in June 1941.[8] At first sight, and by just about all accounts, he appears to have had a stroke of inspiration that marked him out as one of the military geniuses of World War II. Indeed, given the repercussions of the SAS's inception on the style of warfare that has characterised much of the post-war world, Stirling's idea has been seen as a turning point in modern military history. While the SAS and their kind have been sniped at over the years by critics of special forces for failing to make an impact on the enemy commensurate with the resources expended on their activities, special forces, and the SAS in particular, have proven themselves central to the development of post-war counter-insurgency forces and operations. The SAS has shown itself – not least in the early twenty-first century 'long war' or 'war on terrorism' – to be a key player in maintaining the global order.

So, how could it be that a 25-year-old subaltern, Stirling – who had no battlefield experience and enjoyed a reputation for indulging in a lazy, playboy lifestyle, even being dubbed by friends 'the Great Sloth', came up with a ground-breaking scheme for a strategic behind the lines special force, purportedly off the top of his head? Could there be more to his proposal than a 'eureka!' moment?

The more I pondered it, the more I was convinced that there might be an untold story that had yet to be uncovered by historians. My suspicion was confirmed by the fact that, in 1984, Stirling stated that he was but one of several fathers of the regiment. He commented that he regarded his wartime colleagues Jock Lewes, Paddy Mayne and George Bergé of the French SAS (formed in 1942), and post-war comrades such as Brian Franks and John Woodhouse, as vital to the SAS's overall evolution. Stirling's magnanimity was both well placed and, as it transpires, rather too narrowly defined.

In fact, there were many others who contributed to the development of ideas about unconventional warfare that would coalesce in Egypt during the summer of 1941 as the strategic raiding concept outlined to his superiors by Lieutenant Stirling. As will be shown, it was fortuitous that he was in the right place at the right time for such heterodox thinking to be accepted by top-level decision-makers in both his own military theatre and in the UK. But then, as the Roman writer Terence posited, fortune favours the brave – or to paraphrase, those who dare.

Stirling, as will be seen, was both the leading co-originator of the conceptual *modus operandi* of the SAS and, as significantly, the focal point for the gathering and refining of shared and individual ideas about the style that future special force operations should take. From his hospital bed, he was able to mould these into a more convincing, fully-formed paradigm than had hitherto been presented to the Command HQ, affording his proposition a greater chance of acceptance by the traditionally special forces-agnostic military brass. Thus, Stirling made a unique, invaluable contribution to the genesis of the SAS and should be considered, at least, to be its prime godfather. But he was not alone.

To draw an analogy with fertilisation, Stirling was not the only party involved in the SAS's conception, birth and growth, let alone its subsequent nurturing during and after the war. This was down to a team of conceptual donors, whose seeds, when taken together, created the environment in which a newborn force could be established. The concept of a strategic small unit raiding force stemmed from their combined knowledge and experiences of, and/or their service in, other wartime and pre-war special forces and unorthodox military units. That Stirling oversaw the delivery of their own embryonic special force and fought to ensure that it would not be still-born, meant that he rightly came to be regarded as its true father.

The aim of this work is to recount just how he and those other participants involved in the complex process of the SAS's birth – one that has been shrouded in mystery for over six decades – developed their ideas about unconventional warfare, and to pin-point the main factors that shaped their strategic and tactical thinking. These led, by July 1941, to the creation of L Detachment, SAS Brigade – a title adopted as a means of deceiving Axis forces in North Africa into believing that an Allied parachute brigade was stationed in the region.[9] It was to be the beginning of a legend.

But before addressing the circumstances that conspired to bring this situation about, many strands of the story need to be unravelled, identifying both contemporary and historical factors that came into play during the critical period in mid-1941. Once these are marshalled in context, they provide a fresh historical viewpoint about the origins of the SAS.

Unsurprisingly, among the first critical factors that must be examined are the character and past experiences of Stirling himself, not least his military background, acumen and pedigree, which, in tandem, placed him in a position where he would be able to champion a revolutionary military concept.

Acknowledgements

This book is the culmination of seven years' research and would not have been possible but for the valuable assistance kindly provided to me by numerous individuals and institutions. My thanks go to Kevin O'Gorman, Archivist, Scots Guards HQ, Wellington Barracks, London; Gordon Stevens, Alex and Ed at Ebury Press for access to *The Originals* m/s; Royal Marines Museum, Southsea, Hampshire; Chris Hughes, Household Cavalry Museum, London; John Hodgson, Archivist, John Rylands Museum, Manchester; A. S. Brown, Airborne Forces Museum, Aldershot, Hampshire; David Parry and Yvonne Oliver, Imperial War Museum, London; David Fletcher and Janice Tait, Tank Museum, Bovington, Dorset; Kate O'Brien, Liddell Hart Centre for Military Archives, King's College London; Maggie Johnstone and Lesley Junor, Am Baile; British Library, London; Simon Moody and Teresa Watts, National Army Museum, London; Hugh Alexander, National Archives, Kew, Middlesex; Andrew Renwick and the Society of Friends, RAF Museum, Hendon; Lieutenant-Colonel G. S. Johnston, RHQ Highlanders; Roni Schnable and Maggie Lindsay Roxburgh, Royal Engineers Museum and Library, London; A. R. Smith, Historical Manuscripts Commission, London; N. Mithani, British Library Oriental and India Office Collections, London; D. Nunn, British Resistance Organisation Museum, Parham Airfield, Framlingham, Suffolk; Museum of Army Flying, Middle Wallop; University of London Senate House Library; King's College London Library; Ministry of Defence, London; SAS Regimental Association, London; Sir Ranulph Fiennes; Major-General Julian Thompson; Major A. N. B. Ritchie; E. P. Horne BEM; Brian McMorrow; Company Sergeant-Major Ronnie Gamble; Geoffrey and Mike Grierson; Skip Kippax; Image Analysis Laboratory, NASA Johnson Space Center, Houston, Texas (http://ed.jsc.nasa. gov); Sergeant Peter Verney; Charlie Delta; Neil

Smith, www.3squadron.org.au; Keith Hansen, 113squadron.org; Kieron Michelle; Andre Boucher; Francine Bailey; Les Delamere; Don Clark, www.211squadron.org; Nancy Spiegeland and Marlis Saleh, Middle East Department, University of Chicago; Jim Devlin and Group Captain Mike Devlin; Nate Hicks, 40 Bomber Group; Phil Verbena; Seymour Balkin; Karen Humphries, Tatton Park; James Masterson; Alan Lewis; Jono Scott; Paul Bowler; Sarah Rogers; Jake Kennedy; David Watkins, Michael Leventhal, Henry Alban Davies and all at Greenhill Books; and especially all my family and friends, notably Howy (especially for IT and illustrations), Ed, and Bill (particularly for postcards).

Thanks for information on the American Revolutionary War to Todd W. Braistead (4th Battalion, New Jersey Volunteers), Michael Davies (Re-created 23rd Regiment of Foote), Don Beale (Commander of the Re-created 16th Queen's Light Dragoons [Dismounted]), Pete Garrison, John Lea and Julianne Dombrowski. Finally, my thanks for access to papers in their care to the Imperial War Museum, London; Liddell Hart Centre for Military Archives, King's College, London; John Rylands Museum, Manchester; the National Archives, Kew, Middlesex.

Tim Jones

Abbreviations

ADC	Aide-de-camp
AOC	Air Officer Commanding
BEF	British Expeditionary Force
CIGS	Chief of the Imperial General Staff
CINC	Commander-in-Chief
CTC	Combined Training Centre
DCGS	Deputy Chief of (the General) Staff
DCIGS	Deputy CIGS
DMI	Directorate/Director of Military Intelligence, War Office
DMO	Directorate/Director of Military Operations, War Office
DZ	Drop Zone
GOC	General Officer Commanding
G(R)	MEF HQ Raiding section
GSI	General Staff Intelligence
GS(R)	General Staff (Research), War Office
IRA	Irish Republican Army
ISTDC	Inter-Services Training and Development Centre
IWTC/S	Irregular Warfare Training Centre/School
LoC	Line(s) of Communication
LCP	Light Car Patrol
LRDG	Long Range Desert Group
LRP	Long Range Patrol
MEF	Middle East Forces
MI(R)	Military Intelligence (Research), War Office
MI5	Military Intelligence section 5, or Security Service
MI6	Military Intelligence section 6, or SIS
MoI	Ministry of Information
MO9	War Office DMO section 9
PT	Physical Training

RASC	Royal Army Service Corps
SAS	Special Air Service
SBS	Special Boat Squadron (later Service)
SIS	Secret Intelligence Service, or MI6
SNS	Special Night Squad(s)
SOE	Special Operations Executive
SO2	SOE operations section
SSB	Special Service Battalion
VCIGS	Vice-CIGS

'The one duty we owe to history is to rewrite it.'
Oscar Wilde, *The Critic as Artist*

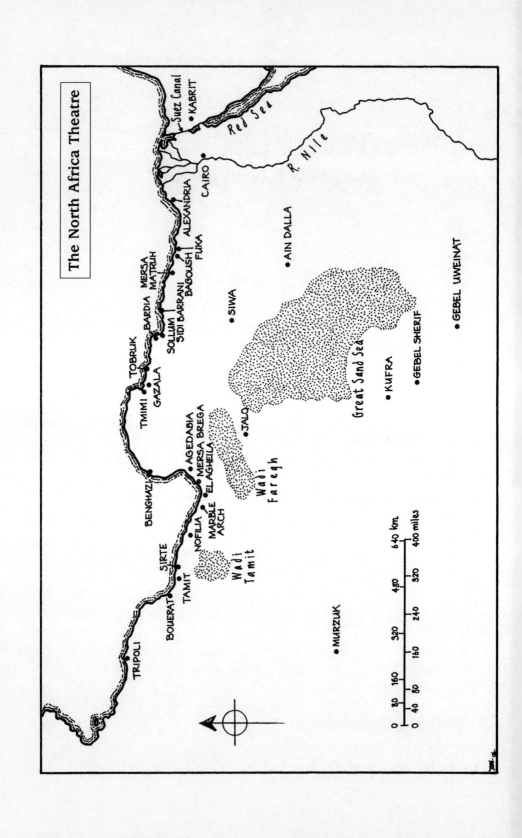

The North Africa Theatre

Chapter 1

The Legend
and the Man

The Legend

Scores of books have scrutinised the events of mid-1941, including wartime accounts published in the 1940s and 1950s by SAS soldiers – Andy McNab was by no means the first. But the essence of the legend that built up over the years was described in detail for the general public for the first time in 1958 by the war correspondent Virginia Cowles. Her best-selling *The Phantom Major – The Story of David Stirling and the SAS Regiment* was subsequently issued as a Fontana paperback and, in recognition of its status, as a Cassell Military Classic some forty years later.

Cowles – who interviewed Stirling for her account – relates that, his 'private army was born on paper in a hospital bed in Cairo and . . . brought to the attention of Middle East Headquarters . . . by unusual means'. He reportedly set off for Middle East HQ in Cairo to present his hand-written proposals to the Commander-in-Chief, Middle East, General Claude 'the Auk' Auchinleck.[1] The injured lieutenant from No. 8 Commando – part of the 'Layforce' special operations formation – was reportedly dropped off by a taxi with his pair of crutches outside the Grey Pillars HQ in the Garden City district of Cairo, not far from the Nile. There, he proceeded unsuccessfully to try to bluff his way past the sentries at the gate, by professing to have forgotten his pass, while simultaneously being late for an urgent appointment within.

Undaunted, Stirling is said to have propped himself up against a tree by the perimeter enclosure, where he had spotted a small gap in the barbed-wire fence. As two staff cars drew up at the main gate checkpoint, carrying half a dozen officers whose identities would have to be checked, Stirling slipped through the wire and, joining the visiting party, made his way towards the steps of the HQ. However, as the hobbling 6 ft 5 in officer neared its entrance with, quite literally, hardly a leg to stand on, he was apparently spotted by one of the guards, who had noticed the discarded crutches resting on the wire (acting as an improvised ladder). Ignoring an NCO's shouts to stop, Stirling made through the doorway and into the HQ's labyrinthine corridors.

One of Stirling's subsequent SAS brethren, Malcolm James Pleydell, wrote in a memoir of 1945 that Stirling was 'well known at Headquarters and a friend of ... Auchinleck'.[2] But his assertion has not been corroborated by any other source and was likely made in hindsight, in the light of Stirling successfully convincing the powers-that-be of the worth of his proposals. Indeed, as Cowles notes, Stirling had to resort to subterfuge to enter the HQ and, as the cries of his pursuers echoed through its hallways, Stirling swiftly and unceremoniously entered the office 'marked Adjutant-General'. Stirling surprised Lieutenant-General Arthur Smith, who was less than impressed by the intrusion, enquiring 'What the devil do you want?' The young officer reportedly made a hurried explanation of his membership of Layforce, which was in the throes of disbandment due to the 'arrival of the Germans in Africa and the urgent need for replacements' for Britain's hard-pressed front-line forces, in order to stem General Erwin Rommel's rapid advances. However, before Stirling had the chance to elaborate 'a scheme of his own' to form 'a small command of hand-picked men and officers' that could 'parachute behind enemy lines and destroy the whole of the German air force on the ground', he was cut short.[3] Smith had already formed a dim opinion of Stirling as 'one of the least desirable officers in the ... regiment', having encountered the uninterested Scot dozing during a lecture course about tactics that he had delivered while attached to the Guards at Surrey's Pirbright Barracks in 1939. Unsurprisingly, he rejected Stirling's advance outright – 'you were a fool then and you're a fool now' – and, after being lambasted as a member of 'a crackpot outfit', Stirling retreated from Smith's room, just as his unimpressed host was informed by telephone of the presence of an intruder in the headquarters.

Apparently eluding the pursuing sentries once more, the shuffling Stirling barged through the door of the Deputy Chief of Staff, Major-General Neil Ritchie. Although the door was clearly labelled 'DCGS', purportedly 'the letters meant nothing' to Stirling, although he soon 'found himself facing a man he knew well' by virtue of having seen his photo, so that Ritchie 'was very familiar' as a member of the staff of the previous commander-in-chief, General 'Archie' Wavell.[4] Although most historians have failed to see the significance of this fact, it shows that Stirling was well aware of Ritchie. Furthermore, Ritchie was from an aristocratic Scottish family that was well known to the Stirling clan, not least the latter's kinfolk, the renowned Lovats.[5] Military writer Arthur Swinson speculates that it was 'perhaps because of the bond between Scot and Scot, or . . . because he recognised Stirling's unusual air of authority Ritchie asked him to be seated'.[6] It was far more likely the fact that, 'In the British Army, families and family connections count for a good deal.' Hence, Stirling was able to prevail on Ritchie to attend to some 'vital business'. As a member of Ritchie's Highland set, Stirling's credentials (and those of his father, the Great War veteran, Brigadier-General J. Archibald Stirling of Keir) would have counted for much. Hence, David Stirling was allowed to 'pull . . . a pencilled memorandum out of his pocket' and hand it to his superior for perusal.

Reportedly, it took Ritchie ten minutes to read Stirling's paper *three* times, 'without moving'. This considered response to an interloper hardly squares with the reaction one might expect if Stirling lacked any credentials to recommend him to Ritchie, let alone warrant the general's undivided attention. Hence, it is likely that Ritchie was familiar with Stirling's family, either from the subaltern's own elaboration of the fact, or simply from his surname. After all, if Ritchie had not been aware of Stirling's pedigree and had been apprised of the opinion of the adjutant-general just down the corridor, things could have turned out very differently.

Ritchie's response to Stirling's memo was equally positive. He is said to have declared that, 'This may be the sort of plan we are looking for', and that he would 'discuss it with the commander-in-chief and let you know our decision in the next day or so'.[7] The speed with which he promised to address the issue again indicates that he was *au fait* with Stirling's background, cutting out the bureaucratic machine as one would for a member of one's circle, albeit a junior, which would hardly have been the case if Stirling was a wholly unknown quantity to Ritchie.

Over the next forty-eight hours, Cowles relates that Ritchie made enquiries about his uninvited guest and 'learned that David came from an old well-to-do Scottish family, whose ancestors had often distinguished themselves in the border wars of other days'. Exactly how much Stirling told Ritchie about his kin is a matter of conjecture, but Ritchie would have known soon enough that two of Stirling's brothers, Bill and Hugh, had been in the Scots Guards (Bill was still serving but Hugh had been killed in action), and that their other brother, Peter, was third secretary at the embassy in Cairo. Moreover, Ritchie had often gone shooting with the Stirling boys' uncle, Simon Joseph Fraser, the 16th Lord Lovat (who had died in 1933), who had an acclaimed record of conducting unorthodox military operations (*detailed later*). Whatever Stirling's background, though, his plan had to appeal both to Ritchie and the Auk, as well as the high command in London – the crux being its potential value to the hard-pressed Allied forces in northern Africa.

As Cowles relates, Stirling's memo 'suggested that a force of sixty men be raised . . . divided into five groups of twelve men each'. They should 'attack the five advanced German airfields' dotted along the north African coast and its hinterland. As Cowles goes on, the proposal 'was wonderfully economical. It promised much and risked practically nothing.' Auchinleck 'was an efficient, thorough, cautious [Ulster] Scot' – another coincidence that might have worked in Stirling's favour – and, while Auchinleck's 'temperament would not allow him to take chances . . . here was a proposal that required only a handful of men'.[8]

Immediately upon taking over Middle East Command in mid-1941, Auchinleck was put under pressure by Prime Minister Winston Churchill – a life-long advocate of the unorthodox in military affairs – to relieve pressure on the isolated garrison at Tobruk, which was under siege from Axis forces. Hence, Auchinleck agreed to sanction the venture proffered by Stirling via the general's old Wellington School colleague, Ritchie, in which 'something might be gained and nothing would be lost'.[9]

Consequently, three days after his encounter with Ritchie, Stirling's proposal was sanctioned and he was promoted by his fellow Scot to the rank of captain. Stirling was instructed to recruit six officers and sixty men – a manpower ceiling equivalent to a Commando sub-unit – from the depot at Geneifa in northern Egypt, in order to carry out the tasks spelled out in his memo.[10] Thus was the SAS born.

The Plan

In the light of the importance of Stirling's memo on special force operations, a central question about it that historians of the SAS have failed to answer must be addressed – what were the precise factors that led to its formulation?

Stirling's experiences prior to the summer of 1941 doubtless played a role in the development of his thinking on the subject, and these are related in subsequent chapters. Most recently, following a stint in the Scots Guards, he had become an Army Commando and joined the Royal Horse Guards' 32-year-old Major Robert Edward 'Lucky' Laycock in his Layforce. At first glance, one might assume that Stirling's service in the Commandos would be a key factor shaping his ideas about small-unit behind the lines operations. But, as will be seen, Layforce conducted comparatively little in the way of this type of raiding, and Stirling and his associates even less.

Indeed, after only a few months in existence, by May 1941 the writing seemed to be on the wall for Layforce. As Cowles was the first to point out at length, 'Stirling sat in Alexandria fuming' at the decision to disband it. 'He refused to accept the fact that there was no place for "special operations" in the desert battle.' He argued that, while the 2,000-man Layforce had been too immobile to prosecute successful seaborne raiding operations against the enemy-occupied coast of North Africa, Commando troops could be 'dropped by parachute' behind enemy lines, the Germans having used this novel technique of troop insertion during their recent occupation of nearby Crete.[11]

Stirling was fully aware of the problems that would arise from pursuing such a plan, not least that there were no British parachute schools in the Middle East, nor was there 'a single parachute expert' available to conduct training there. However, Cowles observes that

Stirling had 'heard that a fellow officer in No. 8 Commando, Jock Lewis [*sic*] had laid his hands on fifty parachutes which had been intended for India but had been unloaded in Alexandria by mistake'. Reportedly, Lewes had 'received permission and encouragement from Brigadier Laycock to experiment with them'.[12] Hence, the received wisdom about events in mid-1941 states that Stirling and Lewes were fortuitously on the same wavelength in seeking to experiment with Commando parachute operations, and that fate conspired to bring them together to try out this novel concept. However, in reality, there is far more to this reported happenstance than at first meets the eye.

Suffice it to say for now that Stirling 'at once asked if he might join' Lewes in the experimental parachute jump that he was due to make over the desert, the erstwhile Welsh Guardsman having acquired 'an old Valencia aeroplane' – in reality a Vickers Valentia mail delivery aircraft – which was 'wonderfully unsuited for parachute jumping'.[13] Despite this impediment, the two officers, accompanied by six other ranks, carried out trial jumps from an airfield near Mersa Matruh on the Egyptian coast.

Cowles recounts that 'Stirling was the [only] unlucky one' during the jumps, as his parachute ripped away from its static line – which had been attached, Heath-Robinson style, to the Valentia's seats – snaring on the tail of the aircraft as he exited. This precipitated an overly rapid descent, resulting in a 'severely injured ... back' for Stirling. 'For some days, both his legs were paralysed, and for some weeks he was unable to move from his bed at the Scottish Military Hospital in Alexandria' (most of his recuperation was actually in Cairo). In spite of this setback, in mid-June 1941, Cowles points out that Stirling's time 'was not wasted. He began to work on his scheme for special operations.'[14]

During his convalescence, he concluded that Commandos as they were constituted in the Middle East were both too immobile and too unwieldy – usually operating as they did in parties of at least 200 men, and often more – to undertake successful raids, which required the retention of surprise. This stemmed from their conception and constitution as a large-scale seaborne raiding force. In this scenario, Stirling realised, at least one-third of the attacking force had to adopt a static posture, securing a beachhead in order to cover the departure of the offensive elements of the Commando once their mission was over. Further, the involvement of such large numbers of men meant that they created too much noise and were consequently easily detected by the enemy. Stirling concluded in the light of his colleagues' previous, usually abortive raids, that it would be 'much better to drop half a dozen men, use every one of them, and . . . retain surprise until the demolition fuses went off'.

In hospital, Stirling pored over maps of the Western Desert and decided that its unpopulated, mainly road-free expanses were ideal for the undetected infiltration of small units of specially trained and equipped men. They could retain surprise by remaining undetected until and even during their raids on enemy airfields, supply dumps, vehicle parks, repair shops and camps. 'If a handful of men could be dropped by parachute miles behind the enemy lines', Stirling asserted, 'they could hide in the desert by day, then at night creep onto the unguarded and exposed airfields and place their bombs on the aircraft.' They could then exfiltrate using friendly desert motor patrols to escape any pursuers.[15]

As outlined by Cowles, this was, in essence, Stirling's ground-breaking plan for strategic small-unit behind the lines hit-and-run raiding – a milestone in British military thought and an apparent stroke of genius. Yet, to draw another analogy, many roads had been traversed to get to the crossroads signposted by Stirling, while many more bridges would have to be crossed before such a unit could prove itself on the battlefield. Before retreading the steps taken by Stirling and his fellow travellers, however, more needs to be said about the growth of the legend surrounding Stirling's plan and its genesis.

Official History

It was another thirteen years after Cowles's book before the public was presented with an official version of these seminal events by Philip Warner's *The Special Air Service*. While he noted that his book could 'not, of course [be] a complete account' of all its activities, its opening Guideline stated that Stirling was the 'founder of the Regiment'. Warner added the caveat that 'J. S. "Jock" Lewes . . . probably had more influence on the formation of the SAS than anyone except David Stirling', but he also stressed that Lewes's conceptual influence was less important than his 'practical enterprise' and role in training the SAS's first recruits and devising some of their essential weaponry. Additionally, Lewes purportedly took the initiative in acquiring the parachutes needed to experiment with air-dropping over the desert, though Warner notes that the vital 'acquisition of the parachutes seems to be enshrouded by a little of the mystery that sometimes accompanies unorthodox enterprises'. Following Cowles's line, he notes that, 'There were no plans for parachute training in the Middle East', but that there were 'plans for parachuting in India, and a consignment of fifty parachutes destined for that country were unloaded by mistake in Alexandria.'[16]

Yet, neither Warner nor any other historian has explained how fifty bulky, rare and conspicuous packages were transferred from the Alexandria docks into Lewes's custody and thence to Layforce's camp. Nor does Warner explain who gave permission for such a cargo to be requisitioned, who was involved in its transportation, or how and why Lewes – who had no parachuting experience – suddenly became so interested in the parachutes in the first place? Or to put it another way, why was Lewes *in particular* made aware of the parachutes' arrival, by whom, and for what reason? Questions, questions and, at least in the official history, no answers to this 'mystery'.

Warner says simply that the parachutes 'found their way into the custody of Lewes, who decided to find out how to use them, and was encouraged in this by . . . Laycock'. This does not begin to address the questions raised above and, as will be shown, there is far more to their crucial acquisition by Lewes – the crux to any plan for Commando parachutists – than has been supposed by other historians.

Indeed, in rather contradictory terms, Warner asserts that Stirling and Lewes 'were not concerned with the methods being developed by British, German, Russian or Italian airborne units', because these were 'for larger and different operations'.[17] But if they had no knowledge of other parachute forces, how can they have been inspired to carry out their experimental parachute jumps? In fact, the broader development of paratroop operations and various examples of their use in the Middle East theatre and elsewhere will be shown to be significant factors in the pair's endeavours and, consequently, in the formation of the SAS parachutists.

With regard to Stirling's and Lewes's trial drops, Warner relates that Stirling was hospitalised for two months. In reality, his convalescence lasted for about half that time, but he *did* use his time constructively to work out and prepare a plan for the conduct of a new form of special operations. Stirling's memo on the subject is outlined by Warner and can be summarised as follows:

1. The Axis forces' lines of communication and infrastructure are vulnerable to offensive action both on the North African coast and in the transport parks and airfields in its hinterland. These were targeted by No. 8 Commando/Layforce raiders and should be again, in order to disrupt Axis operational planning and activities.

2. The large size of Commando units, along with the mass of ancillary equipment that they require to raid the North African coast and its hinterland, prejudice the vital element of surprise. This offsets any advantage that can be gained from such a force's enhanced firepower. Further, Royal Navy vessels and personnel transporting and supporting the raiders are put in considerable jeopardy while they are engaged on such tasks. This risk is disproportionate to any damage that can be inflicted by these raiding parties.

3. A unit with minimal manpower can retain the element of surprise by operating in parties of five and assaulting targets that had previously been assailed by a Commando of 200 or more men. As a result, fifty aircraft on an airfield could as easily be destroyed by a handful of raiders as by a whole Commando unit. Indeed, a force of 200+ men *in total*, from which small parties would be drawn, could prove an effective force-multiplier, achieving disproportionately effective results – 'Properly selected, trained and equipped men, organised into sub-units of five, should be able to attack at least thirty different objectives on the same night as compared to only one objective using the Commando technique.' Furthermore, Stirling argued that, even if these small units achieved only a twenty-five per cent success rate, this would be in excess of what could be achieved by established Commando practices. He explained that his new unit's personnel should be trained for insertion to target areas by various means – by land, sea or air. Hence, their infiltration should be made possible by

parachuting from any type of aircraft, by landing from any kind of sea vessel – including caiques, 'folbots' (toughened canoes) and submarines – or either by marching on foot to a target or being transported by motor vehicles. Indeed, he cited another special force that was operating in the Axis' rear, the Long Range Desert Group (LRDG), as one possible means of assistance.

4. The new unit must have its own training and operational planning staff, so that it can conduct its activities without interference from or diversion by other authorities. Hence, its commander must be directly under the auspices of the theatre commander. This would prevent the force from being re-assigned to tasks in which it would be less productively employed – as had been the case with the Commandos – or from being absorbed by the Special Operations Executive (SOE).

5. The unit's first operation should be a paratroop raid by five parties, prior to the next Allied offensive (which would be in November 1941). Two of these parties should attack the five main Axis forward-area airfields near Tmimi and Gazala, with each landing twelve miles south of their objectives, marching to them, then recconoitring their specific targets. Each party would attack at night using sixty incendiary/explosive charges, fitted with two-hour, half-hour or ten-minute time-pencils, or with twelve-second fuses. These devices would be placed on aircraft and timed to detonate simultaneously, thereby assisting exfiltration.

Warner notes that, 'Even at this early stage, Stirling was bursting with ideas for the organisation and use of the unit.' But, as will become clear, he was not thinking and acting in a conceptual vacuum.[18] The thrust of Warner's account is reiterated by Strawson's *A History of the SAS Regiment*, 'Anyone *might* have thought of it, but it was David Stirling who did.' It was *his* 'great idea'.[19] Stirling added in his recollections for Alan Hoe that, when it came to the development of his concept, 'I had these loose thoughts in my mind' already, and Hoe observes that 'Stirling instinctively thought that he was on to something.' But Stirling confirmed that it was teaming up with Lewes and 'the parachute incident that was the real trigger'. However, while Hoe asserts that Lewes acquired the parachutes simply as 'a way of relieving the boredom of waits between operations', Lewes and Stirling did *not* undertake their hazardous drops simply because 'inactivity was anathema' to them. There are hitherto undisclosed reasons for their actions.

Before delving further into this issue, however, it is noteworthy that, also according to Hoe, 'Auchinleck made enquiries about Stirling', and 'as a Scot, would have had knowledge of Stirling's pedigree'.[20] Whatever the case, Stirling's background certainly requires closer attention, in order to assess just how it affected his thinking about unorthodox methods of warfare and, ultimately, his proposals for the SAS.

The Man

Stirling was born in November 1915 to a 'well-known distinguished' family of the Scottish landed gentry. His mother, the Honourable Margaret Fraser, was a daughter of Simon Joseph Fraser, Baron Lovat, owner of vast Highland estates. Indeed, David's uncle was a South African War hero and founder of the celebrated unorthodox military unit, the Lovat Scouts (*described later*). Thus David shared with his brothers and cousins a proud military heritage. According to Hoe, the young David was close to his brothers Hugh, Peter and William (known as Bill), the last of whom would become a central player in David's wartime SAS, progressing from youthful expert poacher to founder of the 2nd SAS Regiment. Peter's role in the story has been ignored hitherto, a matter rectified in due course.

While they were children on the Keir estate near Dunblane, the Stirling boys honed their hunting skills – stalking, shooting and fieldcraft – in the glens around Ardchullary lodge, with David rated an 'expert' shot and said to possess a 'countryman's sense of tactics'.[21] At boarding school in Ampleforth, North Yorkshire, where his brothers and his cousin, Simon Christopher Joseph 'Shimi' Fraser (later Lord Lovat), were fellow pupils, David did solitary cross-country rambles that demanded self-reliance, organisation and planning. This environment, in which the virtues of the outdoor life (sharing much in common with the rigours of the military) were emphasised, proved valuable for his future Army career. It also doubtless played a part in his development of the idea of operating in very small parties, or even alone, stealthily tracking the enemy and striking with speed and surprise.

The brothers spent numerous summer holidays at the Lovats' lodge by Loch Morar, shooting deer and other game, fishing, and hill-walking. While David's family connection with the Lovats is well known, it has never been suggested that his ideas about military operations could have been informed by his family's own military heritage. Yet, the adventurous boy had a professed interest in history and would undoubtedly have taken a keen interest in the exploits of his uncle and other relatives who had borne arms for their country. Hoe notes that David 'mixed with famous fighting men throughout his young life, and clan chiefs (his uncle Lord Lovat was both) were constant visitors to Keir'.[22] David must have heard tales about his uncle's derring-do on the South African *veldt*, fighting against the Boer *Kommandos* between 1900 and 1902, and raising his own unit in the process.

Then, when Stirling went to Cambridge University, he took up another risk-laden pastime at the nearby Newmarket race course – gambling. It was another characteristic of his personality that informed his future conception of military action: the acceptance of calculated risk based upon prior knowledge, preparation and intuition. In other words, who dares wins! Then, after an interlude working as an artist in Paris – which at least taught him the benefits of close observation and being multi-lingual (another tenet for personnel serving in his future military unit) – David acquired a post as a trainee architect (demanding attention to detail) in Edinburgh. This came about through family connections, demonstrating that Stirling was not averse to a bit of string-pulling to advance his cause, as would be the case with regard to the presentation of his plans at Middle East HQ. By 1937, however, he had shifted his focus to a far greater challenge – to become the first man to conquer Mount Everest and return to tell the tale.[23]

In order to achieve this, Stirling embarked on a period of intense preparation, sharpening his mountaineering skills and building up his fitness. He crowned Scottish peaks like the knife-edged Cuillins of Skye, before making his way to the Swiss Alps. There he spent six months honing his mountaincraft, not least his navigational and logistical nous. He returned to Keir in the summer of 1938 and decided to embellish his training by keeping up the family military tradition. He enlisted in the Supplementary Reserve of his father's regiment, the Scots Guards, which required his part-time attendance at Pirbright camp. After attending several mundane sessions in tactics and drill, however, he decided that his time would be better spent in the Canadian Rockies. He arrived there in the autumn of 1938 and, to raise funds for his proposed Himalayan expedition, he took on work as a cattle-drover, resulting in further hardening-up thanks to overnight bivouacking.

After a seven-month stint ascending several peaks, including Mount Stimson, Stirling retired to the Blackfoot Reservation on the USA–Canada border. There, a Texan prospector known as 'Panhandle Pete . . . fired Stirling's imagination' with tales of the Amerindians and their resistance to the white invaders. The 23-year-old Scot became 'fascinated by the folklore of the Indian nations', and Hoe observes that 'distant ancestors of the Stirlings had been involved in the Indian wars'.[24] But what Hoe does not add – and other historians of the SAS have overlooked – is that the campaigns of the Amerindians and their foes provided examples of unorthodox military operations that would be referred to by Stirling's colleagues at the time that his SAS plan was being drawn up in mid-1941.

Indeed, while Stirling claimed in 1985 that 'as a young man I didn't read military history',[25] as Lovat noted in his memoir, 'raising special troops for battle is in the Lovats' blood'.[26] In 1779, one of the laird's ancestors, Colonel Thomas Lister, raised Lister's Light Dragoons, and it is quite feasible that Stirling – Lovat's perennial holiday-time shooting partner – learned from him about the family tradition of raising heterodox units in both America and South Africa. Such knowledge could have encouraged Stirling to uphold that tradition and also made him more predisposed to taking counsel from his colleagues about past unorthodox military units in mid-1941.

Although no detailed account of Lister's Light Dragoons appears to have been published, it seems that they were raised during the American Revolutionary War of 1776–84 as a British provincial reserve force that could be called on to confront opposition either from France or within Britain. The regiment was not deployed to America, though its colleagues in the 16th (Queen's) Regiment of Light Dragoons and the 17th Regiment of Light Dragoons saw action there.

The 16th Light Dragoons arrived in New York in September 1776 and moved to Philadelphia in 1777, fighting at Brandywine and Paoli. On returning to New York in 1778, they were engaged at Monmouth Court House, after which, under strength, they were amalgamated with the 17th Regiment at the end of the year. The 17th had arrived in Boston in May 1775, before moving to New York in 1776 and fighting at Long Island, Fort Washington and Princeton, with elements making for Philadelphia and New York. After mustering there in 1778 and skirmishing at Monmouth, the 17th marched on Pound Ridge. One troop then moved south with the British Legion to Cowpens, Guilford Court House and Yorktown, before the regiment departed for Britain in 1783.

While there is no evidence that Lovat or Stirling was familiar with these particular operations, it is worth noting that, from August 1776 to May 1777, Colonel Robert Rogers – the creator of a force of Rangers in the American war of the 1750s (*see Chapter 10*) – led a brother unit, the Queen's Rangers, which was 'active between the lines' up to 1782. 'They attacked outposts, skirmished along lines of battle, and patrolled the outskirts of the main army or posts.'[27] Rogers's feats were referred to when the creation of the SAS was mooted, and Stirling's interest in the American wars, in which another Lovat forebear led Fraser's Highlanders in 1759, at least made him well disposed to discussing the tactics used there.

In September 1939, Stirling's bid to ascend Everest was put on hold as Britain declared war on Nazi Germany, requiring him to return to Pirbright and the Scots Guards, in which his brothers Hugh and William had also enlisted. (Their 28-year-old cousin, Simon, had served in the Guards with Bill before the outbreak of hostilities, but he joined the Lovat Scouts on the declaration of war.)

Back at barracks, David did his damnedest to ignore the outmoded tactics taught by instructors such as 'Major Smith', which would lead to their infamous run-in at Middle East HQ in mid-1941. Still, this meant that Stirling retained an open mind about military operations and he was more than willing to volunteer for anything that would break the monotony of parade-ground life. He soon got a chance to do so at the turn of 1940.[28]

Chapter 2

Stalin's War

Apparently, when David Stirling left Pirbright, he was rated by his superiors as 'an irresponsible and unremarkable soldier'.[1] But in the circumstances that faced the United Kingdom, the country needed all the military men, and the friends and allies, that it could get. Hence, when the Soviet Union invaded Finland on 30 November 1939, Britain offered the Finns moral support, and the prospect of a limited deployment of military manpower in the shape of a British Expeditionary Force. Stirling wanted to be part of it.

The proposal for a force of skiing Arctic warriors who could operate as guerillas behind enemy lines – hitting Soviet communications, installations and other assets – came from the War Office.[2] The military establishment's attitude to unconventional warfare is discussed in more detail in my previous book *A Special Type of Warfare* but, to summarise the position, after the First World War, while the War Office retained files on 'guerilla raiders' such as the Boer Kommandos – 'hit-and-run troops who raided installations, sabotaged machinery and communications, and attacked enemy troops'[3] – it rather sniffily argued that, if the British military needed to raise such a force in the future, this should be done by the Royal Marines. In fact the sum of the Marines' recent raiding experience was their action at Zeebrugge in April 1918.

In 1924, when the government's Madden Committee investigated the question of specialist raiding establishments, it too proposed the formation of a 3,000-man Royal Marine Brigade that could 'undertake raids on enemy coastlines and bases' during any future 'general war'.[4] But, due to a lack of both foresight and financial resources, those in authority failed to act upon these recommendations, and it was not until war loomed again in the mid-1930s that the War Office stepped up its own interest in unconventional military operations.

Following 'several studies by British military strategists in the inter-war years', in 1936, the Deputy Chief of the Imperial General Staff, General Adam, created an army think-tank, the War Office Directorate of Military Operations' (DMO) General Staff (Research) – or GS(R) – section, later known as Military Intelligence (Research), or MI(R). It was charged with, among other things, 'the task of studying guerilla tactics of . . . special groups' that the Army had encountered during its Imperial policing operations, such as the Boers, many of whom operated as guerillas during the South African War in 1900–2. In addition, GS(R) studied guerillas active during the civil wars in China and Spain during the 1930s. GS(R) was ordered to report to the DMO on how such activities could impact on the future conduct of Imperial policing. However, with another major war threatening Europe by the autumn of 1938, the General Staff sought to identify the potential for insurgent forces in occupied territories, should Germany attack any of its neighbours.[5]

In October 1938, Lieutenant-Colonel John Charles Francis 'Joe' Holland, a Royal Engineer and ex-pilot, took command of GS(R). He had personal experience of unconventional warfare and unorthodox military forces, having flown Colonel T. E. Lawrence about during the time that he was trying to assist anti-Ottoman forces in southern Arabia during the Great War. Holland had also fought against the urban terrorists and rural guerilla units of the Irish Republican Army (IRA) during their insurgency of 1918–22.

The forty-year-old Holland and his colleagues studied the activities of the Boers, the Pathans of the North-West Frontier of India, guerillas operating in Russia and its neighbouring territories during its Revolution and Civil War of 1917–22, as well as those in the Spanish Civil War of 1936–9, the 1930s' Sino-Japanese conflict (especially after 1937) and events in Palestine from 1936 onwards. In January 1939, GS(R) circulated a preliminary report on 'special warfare' and its potential utility during another war. It also welcomed two new recruits who were given responsibility for overseeing preparations for resistance demolitions and the organisation of partisan forces: Lieutenant Millis Jefferis, and Lieutenant-Colonel Colin MacVean Gubbins, respectively.

Jefferis came from Royal Artillery Major Lawrence D. Grand's 140-

strong Section D of the Secret Intelligence Service (SIS or MI6), which was busy drawing up its own plans for sabotage and subversion in continental Europe, both by its own agents and local partisan forces. Gubbins was already 'very well' known to Holland. Following service in Russia in March–December 1919, Gubbins served alongside Holland in Ireland and remained there for three years. As an Army intelligence officer in 1920, Gubbins had attended a three-day course on guerilla warfare run by the 5th Division HQ, before gaining practical experience in the field confronting the IRA. Following later service in India, he moved, among other places, to the War Office Directorates of Military Intelligence and Training, before joining GS(R), aged forty-four. Noting his breadth of knowledge, including familiarity with the Spanish Civil War, Holland set Gubbins to work writing pamphlets on special warfare. Then, as the Czech crisis flared up early in 1939 and war with Germany loomed large, on 20 March, the CIGS, General Lord Gort, authorised sabotage and propaganda against pro-Nazi elements in Czechoslovakia. GS(R) became MI(R) under the auspices of the Deputy Director of Military Intelligence, Major-General F. G. Beaumont-Nesbitt. He encouraged Holland's ongoing studies of sniping, ambushing and sabotage operations, with a view to future action against German occupation forces. By 23 March, the ground was being prepared for what would become SOE, which, at its inception in July 1940, would bring together personnel from SIS Section D, MI(R) and the Foreign Office's propaganda and information management department, Elektra House. Its activities lie largely outside the scope of this work but, in April 1939, Gort requested the production of 'guerilla *Field Service Regulations*' and, by that June, Gubbins had written both *The Art of Guerrilla Warfare* and *The Partisan Leader's Handbook*, which became the basis for early SOE training.

Additionally, Holland was 'authorised to expand his section and to earmark suitable staff for special employment'. Assisted by Major Gerald W. Templer – the future 'Tiger of Malaya', who fought Communist insurgents there from 1952 (detailed in *A Special Type of Warfare*) – an Emergency Reserve of officers was created, with Gubbins recruiting polar explorers and others with potentially useful specialist skills into its ranks. By June 1939, he had drawn up pro-grammes for training in guerilla warfare and sabotage, and three courses were up and running for sixty 'very carefully selected individuals who would be sent abroad' as the foci around which local partisan forces could be raised.[6]

Following the outbreak of war in September 1939, Gubbins focused his thoughts on Poland, then France, while a paper on the future infiltration of officers into China was written by his colleague, Peter Fleming, a Grenadier Guards reservist and brother of future James Bond novelist, Ian. However, in November 1939, the attention of Holland and the War Office hierarchy was taken up by Stalin's invasion of Finland. Holland proposed that a guerilla force of mountain warfare specialists could assist the Finns and undermine the Soviets' efforts. His desire was shared both by Beaumont-Nesbitt and the First Lord of the Admiralty, Winston Churchill, who had proposed the formation of a battalion of ski troops before the war. He pressed the CIGS and the Imperial General Staff to do just that now and, reasoning that they might deny Swedish iron ore to Germany and hinder the movement of its Baltic fleet, the military authorities backed MI(R)'s plan. In December, the War Office proposed the creation of what author Eric Morris has dubbed 'Britain's first special force', the 5th Battalion (Special Reserve), Scots Guards. A circular calling for 'experienced skiers' was despatched to all Home Forces commands and HQs in January 1940.[7]

David Stirling was among those who volunteered for the 'Snowballers', who were 'specially recruited from the Brigade of Guards and included a number of veterans of the 1935 Everest expedition'. There were also Arctic explorers who had been on Gino Watkins's 1931 British Arctic Air Route Expedition to Greenland. Designated as instructors, they were led by Captain Martin Lindsay, Royal Scots Fusiliers, and joined by one-time participants in the Spanish Civil War, several mercenaries who had fought in China and Latin America, and 170 Territorial Army and regular officers 'who had laid aside their commissions to serve in the ranks of this highly qualified specialist unit'.[8]

Among Stirling's fellow 700-plus Guardsmen and other uniformed volunteers were some prominent figures in the SAS's future story. One was a future wartime SAS commander and a member of the War Office MI(R) branch who was already regarded as a demolitions expert

– Lieutenant J. Michael 'Mike' Calvert, Royal Engineers. There was also his future colleague in the Far East, who would become an equally legendary commander of guerilla forces, Lieutenant Freddy Spencer Chapman, Seaforth Highlanders. He had been part of the 1931 British Greenland expedition and was an associate of Lord Lovat. Indeed, Spencer Chapman accompanied Lovat later in 1940 to the new Irregular Warfare Training Centre (IWTC, later School – IWTS) in Scotland, to work as a Commando instructor.

There was also a future leading light in the Small Scale Raiding Force and a participant in SAS-led operations in southern Europe, Captain Philip Pinkney; a future member of Layforce and confidant of Jock Lewes, Carol Mather; Mather's Klosters skiing colleague and a future leader of the Special Boat Section, the Right Honourable George, the Earl Jellicoe; post-war SAS stalwart, Major Eric 'Bill' Barkworth; and one of Stirling's originals, teenage Scots Guardsman Johnny Cooper – quite a group of future celebrities!

In February 1940, the would-be ski troops were transferred to the Quebec and Martinique Barracks at Bordon camp, Aldershot, Hampshire. They were joined by their CO, Lieutenant-Colonel J. S. 'Jimmy' Coates, Coldstream Guards, an accomplished St Moritz skier and a 'distinguished winter sports expert', and his second-in-command, Captain W. D. M. Raeburn, 'a well-known skier' from the 2nd Scots Guards, who had transferred from their camp at Mersa Matruh in Egypt (later used by the SAS).

Possessing considerable skiing experience of his own, Stirling was immediately made a sergeant instructor by Coates. Most of the 700-plus officer volunteers received their call-up telegrams on 3 February 1940 and arrived at Bordon three days later. There they were organised into four ski companies (Left, Right, W and X). The recruits attended frequent lectures on Arctic survival and snow camping, and carried out drills and route marches. However, any swift deployment was hindered by a lack of co-operation from neutral Norway and Sweden in affording passage to the force. By March, only 429 other ranks were available for service with it, so the Brigade of Guards was called upon to provide two companies of newly trained Guards from Pirbright to make up the battalion's numbers. (They became known as Training Battalion and, later, Y Company.)[9]

On 2 March 1940, the 5th Battalion was put on active service and sailed from Southampton to Cherbourg and Dieppe. Their destination was supposed to be known only to their commander, but their impending arrival in Chamonix was reported in the *Daily Telegraph*! After transferring to trains, they made for Mont Blanc in the French Alps for ten days of special training authorised by the Paris government. This was meant to involve mountain climbing and ski descents in the Haute Savoie under the tutelage of the 199th Battalion of the Chasseurs Alpins, Des Chausseurs de Haute Montagne. However, its soldiers felt that the avalanche risk was too great to undertake serious training, and they carried out only demonstration attacks, two platoons of ski troops assaulting a position held by a third. The battalion subsequently did its own skiing and sledge-pulling before being shipped back to Southampton on 11 March.

Back in Britain, Calvert for one was ordered to prepare for travel by ship (in his case, the Polish liner *Batory*) to Gairloch on the River Clyde in Scotland, while another, Mather, travelled via Birmingham up to Glasgow. However, just before the battalion's members mustered, ready to sail across the North Sea on 12 March, news came through of the Finns' capitulation and a treaty with the USSR. This brought the Winter War to an end. Consequently, the War Office's Plan R4 to relieve the Finns by behind the lines guerilla operations was shelved. The 5th Scots Guards – dubbed 'the Phoney Fifth' – were unceremoniously disbanded under the supervision of Colonel E. W. S. Balfour (although they remained on stand-by).[10]

Stirling learned little new from his time with the battalion, but bearing in mind the potential influences on his thinking about special operations, it should be noted that he retained an interest in the Scandinavian cauldron. His brother Bill was at the heart of the first attempted raids there.

With the German advance on Norway progressing from 9 April, some of MI(R)'s 'ideas gained acceptance' among the top brass and 'a number of officers', among them several former 5th Scots Guards, 'persuaded the authorities to allow them to raid the Germans in southern Norway. Their plan, "Jack Knife", was to' land at Sogne Fjörd by submarine and 'sabotage the railway line and bridges' between Bergen and Oslo. Then, they would arm partisans and carry out intelligence gathering and demolitions, before making for Sweden. The raiding party was to comprise six officers, led by an expert skier, the 5th Scots Guards' Captain Brian Mayfield (who would go on to serve with the Commandos). Moreover, the team included not only Royal Engineers demolitions expert and mountaineer, Jim Gavin, MI(R)'s Peter Kemp and skier Peter Fleming, but three 5th Scots Guards volunteers including Captain Bill Stirling.

The expedition was briefed at MI(R) by Captain F. Tommy Davies and Captain Kennedy, before joining the submarine HMS *Truant* at Rosyth. However, soon after leaving, Lieutenant-Commander Hutcheson's vessel was damaged by a mine in the North Sea and had to limp back to port for repairs. While these were carried out, Bill Stirling arranged for the raiding party to stay at Keir, where new plans for 'Operation Knife' were drawn up. These included working alongside a new unorthodox British force set up by Holland and Gubbins, the Independent Companies (*see Chapter 3*), which were meant to relieve some of the pressure on the Norwegians.

Among those who sought to participate in the upcoming Knife raid was Shimi Lovat, who arranged to be posted back to Scotland to join his cousin Bill. However, while the would-be raiders enjoyed 'superb hospitality with the Stirlings', a decision was made in London to pull British forces out of Norway and the mission was aborted. The party returned to London,[11] where David was ensconced, having returned there via Pirbright. He reportedly spent most of his time in hostelries such as White's Club,[12] and it was there that, in June 1940, he first learned of another new special force being established by the War Office – the Commandos.

Their genesis and impact on him is another important piece of the jigsaw regarding the SAS's origins, and the Commandos, in turn, owed their formation to various factors. These included both the recently planned British special force missions to Norway, and pre-war unorthodox military operations.

Chapter 3

The Independent Companies

Many of the officers who recruited men into the Commandos had themselves experienced 'Special Service' in the five Independent Companies that were sent to Norway in the spring of 1940. Given that they would be passing on their knowledge to those under their command – including David Stirling and others – an understanding of what the 3,000-strong Independent Companies were about is instructive.

They were established with a view to operating as raiders on the Norwegian coast and its hinterland in the event of a German invasion. This had been foreseen by Joe Holland by March 1940, when he instructed Gubbins to begin 'preparing and training ... selected assault troops' for a North-West Expeditionary Force (later styled the Allied Force in Norway). Plans were drawn up by 20 March, but before any action could be taken, Operation Weserübung was instigated and the Germans invaded Denmark and Norway (partly in order to secure Swedish iron ore supplies and to forestall any pre-emptive British military action to protect them). The Axis assault was led by Nazi paratroopers on 9 April 1940 – the first major wartime paratroop operation.

In Denmark, a German parachute battalion captured the airfields at Aalborg, as well as the Vordingborg bridge between the Falster and Zealand islands. In Norway, five companies of German paratroopers secured the country's major airports at Oslo and Stavanger, although major casualties were sustained due to bad weather. Additionally, an assault on the Dombas Pass on 17 April (which, incidentally, was noted in his diary by one of the founding fathers of the Commandos, Captain Dudley Clarke, Royal Artillery) was handicapped by a combination of overly low air-dropping, malfunctioning parachutes and the dispersal of essential equipment in the snow-covered mountains.[1] Even so, with the Finnish domino fallen, Norway, with its eight strategically important ports, looked set to follow.

In the light of the Finnish example, by 13 April, Holland had urged his superiors to draw upon the expertise of the Lovat Scouts, who had been training for operations since September 1939 and had been ear-marked for use in Finland. Holland argued that the Scouts, who had 'a high proportion of stalkers, keepers and ghillies . . . should be re-organised and specially trained to operate as raiding parties', alongside remnants of the 5th Scots Guards. The Scouts' commander, Lieutenant-Colonel Leslie Melville, however, blocked this. Con-sequently, on 15 April, MI(R) suggested the formation of ten new 'Guerilla Companies' to carry out raids in Norway, plus a corps of sniper 'experimental riflemen' (following Manningham's precedent of the previous century, the 95th Rifles).[2]

The Norwegian government had now requested British military assistance and the authorities took up MI(R)'s proposal, promising the Norwegians 'guerilla forces', while a main force landing was made at Narvik by units under the overall command of Major-General P. J. Mackesy, followed by one at Namsos on 16 April. The Guerilla Companies were redesignated as 'Special Infantry Companies' and, not long afterwards, 'Independent Companies'.

John Parker, author of *SBS* and *Commandos*, notes that the Boers inspired the Independent Companies,[3] though their particular nomen-clature may have been drawn from another historical precedent – units of that name operated in the wars of the American colonies in the eighteenth century. Whatever the case, each of the Independent Companies was to comprise 268 Territorial Army officers and men, plus twenty-one regular officers, hand-picked by the Company leaders. From 20 April, the units came under the command of Gubbins.

Every Territorial brigade was directed to provide a platoon for the Companies and every battalion a section for that platoon. Gubbins chipped in that there was in the Army a considerable 'untapped reservoir of officers and men with the necessary qualifications and experience' who could 'act as instructors', and he proposed that the

Independent Companies (2,000 of whose number would go on to join the Commandos) should be led by soldiers with experience of combat against irregular opposition. He held that regular officers with service in the mountainous North-West Frontier Province of India should be recruited, along with bush-whackers from the West African Frontier Force and the King's African Rifles. Gubbins also wanted to cast the net wider to soldiers with particular skills and backgrounds, such as polar explorers, blood sports enthusiasts, and individuals grounded in the outdoor life, like the ghillies of the Lovat Scouts (who had manned trench observation posts in the Great War).[4]

Another Whitehall figure who recommended the Lovat Scouts' deployment on raids, and who crops up subsequently in Middle East special operations, was MI(R)'s Scandinavian desk officer, Captain Peter Fleming, a veteran of the Spanish Civil War, where he and Gubbins 'had friends in common'. Earlier in April 1940, Fleming was ordered, along with some Norwegian-speaking officers, to make a reconnaissance of Namsos as part of No. 10 Military Mission, returning by submarine to the Shetlands on 27 April. Fleming's brother Richard was a friend of Lovat, and Peter understood the Scouts' potential value. Even so, the War Office posted most of them to the Faroe Islands on guard duties, though, in July, Fleming attached some Scouts to another formation that Holland was establishing 'as [a] guerilla [force] in the enemy's [potential] beach-heads' in southern England. In this regard, Fleming urged XII Corps' Lieutenant-General Andrew 'Bulgy' Thorne to ask the War Cabinet Secretariat chief, General Hastings Ismay, to provide 'an officer who would raise and train a body of troops to stay behind . . . in the wake of the German advance and harass the raiders'.[5]

Mike Calvert would advance from Commando demolitions training instructor to leader of the 'small experimental . . . XII Corps Observation Unit'. In the 'utmost secrecy, he began to raise and train a clandestine army' from the newly formed Local Defence Volunteers (later redesignated as the Home Guard), who provided 3,000 personnel for mining and booby-trapping by October. Calvert recruited farmers, gamekeepers and foresters for training at Garth, near Bilting in Kent, not far from the Army Intelligence Corps HQ at Ashford. They were drilled in 'sabotage attacks at night', using improvised explosive devices to blow up bridges, and the 'mopping up [of] odd parachutists'.[6]

Lord Lovat avoided the Faroes by taking up an offer to become a sniper instructor with the 61st Division in London, prior to transferring back to Scotland. While in the metropolis, he met friends at the Parson's Rest pub, among whom were such notables as Freddy Spencer Chapman, Phil Pinkney and David Stirling.[7] Doubtless they discussed the latest developments, among them the formation of the Independent Companies.

Of the ten set up in April 1940, five were designated for use in Norway, while the remainder were directed to train in Scotland. No. 1 Independent Company was formed from 52nd Division and shipped off to Norway within days of its formation, setting off from Rosyth on HMS *Arethusa* on 27 April, before being recalled the next day and re-embarking for Mo on the RMS *Orion* and SS *Royal Ulsterman* on 1 May. It was soon followed by Companies 3, 4 and 5, while No. 2 Independent Company remained on standby under the command of Gubbins's future successor, Major Hugh C. Stockwell (another subsequent supporter of the SAS). No. 5 was led by Major A. Charles Newman (a future VC winner with No. 2 Commando in the raid on St Nazaire in 1942, and then commander of the post-war Territorial SAS Regiment, 21 SAS). No. 5 was based in Scotland alongside the 1st Battalion of the Scots Guards and assigned to Colonel Trappes-Lomax as the vanguard of a larger BEF, which was due to relieve the Norwegians by landing at Namsos and Andalsnes. Of the other Independent Companies forming at that time, No. 6 was led by Major R. J. F. 'Ronnie' Tod of the Argyll and Sutherland Highlanders (a future Commando leader and staunch supporter of the wartime and post-war SAS).

The five companies under Gubbins's command were due to head for Norway as 'Scissor Force', equipped with rudimentary Arctic kit. They were 'expected to live off the land' and 'strik[e] at German forces . . . as the opportunity arose', operating in 'sub-sections of three or four men'. They were ordered by the BEF command staff's General Hugh R. S. Massy, 'to harass the enemy's flanks and LoCs' in the vicinity of Mo, Bodo and Mosjöen. However, as the force was put together so hurriedly, its volunteers lacked Arctic warfare training and had to rely on the specialist knowledge of some of their officers. These included twenty seconded from the Indian Army to disseminate their wisdom about mountain warfare, eight of them possessing first-hand experience of fighting on the North-West Frontier.[8]

The bulk of Independent Companies 3, 4 and 5 left Gourock aboard the SS *Ulster Prince*, while Scissor Force's HQ in Norway was set up by a party from No. 5 Independent Company on 4 May. Major Newman and his subordinates were instructed to 'maintain themselves on the flanks of the German forces and continue harrying tactics against their [communications]'. Nos. 3 and 4 eventually joined them on 8 May after a spell of bad weather, just as a company of French Chasseurs Alpins departed. It was two days before the German onslaught into Western Europe, which resulted in Britain's withdrawal via Narvik from 3 June. But for nearly a month until then, the Independent Companies 'moved up and down the western coastline of Norway, engaging the enemy . . . and . . . harrying' him.[9]

One of the officers involved in Scissor Force planning who would figure in the SAS's story was General Auchinleck. A student of history, Auchinleck graduated from the Royal Military Academy Sandhurst in December 1902 and was conversant with the South African War both from his academic studies of it and informal mess discussions. He went on to serve in India and Tibet before the outbreak of World War I, gaining an insight into mountain warfare in the process. After serving in wartime Egypt, Mesopotamia and Kurdistan between 1914 and 1918, he returned to the Raj. There, he 'treated everyone in exactly the same manner, whether officer or private [and] he preferred to listen rather than talk'. This commendable trait afforded his subordinates the latitude to approach him with ideas rather than face the prospect of an instant brush-off, and the fact that 'officers and men found him extremely easy to talk to and confide in' would prove important for Stirling when he proffered his SAS concept.

In 1927, Auchinleck was posted to the Imperial Defence College, where he met future general and CIGS, John G. 'Jack' Dill, who 'became a good friend to Auchinleck', as well as to Wavell, and who also went on to play a part in the creation of British special forces in the Second World War. After returning to India in 1928, Auchinleck 'stood out' among his fellow officers at Quetta Staff College, commanding great respect from them. After seeing action against native irregulars in Peshawar district in 1933, he experienced six weeks of skirmishes and night patrols in the Mohmand campaign of 1935, commanding a brigade against the Haji of Turangzai. He next joined the New Delhi HQ's Modernisation Committee and impressed colleagues with 'the breadth of his mind, his receptiveness to new ideas, and his capacity to translate novel theories into practice'.

On returning to the UK, Auchinleck was posted to IV Corps HQ in January 1940 and, after a short inspection tour of Lille in France – his corps' prospective forward base, on 14 April, he was assigned to command the land forces in Norway. His views about the Independent Companies bound for Narvik, Namsos and Alesund – which he related to Dill, among others – make for interesting reading in the context of his ideas about special forces.[10]

Auchinleck set off for Norway on 6 May with 'doubts about the value of the Independent Companies', later confiding to Dill that he felt, 'to be a successful guerilla, you must [operate] in your own country'. He added that 'the maintenance of small forces [is] almost impossible unless we can provide an adequate counter' to opposition both 'in the air or on the ground'. Indeed, after landing at Harstad on 11 May, he witnessed the Nazis' consolidation of their grip on the country, with British forces penned in at Mo and Bodo. Still, the Auk was impressed by Gubbins and determined to try to stall the enemy's advance by directing operations with his grab-bag of forces, while noting 'the danger of having too many small independent units in the field'.

Hence, Auchinleck relied on the 1st Scots Guards, and the untrained Independent Companies were not deployed as initially envisaged. Instead, they had mainly conventional reinforcement duties and precious little time to make an impact. When they were evacuated from the positions south of Narvik on 25 May, Auchinleck reiterated that 'guerillas could only work inside their own countries, which they would know better than the invading enemy', whereas 'guerillas in a foreign country' were unlikely to prove 'productive'.[11]

By 7 June, the whole Allied force was obliged to vacate Norway. The Independent Companies returned to Scotland having conducted few guerilla raids. Even so, they would prove a useful template for the recruitment of Special Service personnel and had laid the foundations for a broader acceptance within the British military establishment of special forces in the wartime order of battle. Further, the first active Special Service force of the war provided inspiration and some key personnel for those that followed.[12]

On his return home in June, Auchinleck took command of V Corps in southern England and was instructed by Churchill's confidant, the Secretary of State for War, Oliver Stanley, to be ready to stem Axis 'raids or attempted landings by parties carried in coastal vessels; sabotage, especially of the railway', and behind the lines parachute landings.[13] These were all operations that British forces like the Commandos and SAS would soon conduct.

Clarke, Wavell and Special Forces

One officer in Whitehall who was most active in the preparation of the Independent Companies was Captain Dudley Clarke. On their inception in April, he was at the centre of DMO planning. He had previously served in Mesopotamia in 1920 and on the staff of the Palestine Army HQ in 1936–9, before going on to Middle East HQ. On arriving in August 1937 to take command of British forces in the Holy Land, Wavell told his former aide-de-camp, Captain Bernard Fergusson (who would become a wartime Chindit and friend of future SAS commander, Mike Calvert), 'Never let yourself be trammelled by the bounds of orthodoxy . . . the herd is usually wrong.' This set the tone for Wavell's HQ staff, including Clarke, and afforded them the opportunity to think beyond the familiar and embrace innovation.[14]

As will be seen, Wavell nurtured some of Lawrence's ideas about unconventional warfare and, when Wavell and Clarke confronted Arab rebels in Palestine in 1937–8 (*also detailed later*), they used both tried-and-tested British internal security techniques[15] and encouraged adaptation. Indeed, before departing to take over Southern Command in the UK in mid-April 1938, Wavell made a special note of Clarke, whom he 'recognised [had] an original, unorthodox outlook'. He 'pigeonholed' Clarke's name 'for use should' he 'ever command an army in war'.[16] This would have a great bearing on the creation of the SAS, as the duo went on to play a key role in preparing the ground for it: Clarke proving instrumental to the formation of the Commandos, as well as – along with Wavell – providing Stirling the opportunity to develop his ideas about special forces in 1941 (not to mention devising the SAS's nomenclature).

Wavell's pivotal role is expounded in due course, but when the Commando concept came to the fore in the late spring of 1940, he is said to have been a sceptic, worrying that they would take the best 'men from . . . units'. His concern was shared by the CIGS, General Dill. Even so, Wavell – from 2 August 1939 Commander-in-Chief, Middle East – fostered special forces in his own backyard that would, in turn, make a major impression on Stirling and his colleagues.[17]

But, before unravelling the developments under way in the Middle East and the role played by Wavell and Clarke there, the latter's involvement in the formation of the Commandos should be considered, as they also had a big impact on Stirling and his friends.

Dill had commanded in Palestine before Wavell and Clarke worked on his Jerusalem staff and impressed him. Dill handed command to his friend, Wavell, on 12 September 1937, sharing his fellow officers' view that Wavell was 'something of a prophet' of military thought. Indeed, one contemporary, General Gordon Young, wrote that, 'In the British Army today there is only one good general . . . Wavell [and] he may well prove the dominant personality', as he was possessed of a 'freshness of conception which is the hallmark of all true thinkers'.[18]

The same could be said of Clarke, who, after the Arab Revolt petered out in 1939, travelled across Egypt and the Sudan before transferring to the DMO in London. By May 1940, he was once more working for Dill as the newly appointed CIGS's Military Assistant. Clarke travelled to Dublin to discuss the possibility of German parachute landings there and, fortuitously in the context of creating new British raiding forces, both of them had dealt with the threat of unconventional warfare in inter-war Palestine. On 30 May 1940, Clarke wrote a draft memo about raiding, noting that the enemy had 'air bases . . . communications [and] tired and hungry troops' that could be targeted by raiders. He continued that, 'History shows many examples of the damage small bodies of determined men can inflict' by guerilla action. This was exemplified by 'the Boers and' those resisting 'the Turks . . . in recent years' (who included the likes of Lawrence), and Clarke identified the 'enormous possibilities of creating havoc' with them.

On the final day of the Dunkirk evacuation – 3 June – the new Prime Minister, Winston Churchill, called on his War Cabinet to take the offensive against the all-conquering Germans. As a result, Clarke later noted that he 'tried to search through scattered memories of military history to find some precedent' of successful resistance against invaders. At his Stratton Street flat in London's Mayfair, Clarke mulled over the sporadic guerilla war, terrorism and other militant operations of Arab rebels in inter-war Palestine, and recalled those of the Spaniards who resisted Napoleon's forces during the Peninsular War of the 1800s.[19]

During that campaign, Spanish guerillas carried out hit-and-run attacks on French garrisons, ambushed their couriers, and interdicted their communications. The Peninsular War was a conflict about which Wavell is also said to have had a 'deep knowledge', and he and Clarke may well have discussed their shared interest before the war. Certainly, when it was over, Wavell wrote: 'I have always had a liking for unorthodox soldiering . . . Perhaps it was inherited [from] my grandfather . . . a soldier of fortune who fought with the Spanish in the Peninsular War'. He added that his own 'father did some of his soldiering in command of irregulars in expeditions against natives in South Africa' in 1880, while a cousin had raised an irregular corps of Arabs in 1914. Likewise, the South African example came to the forefront of both Churchill's and Clarke's thinking about irregulars early in June 1940, both having an intimate knowledge of that protracted conflict.[20]

Chapter 4

The Kommandos

Clarke and Churchill were among those most responsible for breaking the ground in which the seeds of Stirling's SAS idea could grow. Churchill's forward-looking approach to special forces stemmed both from discussions with his military advisors and his own grounding in unconventional warfare. A full account of the prime minister's character and military thinking lies outside the scope of this book, but it is worth noting that he visited Spanish forces fighting insurgents in Cuba in 1895 and fought at the Battle of Omdurman in Sudan in 1898. Moreover, as a war correspondent with the *Morning Post*, he covered the first months of the South African War of 1899–1902.

Soon after his arrival in the Cape Colony in October 1899, Churchill was hoisted from an armoured train by the Boer enemy. Held captive between mid-November and mid-December, he escaped and arrived in Ladysmith at the end of February 1900. He additionally witnessed the operations of both the Lovat Scouts and imperial mobile columns operating in April and May 1900, as well as eight small actions during a 400-mile advance over forty-five days alongside General Ian Hamilton. Churchill made Pretoria on 5 June and left the country on 4 July 1900.

Thanks to this adventure, Churchill was well aware of Boer guerilla operations from that spring, and he 'ever after admired the Kommandos for their courage and skill at arms'. Indeed, on his return to the UK, he wrote a best-selling 400-page tome, *The Boer War*, covering its first five months. He followed events thereafter 'closely' and lectured on the 'technical aspects of the war' at the United Services Institution in April 1901.[1]

Likewise, Clarke reflected in the late 1940s on the genesis of the British Commandos and noted how he had ruminated on the fact that the struggles of both the Boers and the Palestinian Arabs were 'the story of the Spaniards over again'. He remembered that, at that vital juncture in the summer of 1940, he jotted 'on a single sheet of paper' a memo for Dill that proposed 'the formation of a mobile, highly trained fighting force that could strike at widely dispersed targets on land or by sea [using] men armed only with weapons they could carry'. The Ministry of Information asserted in 1943 that Clarke 'produced the outline of a scheme which had been long in his mind',[2] but while details had yet to crystallise in his thoughts in mid-1940, Clarke had ample knowledge of past guerilla operations.

One writer avers that Clarke, like Churchill, was familiar with the operations of German stormtroopers during the spring offensive of March 1918, when the Allied line was breached by small units using 'shock tactics'. But Clarke's main focus was on the Boers, noting that they had 'found the same solution' to invasion as the Spanish had nearly a century earlier – guerilla missions against superior conventional forces. 'Their record I knew well enough', Clarke later recounted – he had been born in the Transvaal just before the war broke out. Indeed, his father had taken part in the infamous Jameson Raid of 1895 that helped spark it.[3] Additionally, a number of Clarke's colleagues shared his interest in the war, not least Wavell.

Wavell joined the Army in September 1901 and went to South Africa with the Black Watch that November. He became part of a mobile column led by Colonel 'Mike' Rimington that fought the Kommandos, whom Wavell acknowledged were 'adept at conceal-ment and surprise' attacks and 'capable of moving long distances by night and striking suddenly'. Rimington himself 'raised and com-manded an irregular corps' in the early stages of the war and, 'There was little . . . Wavell's first commander didn't know about the war of the veldt.' Wavell took part in extended night marches, 'endeavouring to hunt down and round up . . . Boers', as well as participating in large-scale drives against the Kommandos in the spring of 1902.

Wavell returned to Britain that October and subsequently reflected that, 'There was a great deal of trekking after the very mobile [Boer] columns, but the infantry seldom got a chance at the enemy.' Clarke shared Wavell's view that the Kommandos offered a fine example of the guerilla soldier and, when it came to considering how the British Army might resist the German onslaught in 1940, Clarke thought that the Boers 'seemed to provide a starting point for further thought'.[4]

On 4 June, Clarke outlined in a draft memo some of the key points about the Kommandos and their two-year resistance to the British. He knew that each Boer unit was an armed band of hand-picked men and he tapped into 'memories of their exploits [that] had long lingered' in his mind and were in part derived 'from the thrilling accounts of Deneys Reitz'. According to special forces author Robin Neillands, Clarke 'had read all the books on irregular warfare in the 20th century' up to that point. Neillands adds that Reitz's memoirs of the South African War 'inspired British soldiers' down the years, and a brief outline of the contents of Reitz's best-selling *Commando* – written in 1903, but published in the UK by Faber in 1929, followed four years later by *Trekking On* – offers an illuminating insight into how Clarke arrived at some of his conclusions about unconventional operations and incorporated them into his plan for 'Commandos'.[5]

Reitz's *Commando* emphasised that the Boer Kommandos' *raison d'être* was both to inflict damage on the British military, thereby wearing down its resources and will, and to boost the morale of the Afrikaners. They did so by operating in units of 300–500 men (later officially set at 462 all ranks), and Reitz's *Commando* reveals in detail what General Jan Christian Smuts called in its foreword the 'daredevilry' of the Boers.

Like many of his fellow Kommandos, Reitz was brought up to 'ride, shoot and swim' from an early age, and hunting, fishing and camping were second nature to him – as they were to men such as the Stirlings and Lovats. The Boer mounted infantry, who totalled 70,000-plus by 1900, foraged for food, used their exceptional marksmanship to pick off distant opponents, and retained 'superior mobility' over conventional military formations. As Reitz notes, the British 'troops being mainly infantry, their progress was slow and, although they were quickly at us', when spotted 'we were able to retire before them with very little loss'.

After the Boers suffered several major setbacks in set-piece confrontations with the British Army early on in the war, the Boer command altered its *modus operandi* 'to carry on . . . by means of guerilla tactics' rather than conventional positional and mobile warfare. The 'nucleus of a fresh army' of Kommandos was organised by Commandant-General Louis Botha during the spring of 1900, and the difficulty of the task facing their opponents grew exponentially.

Reitz's father was, along with General Smuts, among those in the Transvaal government who felt that 'guerilla war was best suited to the genius of the Boer people rather than regular field operations'. Indeed, tellingly, Reitz's father told his son about 'George Washington and ... other seemingly lost causes that had triumphed in the end', a trans-Atlantic reference that would crop up again in mid-1941.

Consequently, Reitz and his brother emulated the spirit of the American resistance by joining sixty other Boers in a band led by Austria's Baron von Goldeck that was 'grandiloquently called ... the German Corps'. It was a deceptive title for such a small unit and set a precedent for Clarke in 1940 when he emulated it by creating a fictitious 'SAS Brigade' as the cover name for a similarly sized force that formed part of his deception plans in the Middle East.

The Reitzes were soon pitted against their imperial foe in the field, and Deneys's account describes how the corps planned to scout towards Pretoria for Botha and skirmish with Lord Roberts's forces. However, in mid-1900, Reitz left the German Corps and joined the Pretoria Kommando under Max Theunissen. Facing a major sweep by 30,000-plus British infantry, cavalry and artillerymen, the Kommando retreated and, after the Boers' final pitched battle alongside levies such as Gravett's Guinea Fowls, they took to guerilla operations. Reitz recorded that 'it was planned' that the Kommandos would 'break away before the English advance and scatter in smaller bands', under the overall command of Botha. Reitz and his comrades then retreated to 'the mountains beyond Lyndeburg, where the[ir] forces were to be reorganised for the carrying on of guerilla warfare'.

Once his men were assembled, Botha led his guerillas into 'uncharted bush' and, early in September 1900, he began 'a new phase of the war' in which, Reitz asserted, 'each man [was] practically his own commander'. By the end of the year, Botha had 'mobile forces in every quarter of the Transvaal, harrying and worrying the British'. During one excursion, near Warm Baths, Reitz met Lodi Krause's group of hunter-patrol Kommandos, before moving south in December 1900 to attack an encampment under General Clements. There the Boer horsemen moved into position at night and followed their sniping with a dawn assault, under General de la Rey. In the event, the 500-strong camp that they assaulted beat back the Boers and inflicted a hundred casualties. Thereafter, Reitz made for Lichtenberg and Ermelo, 300-plus miles away.

While serving with Krause's Kommando, Reitz scouted the Johannesburg–Pretoria railway, undertook night marches and carried out another large-scale attack that resulted in hefty Boer losses. Consequently, Reitz noted, Botha 'hived us off into smaller bodies', though de la Rey still moved about the countryside in groups of up to 400 men.

In the spring of 1901, Reitz helped sabotage a railway line on the Cunana Reserve and 'toiled away' for several days at a time behind enemy lines. By this stage, de la Rey 'had dispersed his Kommandos into smaller bands, owing to the pressure of converging British columns. These bands ... were by now scattered all over west Transvaal.' Next, Reitz headed for the Cape Colony, and he reported that his 'knowledge of veldtcraft brought our party safely through to the River Vaal'. Avoiding British mobile columns in the vicinity, Reitz enthused that, 'We almost grew to enjoy the excitement of dodging the enemy forces and patrols.' He and his compatriots next made for Wanda Kop, where Botha's forces were conducting 'periodic raids' by 'small private bands' of eight men (interestingly, the standard size to this day of sub-units in both South Africa's special forces and the SAS Regiment, which followed their example).

After fording the Vet River, Reitz and his forty-strong party deployed their 'old tactics' of firing on British patrols and 'falling back to repeat the process'. Following these actions, he and ten colleagues made for the Cape under the guidance of Jack Borrius. En route they came across several groups of Boers who were 'dispersed in small guerilla bands among the mountains' and they arrived in the Cape pretty much unscathed in August 1901. There, they linked up with a unit commanded by Smuts, who planned to undertake a 'flying raid into the central districts' of the British colony, to assess the prospects of 'a large scale invasion later on'. Once in British territory, Reitz and his comrades 'scattered into small parties' and acted as scouts for the Rijk section of the Boer Army, foraging and ranging as they went. On 17 September 1901, Reitz and others carried out a surprise raid, led by Borrius, on a camp lodging 200 British troops of the 17th Lancers. Reitz reports that they were taken unawares by the Boers' 'sudden onslaught' and the capture of the camp was 'chiefly the handiwork of our original storming party', who were sensibly loathe to be 'involved in fighting other than of our own making', when surprise and superior force might be assured.

After forging across the Fish River in a party of five soldiers, Reitz entered the Sunday River Valley, where a skirmish resulted in three deaths among a band led by Ben Coetze. Reitz next headed for the Camdebo Mountains, where Smuts was using small parties to pathfind and avoid large British mobile column patrols. By now attached to a group of eight men under Swartzbergen, Reitz arrived in Oudtshoorn and again joined up with Smuts's forces in the Cape, where 'small bands of local rebels had long been' operating.

While Smuts planned to organise larger units to relieve the pressure on some of his other forces, Reitz made for Commandant Maritz's HQ in Van Rijnsdorp. He was the 'leader of various rebel bands' and, there, Reitz became part of Smuts's staff. By now, Smuts had decided that a major conventional counter-offensive could not be successfully staged by the Boers, and so he divided 'his forces into smaller groups'. In December 1901, he made for the Willems River, where he 'began his work of collecting the various rebels into organised Kommandos'.

In January 1902, Reitz travelled to the Orange River – where Smuts hoped to rally – and thence the Fish River. En route, Reitz participated in raids against encampments to acquire horses, and he received orders to muster with other small patrols at Van Rijnsdorp. Kommandos led by van Dewenter and Bouwer arrived there and, subsequently, launched raids against Windhoek, taking 200 British PoWs in the process, after which Smuts again 'distributed the [Boer forces] . . . in small patrols'.

After travelling to Namaqualand, Kamiesbergen and Springbok, Reitz witnessed a major attack by 400 Boers on a fortified British blockhouse of 120-plus officers and men. Having stormed it, the Kommando made for O'Okiep and the British HQ at Concordia, where two more blockhouses were assaulted. Reitz notes how he and his companions 'crawled stealthily' until spotted by a sentry and, although one of their night raids failed to achieve its objective, the other – involving twenty of Maritz's men, led by Coetze – netted 200 or so British prisoners.

Finally, in April 1902, Reitz was involved in sniping against British units near O'Okiep, when news came through of the peace settlement at Vereeniging, bringing the campaign to an end.[6] Reitz's recollections made a deep impression on Dudley Clarke. And a similar impact was very likely made by the Lovat Scouts on others in the SAS's story, not least David Stirling.

The Lovat Scouts

Formed by Simon Joseph Fraser, 16th Lord Lovat, the Scouts that bore his name originated as a result of the laird's recognition that the Army had insufficient reconnaissance forces to confront the fleeting Boer opposition. Having arrived in South Africa in 1898 in search of new farmland, he admired the Boers for their 'skill and fighting qualities'. In autumn 1899, when the war broke out, he had 'the idea of raising a corps ... skilled in the use of the telescope' for observation and sniping – as he was himself. He 'proposed a scheme to raise 150 stalkers and ghillies from his own and other estates', who possessed extensive experience of stalking prey. He emphasised that 'the high-landers' knowledge of ground and capacity for handling a rifle and telescope' could be invaluable and, on 12 December 1899, Lovat per-suaded his friends at the War Office to accede to his request to create two companies of Scouts – one mounted, one foot. They would be commanded by a War Office appointee, Major Andrew Murray, Queen's Own Cameron Highlanders, a Sudan veteran and 'officer of rare capacity and courage'. Lovat would lead the mounted infantry section, while Captain V. Stewart, Argyll and Sutherland Highlanders, led the Scouts' foot company.

Of 1,500 men who volunteered for the Scouts early in 1900, over a hundred came from Lovat's estates. The Scouts were to comprise a dozen officers and 224 other ranks, and those selected would be trained in mounted reconnaissance work, scouting, day and night patrolling, and fieldcraft. This was done on the Beaufort estate between January and March 1900, while Simon's brother, Hugh Fraser – a fine marksman – offered them musketry tuition. All the Scouts' officers were selected by Lord Lovat, and they and their foot soldiers arrived in the Cape Colony on 31 March 1900. They were followed by the horse on 17 April, and both were thrown into the fray during May, being deployed so as to make best use of their 'marksmanship and special skills in scouting, spying and patrolling' in both large and small bodies.

Following Lovat's proposals to his field commander, General Hector MacDonald, the Scouts 'frequently' operated as 'very small parties of men [who] would go out and, after long periods away, would return having gathered vital information' in their four-man telescope parties. Another British commander, General Sir Archibald Hunter, subsequently noted that, 'in ones, twos and threes, these men crept . . . and spied . . . for days at a time, but always came back safely'. He added that, 'As scouts, spies, guides, on foot or pony, as individual marksmen or as a collective body . . . they are a splendid band.'

In April 1901, Lovat returned to Scotland to raise the 2nd Lovat Scouts from two companies of Imperial Yeomanry. 'The speed with which the Scouts were formed and their enormous popularity', one contemporary commentator noted, 'can be attributed to the inspiration and prestige created by the daring exploits of the contingents' serving in South Africa. Among the successes attributed to them was the capture of Retief's Nek – one of three passes on the Caledon River held by Boer forces – following a reconnaissance conducted by the Scouts.

On another occasion, on 7 July 1901, when a patrol under Captain William McDonald spotted enemy forces at Vaal Krantz, Lovat arranged with McDonald and Major Murray to take a hundred Scouts 'to the top of the ridge through the night' and then attack the position. After a flank reconnaissance by two Scout sections under Captain Evan Grant, they decided to probe the opposition, but MacDonald ruled that the Scouts 'were too valuable to be employed' in this way, and the assault was left to the Highland Light Infantry.

Still, the Scouts had proven their worth and, when their one-year period of voluntary service was over, a second batch of Scouts arrived in South Africa to replace them in July 1901. They were followed by a third contingent formed that October, who saw service in August 1902. By that stage, the Scouts were organised into 500-strong regiments, each comprising eight 'squadrons' of sixty all ranks (a similar size and nomenclature, incidentally, to that adopted by Stirling for the fledgling SAS in 1941).

In the interim, the Scouts took part in numerous engagements and, during the autumn and winter of 1901, Lovat noted that they were 'in constant touch with the enemy'. General Hamilton added that, 'The Scouts were the only troops who ever saw the Boers before they were seen.' The Lovat Scouts suffered one major loss, in September 1901, when Murray's camp was surprised at night at Guadeberg by Kruitzinger's Kommando. Lovat lost two officers and nine men, plus thirty-one wounded. But the Scouts were undaunted and they were 'actively engaged' until the war against the Kommandos petered out in the summer of 1902.

At this point, the Scouts faced disbandment by the War Office, but Lovat fought successfully for a nucleus of his stalkers to be retained, upon which a corps could be built again, should the need arise in a future emergency. However, not unexpectedly, the War Office dragged its feet over arrangements in this regard, though its officials agreed to gazette two regiments of Imperial Yeomanry in February 1903, while a school for scouting was retained at Beaufort.[7] The Lovat Scouts were gone but not forgotten, least of all by Lord Lovat's son and heir or his cousins, the Stirlings, while the likes of Clarke and Wavell were familiar with them from their studies of the Boer War.

Chapter 5

The Desert Raiders

During his ruminations on raiding forces, Clarke referred to the anti-Ottoman resistance, which was catalysed in part by T. E. Lawrence, whose activities impressed the likes of Wavell and Churchill. Indeed, Churchill became one of Lawrence's leading admirers and spent considerable time in his company, not least when Lawrence became his special advisor at the Colonial Office in 1921–2. Hence, his actions and influence require further elaboration.

After 1918, Lawrence was a vocal proponent of behind the lines raiding and, although his eccentricities meant that 'the darling of the literary world' became the 'bane of the officers' mess', his experience with the 'Arab forces of Sherif Hussein and his sons produced both an example and a theory of warfare that became legendary'. While his overall contribution to the war effort is still debated by historians, 'He did provide valuable assistance to the main British forces at very little cost in British resources and Arab lives.'[1]

In December 1914, Lawrence travelled to the Sinai to assess the British position in Palestine vis-à-vis the Turkish foe. He joined the Intelligence section at GHQ Middle East and became a regular at Shepheards Hotel on Cairo's Ibrahim Pasha Street, a military watering hole with a stylish Moorish Hall lounge dating to 1841. It would become a redoubt for many of the SAS's originals, including Stirling, as well as Dudley Clarke.

Lawrence undertook map surveys and the collation of intelligence, mirroring the activities of the 'Great Gamers' of the Afghan–Russian border in the previous century. Then, in March 1916, he left Cairo for Basra in Mesopotamia, with a view to trying to ascertain how to relieve pressure on the hard-pressed British forces in the region. On 5 June 1916, egged on by GHQ Middle East, Arab rebels revolted against their overlords. The 50,000-strong movement based on the Hejaz region of western Arabia knew that the 16,000-plus occupying Turkish troops relied on the Medina–Damascus railway for many of their supplies, and it became a focus for their raids. However, when the revolt 'wavered in the face of Turkish military superiority', Lawrence was sent to decide how the British might furnish further assistance.

In October 1916, Lawrence discussed the state of play with British Army liaison officers attached to the Arab forces, including one at Jeddah (which had fallen to the Arabs that June, soon after the capture of Mecca). Lawrence conferred too with Arab partisan leaders and, by November, he had determined that the Arabs should be assisted by a British military advisory mission. In fact, such a task force was already being constituted and, after making his report, Lawrence was attached to it as a liaison officer.

It was at this time, Lawrence later reflected, that he 'formulated his ideas on the best way for the revolt to proceed'. He saw, as did 'David Stirling and his colleagues . . . 23 years later', that the desert could be an ideal environment in which to conceal small mobile raiding forces who could attack the enemy at will, using local intelligence to hit enemy communications, not least the railway infrastructure. Indeed, Stirling was at least conversant with the desert war of 1914–18, having been apprised by his friend Callum Douglas of Douglas's father's activities in the Libyan desert at that time (where the SAS would itself operate in 1941).[2]

By January 1917, Lawrence was ready to unveil his guerilla strategy, and assaults on the Hejaz railway were conducted until the end of hostilities in October 1918. Although his operations were only an adjunct to the main campaigns against the Ottomans in Palestine and Mesopotamia, the Arabs successfully conducted numerous raids across southern Arabia. Lawrence participated in 'several small-scale ambushes and sabotage attacks against Turkish installations'. Further, by July, he had secured permission from General Allenby (commander in Palestine and himself a supporter of military innovation, not least in developing deception techniques to hoodwink enemy intelligence, such as the use of decoy and dummy forces – which, in turn, inspired the likes of Wavell) to organise raids from Aqaba. The rebel leader Feisal's forces concentrated their attacks on Turkish communications and garrisons and, as the Turks gradually withdrew from the Arabian desert towards Syria, they offered less widely dispersed targets that were more vulnerable to conventional frontal assaults. Their supply routes continued to be interdicted by small rebel forces as well, and Lawrence's strategy of tactical raids proved both psychologically and militarily worthwhile.[3]

Although successive leading figures in the British military establishment criticised Lawrence during the inter-war years – despising his unorthodox style of command, demeanour and lifestyle – Churchill held his military achievements in high regard. This was in no small part due to the colonel's best-selling account of his deeds of derring-do, *Seven Pillars of Wisdom*. Equally significantly, it was required reading for both Wavell and Clarke. Given the impact of Lawrence's account on so many British proponents of unorthodox military operations, an outline of what he had to say about his exploits is enlightening.

By the time that *Seven Pillars of Wisdom* was published in 1926, the legend of 'Lawrence of Arabia' was firmly embedded in the British public psyche, and he has since been called 'arguably the best-known Englishman of the 20th century' (though he was born in Wales, of Scottish and Irish parents).[4] In 1919–20, over a million Londoners attended American journalist Lowell Thomas's slide-and-lecture shows about Lawrence. The *Revolt in the Desert* spectacle at London's Royal Albert Hall, backed by the band of the Welsh Guards (Lawrence's birthplace was Tremadoc, Gwynedd), caused a sensation, and *Seven Pillars* sold 30,000-plus copies within weeks of publication. It was followed by Robert Graves's biography, *Lawrence and the Arabs*, which flew off the shelves at a rate of 10,000 a week. Churchill was one of the admirers who devoured every word about this extraordinary figure, and the former war reporter became 'a hero-worshipper'.[5]

Lawrence himself wrote in *Seven Pillars* that, while the Arabs were armed in 1917 with 'Boer War antiquities', their 'tribal raids' inflicted damage on the Turks everywhere from Medina to the wind-swept hills over seventy miles away. His key role was to 'develop the sporadic raiding activity [into a] self-supporting' campaign of resistance. One of Lawrence's colleagues, Zeid, 'agreed to go down to Rabegh to organise similar pin pricks in the Turks' rear', and Lawrence noted that, 'to exercise my own hand in the raiding genre', on 2 January 1917, 'I took a test party of thirty-five Mahamid' fighters on a camel-back night march through the Dhifran Hills. Lawrence and twenty-five men, with ten left guarding the camels, climbed the dusty slopes and laid up overnight, ready for a hit-and-run raid in the morning. After this dry run, Lawrence called on Sidi Abdullah at Henakiyeh and urged him to organise a raiding party to threaten the Turkish railways north of Medina, before himself heading to Wejh.[6] In a strangely prescient incident that would be mirrored by Stirling's own experiences twenty-four years later, Lawrence was incapacitated for a time and consequently mulled over the current campaign, with beneficial results.

Despite being stricken by 'fever and dysentery ... while lying alone with empty hands', Lawrence was 'driven to think about the campaign [and to] meditate upon the strategy and tactics of irregular warfare'. He recounts in his memoir that this period of enforced 'thinking convinced me that our recent practice had been better than our theory. So, on recovery, I ... went back to Wejh with novel ideas' in mind. He saw that irregulars 'remained incapable of forcing a decision', but that 'their virtue lay in depth, not in force'. He therefore 'decided to slip off to Aqaba' to test out his 'own theory' of non-conventional combat.

Lawrence was keenly aware that, if he was to continue operating with his Arab allies, they would need to prove their worth to the British high command – a situation that the SAS would find itself in during its fledgling months. He noted that, 'In the army our shares rose as we showed profit', and he was determined to maximise the return of the rebels' raiding efforts by honing their *modus operandi*. To this end, he made for another Arab partisan leader, Abdullah, based at Wadi Ais. There, Lawrence sought to deter the Turks from undertaking offensive action in the vicinity 'by making so many small raids on' a nearby railway 'that traffic would be seriously disorganised', obliging the Turks to adopt a defensive posture in the locale.

After travelling through the Jidhwa Hills and falling ill again, Lawrence felt that, during the course of eight days on his sickbed, his mind had 'cleared [and] my sense became more acute' with regard to what was needed to undermine the Turks' position. This enforced period of inaction allowed him to 'look for the equation between my book reading' of military philosophers – such as Clausewitz, Napoleon, Jomini and Foch – 'and my movements' in the desert. He also cited Moltke, Saxe and other military writers, and he began 'to recall suitable maxims' that might be pertinent to his and the Arabs' situation. However, he found that 'they would not fit, and it worried' him. Hence, Lawrence decided to 'find an alternative end and means of war'.[7]

He 'began to calculate how many square miles' the Turks had to defend – a figure of 140,000, by his reckoning. 'Suppose we were,' he ruminated, 'an influence, an idea, a thing intangible, invulnerable, without front or back'. He asserted that the Turks would need 600,000 men to patrol all the land to which they laid claim. Clearly, they could not do this without sufficient supplies, yet in Turkey such things were already 'scarce and precious'. Hence, Lawrence saw that 'our cue was to destroy, not the Turk's army, but his minerals' and manufactured wares. 'The death of a Turkish bridge or rail, machine or gun, or charge of high explosive, was more profitable' than attacking the Turk himself.

Lawrence's and the Arabs' method 'would be a war of detachment', in which 'dispersal was strength', as native forces would 'contain the enemy by the silent threat of a vast unknown desert, not disclosing ourselves until we attacked … against his … most accessible material'. Surprise and the initiative would be retained through this mosquito-bite strategy.

Indeed, Lawrence sought to 'develop a habit of never engaging the enemy' except on his own as opposed to the Turks' terms. The 'aim was to seek the enemy's weakest material link and bear only on that till time made their whole length fail'. The crux was to 'impose on the Turks the longest possible passive defence', by using a 'highly mobile, highly equipped striking force of the smallest size' against widely 'distributed points of the Turkish line'. This would oblige the foe 'to strengthen their posts' or withdraw in the face of 'maximum loss and discomfort'. It was a psychological as well as a physical war that Lawrence sought to wage, aiming to 'arrange the minds of the enemy' by playing the cards of 'speed and time, not hitting power'. He would achieve 'victory without battle', using the desert where 'range was more than force, speed greater than the power of armies'.

At the same time, the rebels boasted 'the virtues of secrecy and self-control . . . speed, endurance and independence of . . . supply', not to mention the Bedouins' 'toughness, self-assurance, knowledge of the country' and 'intelligent courage'. In other words, they possessed the key military virtues of mobility, economy of force, intelligence, fieldcraft and surprise – all valuable ingredients for successful guerilla operations. Later on in his book, Lawrence summarised his raiding ideas and drew an analogy between naval warfare and his 'unorthodox' parties. He argued that guerilla action should mirror that on the sea with respect to 'mobility, ubiquity, independence of bases and communications, ignoring of guard features, of strategic areas, of fixed directions, of fixed points'. Camel-borne groups – literal ships of the desert – would be 'self-contained like ships' on the ocean. He reiterated that, 'Our tactics should be tip and run', and that, 'We should use the smallest force in quickest time at the farthest place.' He added that raiders must be capable of operating at great distances for unusually long periods of up to six weeks, with the 'widest dissipation of force' making 'our battle a series of single combats'.[8]

Following Lawrence's exposition of the foundations of guerilla success, he set out to reconnoitre the Aba el Naam railway station, laying up nearby with his men and overseeing a large-scale raid conducted by 300-plus fighters. Although they failed to assail the targeted garrison, Lawrence left two smaller parties to carry out sabotage in the locality in the following days, and tracks and bridges were hit 'at speed'. Indeed, there were enough 'parties on the railway . . . to do a demolition . . . every day or so'.

Lawrence next headed for Bair with 500 men, using hills and mountains that were 'better suited to our tactics' and where a number of bridges were mined and blown up. After one major skirmish with a Turkish column, Lawrence's forces arrived at Waheida in July 1917 and, that September, he set out to assault a water station at Mudowara with 300 irregulars. Following another major set-to, Lawrence determined to head for targets 'where our weight and tactics would be least expected and most damaging'. Hence, Dera'a was singled out, since it was the junction of the Jerusalem, Haifa, Damascus and Medina railways. At the same time, in order to foment further Arab unrest, Lawrence emphasised the need to 'undertake some operations in the enemy rear'. He identified several bridges in the Yarmuk valley as ideal targets, for a breach of the railway there would isolate the Turkish garrison from Damascus for at least a fortnight. As Lawrence realised, 'The Turks thought the danger from us so remote that they guarded bridges insufficiently.'

Lawrence planned to attack on 5 November 1917, moving with fifty men from Azrak to Um Keis and then the Yarmuk River valley. He, Sapper Woods and thirty men aimed to assault the bridges, which were guarded by only half a dozen sentries, using cover provided by Indian machine-gunners. En route to their destination, they cut Ottoman telegraph wires and, when they got to the bridges, they approached with sacks filled by explosive charges of thirty pounds of gelignite, which they laid on the bridges at night. However, when they were discovered by a guard, a firefight broke out and Lawrence's party was obliged to withdraw from the Tel el Shebab bridge. Still, another party laid a railway mine and undertook a second, successful bridge assault, which was followed by an orderly general dispersal from the area in small groups.

After returning to Cairo, Lawrence experimented with revised demolition techniques and, over the course of a week, developed a 'special dynamite', thereby presaging experiments conducted by Jock Lewes and the SAS in their formative months. After spending Christmas at Aqaba – during which time the Arabs continued to carry out raiding and railway sabotage operations south of Maan and Medina – Lawrence moved to Guweira. There, he planned operations in Tafilah, including hitting the railway station at Jurf, on the Hejaz main line.

Next came a raid on the Turkish forces near the Dead Sea and at Kerak on 28 January 1918, and this was followed by several scouting operations for Allenby in Jordan. Back at GHQ, Lawrence drew up new plans for raids against the Maan garrison, severing of rail supplies to Medina, and even lengthier desert patrols. Indeed, to this end, Allenby provided motor transport for Lawrence, so that, as the desert raider put it, 'we might have longer range and more mobility', setting another precedent for the Desert War of 1941. Subsequent raids were aimed at 'diverting the Turkish effort to relieve its garrisons' from the pressure exerted on them by the Arabs, and to 'draw off one division of the enemy from Palestine', thereby easing Allenby's advance northwards.

By this stage, Lawrence's forces had grown to 3,000-plus and small parties frequently broke off to hit Ottoman railway lines, with numerous raids led by 'Nasir, our best guerilla general'. In addition, the Arabs carried out offensive patrols in armoured cars, as well as some with artillery support. Clearly, Lawrence's expeditions were taking on a more conventional character, and Allenby planned to use the rebels as an adjunct to his main advance in the Holy Land in September 1918. But, to this end, he also called for more diversionary raids by the Arabs as part of a deception plan that incorporated dummy camps, troops and horses. As part of the overall effort, Lawrence was instructed to cut three railway lines and afterwards make for the desert, carrying three weeks' worth of supplies with him to pursue his raiding plans. Better Turkish defences on key bridges prevented a successful strike by resistance forces at Dera'a, but with air support and armoured cars, Lawrence's camel columns made for Azrak and uprooted the railroads at Mafrak, Arar and Mezerib, before joining Allenby's main forces in their ongoing advance.[9]

As part of the gradual reorientation of Lawrence's forces to conventional fighting from the summer of 1918, they acquired the services of a GHQ observer and military intelligence officer, Major Wilfred 'Will' Frank Stirling (a distant albeit unbeknown cousin of David). Will was, according to Lawrence, 'a skilled staff officer, tactful and wise', and had 'worked with Lawrence . . . in Cairo'. Will Stirling later recorded Lawrence's map work and unusual style of leadership, while he was himself regarded as something of a 'swashbuckler', having been brought up at Hampton Court with the renowned Zeebrugge raid commander, Admiral Sir Roger Keyes, as a neighbour, as well as spending summers at the hunting estate of an uncle in Scotland. In 1899, Will Stirling had served in South Africa with the 5th Irish Brigade, before becoming a staff officer at GHQ Ismailia in 1915. He would go on to become chief political officer at the Cairo GHQ in 1919, as well as a military advisor to King Zog of Albania in the 1930s and a member of SOE in the Middle East in 1940 (for which David's brother Bill worked at that time).

Will Stirling travelled with Lawrence's column by Vauxhall motor car until September 1918, when they forged on in armoured cars as part of the final push for Damascus on 1 October 1918.[10]

There is no evidence that David Stirling was aware of his name-sake's activities but, it is interesting to note that, when Will Stirling returned to Cairo in 1940, he met Wavell and subsequently noted that 'Wavell and I were very old friends'.[11] If nothing else, this demonstrates that the family name was known both at GHQ and among the Cairo social set, which might have assisted David Stirling when he made his red tape-cutting visit to Grey Pillars some months later.

On their way to Damascus in September 1918, Lawrence's men once more cut telegraph wires, blew up bridges and hit the Umtaiye aerodrome with their armoured cars, before catching up with Will Stirling at Dera'a and surging into Syria. Soon afterwards, the war in the Middle East came to an abrupt end with Allenby's defeat of the Turks in October 1918.[12]

All this was meat and drink to Churchill and other admirers of Lawrence, and the idea of using motor transport as a means to traverse the desert for offensive raiding operations was taken up in the Middle East from the Italian declaration of war in June 1940, not least by Wavell. Indeed, it is worth noting that, when Lawrence was killed in a motorcycle accident in May 1935, his funeral was attended by only a 'small crowd of mourners'. Among them were both Churchill and the man who would sanction a motor-transported desert special force in mid-1940 – Wavell.

After serving as a staff liaison officer between the CIGS, General Robertson, and Allenby, in Palestine during 1917 – from whom he learnt the value of 'surprise and deception' – Wavell was one of twenty officers who attended a victory parade in Jerusalem in December 1918. Another of that select band was Lawrence, who stood next to Wavell. They subsequently bumped into each other on occasion and, when Wavell was transferred in 1919 to the Palestine HQ, Lawrence 'warmly welcomed the appointment'. Like Lawrence, Wavell favoured the out-of-the-ordinary in military matters, having served in South Africa, faced the Pathan tribes of the North-West Frontier, worked during the Great War for MI5 in France, and operated as part of a wartime military mission to Russia. Indeed, while in Palestine, Lawrence 'strongly supported him, both then and in later years', and he and Wavell sometimes socialised together at Shepheards.

Wavell returned to the UK in the early 1920s but, in May 1923,

Lawrence wrote to him from the Royal Tank Corps at Bovington, Dorset, on the subject of 'raiding techniques', emphasising the value of desert patrolling. By 1930, Lawrence and Wavell had renewed their 'acquaintance and [Wavell] earned the respect of ... Lawrence'. Indeed, when Wavell commanded the 6th Infantry Brigade at Aldershot and Lawrence was serving with the RAF, they enthusiastically 'discussed in talk and on paper' Lawrence's 'theory of irregular warfare'.

Wavell thought that Lawrence was 'a very charming acquaintance' and spoke of his 'greatness', even going so far as to contribute an essay about him for a posthumous published tribute compiled by A. W. Lawrence, *T. E. Lawrence: By His Friends*.[13] As Lord Carver notes, Lawrence had 'a significant influence on Wavell's predilection for irregular methods' and, by June 1940, he, Clarke and Churchill were 'championing a form of war which Lawrence had hoped to render comprehensible and appealing'.[14]

The Arab Rebellion

When Dudley Clarke wrote his June 1940 report on raiding for General Dill, he also drew on the experience, shared by Wavell, of the Arab Rebellion of 1936–9. Clarke wrote that, 'when one came to think of it', the example of the Peninsular War had been 'followed later with some profit by the Palestinian Arabs' in the late 1930s, and he recalled 'how a handful of ill-armed fanatics' had neutralised 'the strength of ... an Army corps of regular troops'. He concluded that similarly organised British raiding forces might be able to divert large numbers of German troops.

On 5 June 1940, Clarke apprised Dill of his thoughts, noting that his ideas were informed by his 'experiences gained as his GSO2 at the time of the Arab Rebellion' in Palestine.[15] While details about its genesis and evolution can be found elsewhere,[16] a brief outline of the situation in the Holy Land will clarify Clarke's thinking about it with regard to his proposals for new raiding forces.

The British Mandatory authority had faced Arab opposition to its rule in Palestine in the recent past – such as major urban rioting in 1929 – but it was only in the spring of 1936 that a fledgling insurgent movement grew in the countryside and towns from of a wave of anti-

imperialist strikes, propaganda, demonstrations and civil dis-
obedience. The turmoil was sparked by economic unrest, along with
underlying racial, religious, clan and land issue tensions, as well as
political pressure from various parties for Arab dominance of the
government's advisory Legislative Council. Guerillas set about
sabotaging railways and telegraph lines and carried out arson and
assassinations, while strike committees demanded an Arab nationalist
government and, critically, a halt to Jewish immigration into and land
acquisitions in the Holy Land. Following anti-Jewish riots in Jaffa, a
general strike in October 1936 was threatened by the Arab Higher
Committee, and Arab irregulars attacked Jewish settlements and
British security forces.

Between May and October 1936, a terrorist campaign targeted
Jewish communities, civil buildings and the British Palestine Police
Force, and groups of irregulars undertook sporadic guerilla raids on
British military installations. The authorities responded by deporting
sixty Palestinian Arab leaders and implementing punitive measures
such as village cordons, searches and curfews. But the turmoil and
anti-British propaganda increased and rival Arab guerilla factions
began to co-operate for the first time. The security forces found it
difficult to deal with the small bands facing them and these soon grew
into groups of up to seventy. In July 1936, the Army undertook urban
cordon-and-searches but terrorism continued. Fortunately for the
authorities, while the number of incidents grew and they were better
co-ordinated, internecine splits soon appeared among the rebels.

In September, the British administration adopted the time-
honoured approach of proposing a royal commission to look into the
troubles, focusing in this case on the question of Jewish immigration.
The GOC Palestine, Dill, simultaneously called for statutory martial law
if the threatened general strike went ahead and, in the face of the
government's carrot-and-stick approach, it was called off by the Arab
National Congress. Thereafter, most of the Arab fighters melted away,
while the newly appointed Peel Commission investigated the issues
that most troubled the Arab community. Its report of July 1937,
however, floated the idea of territorial partition and proposed reduced
rather than curtailed Jewish immigration, sparking renewed rebellion.
From August 1937 – as Wavell prepared to take over as GOC – the

number of attacks on British forces and Jewish settlers rose and more Arab leaders were arrested that October.

Following numerous skirmishes with British conventional forces which resulted in heavy Arab losses – not least due to Wavell's more extensive use of air power, motorised infantry, and radio communications, as well as village occupations by the security forces – by the spring of 1938, the focus of the Arabs' campaign once more shifted to guerilla raids and urban terrorism. By that summer, they again had the run of most rural mountainous districts and, in September 1938, the rebellion peaked, with nearly 200 murders (from a total of 3,000 deaths).

The British reacted with more punitive measures like demolitions, summary courts, collective fines, Army direction of policing, identity cards and over a hundred executions, as well as block-houses and wire barriers to impede rebel movement. In 1939, a political conference in London and unrest among the Arab population about the rebellion, combined with splits between and within groups of politicised urban activists and traditionalist, parochial, feuding rural militants, meant that the rebellion ground to a halt, putting paid to the nationalist cause.[17] However, by that juncture, many senior British officers recognised the difficulties that had faced the British security forces and accepted that traditional methods of coercion were not enough to deal with the insurgent threat.

Special Night Squads

Indeed, early in 1938, in a manner redolent of David Stirling's approach to Ritchie and Auchinleck three years later, Wavell was accosted while GOC Palestine by a British officer who proposed to create an unorthodox military special force.

Captain Orde Wingate – who, as Christopher Sykes notes, was a distant relative of T. E. Lawrence and would himself become a legendary maverick wartime advocate of special forces, by turns influencing the likes of Wavell, Clarke, Churchill and Calvert – had arrived in Palestine in September 1936. An Arabic speaker, he was 5th Division's Intelligence Officer and a recognised expert on Arab affairs. Wavell knew Orde's relation, General Sir Reginald Wingate, and arranged to meet the Intelligence staff officer in the autumn of 1937, along with the commander of the 16th Infantry Brigade in North Palestine, Brigadier John Evetts, who was charged with restoring law and order there. At this meeting, the GOC learned of the pro-Zionist Wingate's close contacts with the Jewish community. With his own 'taste for the unorthodox', Wavell ordered Wingate to locate the trails being used by Arab irregulars to bring weapons into Palestine from neighbouring territories.

Wingate proceeded to do so from a base at Tirat Tsevi, using supernumerary police recruited from the Jewish settlements. By early 1938, he had come up with the idea of 'Special Night Squads' (SNS) that could conduct patrols around Jewish settlements and counter incoming Arab raiders. Evetts supported Wingate's idea but the HQ staff in Jerusalem opposed the establishment of a Jewish military force. Hence, Wingate sought to go over their heads by securing a meeting with Wavell. When he failed to get one, in February 1938, Wingate – who possessed 'a readiness to risk official displeasure' – flagged down Wavell's staff car to present him with his ideas in person. He knew from Wavell's reputation that 'the Chief' was 'always prepared to learn anew and to alter his ideas'. Wingate guessed correctly that, 'He was the last man to be annoyed by juniors jumping into his car, provided that they had something interesting to tell him', and the general allowed his intuition to 'influence his decisions'.

Wavell gave Wingate permission to create the SNS, which were meant to prevent the intimidation of the population, elicit public co-operation, cut the links between the Arabs and their support structure among the populace, and re-establish government writ in these locales. Although Wavell was replaced by General Sir Robert Haining in mid-April 1938, he kept tabs on SNS operations, as did the Palestine Army HQ staff, including Clarke.[18]

Wingate and seven men carried out reconnaissance patrols before reporting early in May 1938 to Evetts in Jerusalem. From then on, the SNS tried to stem Fawzi Kawalyi's raids against the Iraq Petroleum Company's pipelines near Hanita, on the Levant border, and two SNS platoons in rubber-soled shoes and civilian clothes operated in north-east Palestine from four outposts. After a short period of training, the first operations began on 3 June, the SNS comprising about eighty Jewish police and other volunteers, backed by Wingate's second-in-command, Lieutenant Bredin, along with three officers and thirty-six men from 16th Infantry Brigade. The SNS was organised into nine units, two of which mustered in Wingate's base camp at Ein Harod on 11 June. These patrols each had ten men and one officer from the Royal Ulster Rifles, along with ten Jewish policemen (while other SNS units had men from the Royal West Kent and Manchester Regiments).

Using a deception plan including the use of civilian cars and pre-arranged signals, the first patrols made for Beisan, where scouts escorted them in single file onto trails leading to oil pipelines. They marched to Danna and there chased an Arab raiding party that had sabotaged one. Such patrols continued throughout June, each lasting for unusually extended periods of ten days or more. Nightly patrols were undertaken and six engagements were recorded that month. One, on 28 June, involved an eight-man SNS patrol deploying by lorry before hitting an Arab raiding party of seventy and withdrawing to the Jewish settlement at Beit Yosef. During July, the SNS patrolled around their four strongholds, operating on information received about Arab movements. On the 5th, Bredin and eight men routed a hundred Arabs north of Ein Harod, while Wingate was involved in an operation on 10 July at Dabburiya. His party moved into the area by lorry and undertook a night march to their target. This was hit by forty-five SNS men, though one patrol was ambushed and Wingate was hit by 'friendly fire'. A second attack by Bredin dispersed the Arab rebels, while Wingate spent two weeks in hospital recovering.

On 13 July, Bredin's patrol inflicted fourteen fatalities on the opposition at Bira and Wingate went back into action at Um Mejeida, near Beisan, on 30 July, successfully ambushing a group of arms smugglers infiltrating via Trans-Jordan. By this point, Wingate felt that the SNS had proven their worth and, after abandoning the idea of adding a thirty-man cavalry wing, he gained approval to double the size of the SNS by September 1938.

By then, the Arabs had been reduced to a handful of successful pipeline attacks and, at Khirbet Beit Lidd, another fourteen rebels were killed in an assault led by Wingate on Shaykh Tahir's camp. The tally increased by a dozen at Danna on 23 September and more successes followed early in October at Karf Mesha and Tiberias. However, at this stage, General Haining sent Clarke to warn Wingate that he was losing patience with his predilection for 'only obeying orders that suited him'. He was told to mend his ways or face the consequences, and Wingate did so.[19]

In fact, Wingate had already arranged to leave Palestine for London, citing 'personal matters' while arranging to meet Zionist leaders to offer them support. In the UK, Wingate got in touch with Churchill through military scholar Captain Basil Liddell Hart, who 'had read a memo given to him by Wingate on his SNS theory and practice, and had subsequently transmitted this to . . . Churchill, who had expressed an interest' in hearing more about it. On 30 November 1938, the two met, and Wingate related 'for about 10 minutes' how he had formed and run the SNS. Churchill was reportedly most impressed and called his efforts 'great actions'.[20]

The SNS founder returned to Palestine in December 1938, where Bredin had taken charge of the force. However, the authorities had become concerned that the SNS's successes might antagonise the Arab population and add fuel to the fire of rebellion at a time when it was being snuffed out. Hence, after further patrols in January 1939, and amid accusations of mistreatment of some captured rebels, the SNS were disbanded. Still, it was a major departure in British internal security theory and practice, and it made a lasting impression on several players in the SAS story.

Furthermore, following the German onslaught in Europe, on 1 June 1940 Wingate arrived in the UK and met General Sir Edmund Ironside, who had been CIGS until Dill took over from him on 27 May and was now CINC Home Forces. In the face of the Nazi invasion threat, Wingate proposed creating 'a special type of unit to deal with penetration by enemy units behind the lines, either by tanks, parachutists or airborne troops'. Wingate met the Director of Military Intelligence, General Beaumont-Nesbitt, and reiterated the potential value of an SNS-type force to deal with German invaders. The DMI raised no objections and, on 11 June, Wingate travelled to York to discuss setting up such a unit in Northern Command. However, events overtook him and, with Military Intelligence failing to press Wingate's case for a new special force, he eventually flew back to the Middle East in mid-September 1940 at Wavell's behest, to try to apply his talents in that theatre.[21]

Chapter 6

Striking Back: Europe

Following the 10 May 1940 invasion of France and the Low Countries by German land and airborne forces – including paratroops of the 1st and 2nd Parachute Regiments of the 7th Air Division, whose aim was 'surprise and shock', and whose very existence caused widespread fear and numerous invasion scares in Britain from then on – Churchill declared that the initiative had to be wrested from the enemy.[1] On 3 June, he demanded that his Cabinet come up with proposals, while three MI(R) officers landed south of Boulogne and sabotaged fuel dumps before returning to Britain a week later in a stolen boat. On 4 June, Churchill stressed to the Chiefs of Staff that they must be ready to repel German paratroop assaults on Liverpool or Ireland, and he asked them if raids could be done in the west of Europe. He instructed his chief of staff, General Ismay, 'immediately [to] set to work to raise raiding forces [for action] on ... coasts where the populations are friendly', adding that, 'Such forces might be composed of self-contained, thoroughly equipped units of, say, 1,000 men.' There ought, he felt, to be 'up to not more than 10,000 when combined', so that 'surprise would be ensured'.

Such 'self-contained' raiding forces were reminiscent of the German 'shock troops' deployed during the spring offensive of 1918, as Churchill later noted. But they were far from the only precedent. During discussions on 5 June at Dill's Whitehall office, Clarke stated that the Boer Kommandos seemed 'the best exponent of guerilla warfare which history could produce', while 'it seemed conceivable ... that Britain might ... have something to learn from the past tactics of the Spaniard ... and Arab' as well. Consequently, he proposed that 'perhaps the "Commandos" should be reborn in some new form [for] tip and run raids of not more than 48 hours' duration, against German forces in western Europe. He envisaged raids either on a large scale –

81

like the Royal Marines' raid on Zeebrugge on 23 April 1918, when Admiral Keyes's amphibious force assaulted the harbour, inflicted damage on enemy assets, then retreated – or by 'cloak and dagger' units that could conduct 'mosquito sting' operations from Narvik in the north, to Biarritz in the south. 'The thought led,' Clarke noted, 'to an examination of the secrets of success in . . . guerilla' war among Dill's advisors, with the key elements identified as mobility, the swift concentration of force and rapid disengagement after a raid.

Clarke reasoned that, while the Boers had horses that provided them with mobility, and the Arabs had mountains in which to disperse their forces, the British could achieve both mobility and rapid dispersal by using the seas that, to a great degree, they still controlled. He averred that 'there seemed no reason why we couldn't adapt the principle' of using bands of 'specially trained British soldiers' for hit-and-run raids. They would 'throw off heavy equipment and echelons of supply' to live off the land, conducting short-duration raids on the enemy, then withdrawing and disembarking by sea. Although he realised that such a concept would require 'drastic' training compared to standard Army practice, he believed that this held the key to taking the fight to the enemy. Clarke later observed that 'the CIGS showed immediate interest' in his memo.

On 6 June, Churchill stated that the Army ought to form 'Striking Companies' of 'specially trained troops of the hunter class', to 'develop a reign of terror down the enemy coasts', prosecuting a 'butcher and bolt' policy. After they had gained experience in this, he felt that the Striking Companies would be capable of larger-scale raids on ports and inland communications, thereby diverting valuable enemy resources. To this end, he proposed organising UK-based elements of 6th Australian Division into 'detachments of 250, equipped with grenades, trench mortars, Tommy guns, armoured vehicles and the like'. They should be, he proposed, 'capable of acting against an attack in this country, but also capable of landing' on the enemy-held coastline. They might even be able to advance from an occupied port and undertake 'a deep raid inland, cutting a vital communication' link prior to returning to Britain.[2]

Despite Churchill's enthusiasm, Eric Morris (author of, among others, *Guerrillas In Uniform* and *Churchill's Private Armies*) asserts that Dill was 'appalled' by the idea of calling on regular Army reserves to form groups of uniformed guerillas. He was adamant that regular battalions must *not* be drained of manpower at a time when all their strength was required to deter and, if necessary, repel the imminent threat of German invasion. 'There was no existing unit in the British Army which could be made available for raiding', and because 'the number of . . . troops' available for homeland defence 'depended on the number of weapons available', there was in any case little equipment for any new raiding force. Dill therefore authorised only one-year contracts specifically for raiding operations (mirroring the precedent set by the Lovat Scouts in 1900), along with a minimum of kit.[3]

Clarke bowed to these stipulations and the paper presented to Churchill on 6 June was a 'compromise between Clarke's brilliance and Dill's practical constraints'. Still, Churchill's 'fertile mind was ever susceptible to fresh ideas' and, on 8 June, he approved of the plan. Morris notes that the War Office acted on his memo 'surprisingly quickly', but Clarke's, Dill's and Churchill's shared interest in unconventional warfare meant that there was little that it could do to oppose the scheme. On that day, the responsibility for the formation of the raiding units was given to the Directorate of Military Operations, which, on 5 June, had set up the Military Operations 9 (MO9) branch to co-ordinate raiding planning and implementation, under the auspices of its Deputy Director, Brigadier Otto Lund.[4]

On 9 June, the Cabinet backed the creation of 'Commandos' and a DMO circular called for 'Volunteers For Special Service'. It 'proposed to raise and train a special force of volunteers for independent mobile operations', comprising five units; one from each Army Command in the UK. Each would have 1,000 other ranks led by 40 officers, giving a total of 5,000 or so for Special Service. The circular to all battalion commanding officers stated that volunteers would be 'trained in the military uses of scouting', so as to be 'able to live off the country, move unseen by night and day . . . to stalk the enemy, and report on this activity'. They would be given instruction on, *inter alia*, mountaineering, driving, boat work, night operations, demolitions, sabotage and street fighting.

It called for 'only the best type of officers and men', who were 'absolutely fit', could swim, were not prone to seasickness and who could operate motor vehicles. Officers had to possess 'personality, tactical ability and imagination ... [and] should be capable of planning and personally leading raiding operations carried out by parties'. Other ranks needed a 'good standard of general intelligence and independence', plus reliability, and there was a particular need for 'sappers who are well trained in demolition work'.[5]

At the same time, MO9 decided, in consultation with the Royal Navy, to augment the Commandos with the existing four battalions of raiders-in-waiting serving in the Royal Marines. They had their roots in the Duke of Yorke and Albany's Maritime Regiment of Foot, founded in 1664, although a Ministry of Information publicity booklet of 1943 notes that Combined Operations of land and sea forces (from which the modern concept of Commando-style raiding is a spin-off) were pioneered as early as 1585 by Drake in the West Indies, then by Essex and Howard at Cadiz in 1596. These raids 'showed how a combination of sea and land forces could inflict great hurt on the enemy', and the failed amphibious operations at Walcheren in 1809 and Gallipoli in 1915 were balanced by the capture of Gibraltar in 1704, Quebec in 1759 and Cape Town in 1795, as well as the destruction of French shipping at St Malo in 1758. Despite such traditions, however, by 1940 the Royal Marines had all but lost their amphibious raiding *raison d'être* – conducting 'offensives from small raids to large scale assaults'.[6]

Indeed, after World War I, the Royal Marines were reduced to 15,000 all ranks and, in 1923, they were obliged to incorporate light infantry and artillery elements. The Admiralty was still officially required to provide 'a striking force ... for ... raids on the enemy coast' in wartime, but it was not until 1937 that an Inter-Services Training and Development Centre (ISTDC) was opened for the preparation of Combined Operations plans and the forces required to carry them out, while a Combined Operations Training Centre was only established at Portsmouth in 1936. Further, when a BEF was sent to France in 1939, the Combined Operations arm of the military was wound down, and only the German invasions of Norway and Denmark in April 1940 sparked fresh high level interest in coastal raiding capabilities.[7]

From mid-April 1940, Royal Marines based both on ships and with coastal artillery batteries were mustered ready for action and the

Royal Marines Brigade was constituted in anticipation of overseas missions. But MO9 was not authorised by the Admiralty to transfer Marines *en masse* to the new Commando units and it had to rely on volunteers. Thus, Clarke went to Scotland in search of recruits from the rump of the remaining Independent Companies – then based around Glasgow, the last having returned from Norway on 10 June – and from fresh sources such as the Territorial Army. Later that day, he returned to the War Office and secured the co-operation of the Royal Navy in providing 20 officers and 200 other ranks for raiding support duties, with the Assistant Chief of the Naval Staff, Captain R. H. Garnon-Williams, assigned to provide small craft (mostly private launches) for the raiding parties.

On 12 June, Churchill rubber-stamped the scheme for large and small scale raiding operations. On 13 June, his intelligence supremo, Lord Hankey, outlined MI(R)'s plan for a co-ordinating Combined Operations HQ – its motto, 'United We Conquer' – to be located at the Admiralty. This was approved of by both Holland and MI6 Section D's Head, Grand, to avoid duplicating their efforts. On 15 June, Sir Alan Bourne, Adjutant-General of the Royal Marines, became the first head of Combined Operations, while his chief of staff was Lieutenant-Colonel A. H. Hornby, Royal Artillery. He and Bourne were to 'plan and organise raids' and then forward their proposals to the Joint Planning Committee of the Chiefs of Staff for their approval. Bourne was further required to supervise preparations of a new Light Infantry Brigade, as well as of the remnants of the Independent Companies and the newly forming 'Striking Companies' of 'Commandos,' initially totalling 5,000 men.

On 13 June, the DMO, Major-General R. H. Dewing, noted that Commando volunteers must be 'trained to fight independently and [undertake] irregular operations ... initiated by the War Office', which, 'as a rule', would last for no 'more than a few days'. A Combined Operations depot was officially set up on 15 June and elementary Striking Company training began in earnest.[8]

The Future SAS Hub

One of the officers who applied to his local military district to become a Commando leader (empowered to select his own troop leaders, and, via them, his officers and men) was Guards Lieutenant-Colonel Bob 'Chucker' Laycock. Having been 'an adventurer in his youth' (sailing solo from Denmark to East Africa), he sought to lead the London District Commando – No. 8, as it would be designated – in which David Stirling and many of his future SAS colleagues would serve. Yet Laycock's application was initially rejected by Clarke because Laycock possessed much sought-after Staff College-acquired knowledge about chemical warfare defence measures. The threat of chemical attack was taken extremely seriously at the time (with British preparations concurrently undergoing an emergency overhaul, as outlined in my book, *The X Site*), and Laycock was designated Anti-Gas Officer for GHQ Middle East. However, when he and David Niven (to whom he was related through marriage), concocted a false story that they had found a replacement for Laycock's technical posting, Clarke relented. Niven's performance was evidently convincing and 'Lucky' Laycock would eventually head for the Middle East, not as a chemical warfare advisor, but as a Commando leader.[9]

Among others answering the call was the 17th Lord Lovat (who would go on to form No. 4 Commando, taking with him a core of Lovat Scouts). Once David Stirling's cousin 'had volunteered for the Commandos . . . Stirling . . . promptly followed suit', signing up for No. 8. It was comprised mainly of Household Cavalry and Foot Guards, along with some Royal Engineers and Royal Marines. Many of its new officers were recruited directly by Laycock in the bay window bar of Stirling's favourite watering hole, White's Club. Indeed, 'it was while he was enjoying a drink' there in mid-June that Stirling 'got into conversation with . . . Laycock, who was . . . recruiting'. Laycock, himself a 'forceful personality', was known for being able to 'sum up a man quickly', and he 'was quick to see that Stirling had all the qualities that go to make a good Commando officer'.[10]

Others who signed up for Special Service were some of Stirling's future SAS associates, notably the premier's son, Randolph Churchill, of the 4th Hussars, who was 'fired by his father's enthusiasm' for the Commandos. In a politically astute move, Laycock appointed the out-of-shape would-be warrior as his quartermaster. Ran, another White's regular, had spent several summers in the early 1920s on the coast at Frinton with one of his acquaintances, Angie Ward, who, he noted after the war, was 'married to my great friend ... Robert Laycock'. Laycock envisaged the war being 'long and boring, and for that reason deliberately gathered his friends about him in 8 Commando'.[11]

Another old chum who signed up and was well acquainted with the Churchills was No. 8's liaison officer, Evelyn Waugh, Household Cavalry. He had joined the Royal Marines in December 1939, sponsored by Winston Churchill, but in July 1940, he approached his pre-war social acquaintance and, on transfer, fellow Blues and Royals officer, Laycock. In October, he agreed that Waugh could join him.

Others who turn up in the SAS's story who enlisted with Laycock include King's Royal Rifle Corps officer, Palestine Police lieutenant and Narvik veteran, Roger J. A. 'Jumbo' Courtney, who would go on to experiment with small boat raiding later in 1940; Lord Jellicoe; David Sutherland (like Jellicoe, a future SBS commander) who transferred to No. 8 after initially joining No. 3; Brian Morton Foster Franks, a future CO of the post-war SAS; 'Jock' Lewes; and fellow SAS originals Pat Riley, Jim Almonds, Ernie Bond, Bob Bennett and Johnny Cooper. Like Stirling, Cooper had joined the Scots Guards after taking up mountaineering (at Chamonix, in August 1939). He similarly endured training at Pirbright in April 1940, and after Dunkirk was interviewed for the Commandos by Scots Guards Captain Dermot R. Daly. A former boxer who 'was most impressive, squarely built, broad in the shoulders and with a delightfully broken nose', Daly approved Cooper's enlistment, and the youngster joined fifty other volunteers from the Scots Guards (plus Welsh Guardsman Carol Mather) in No. 3 Troop, No. 8 Commando. It would be commanded by Daly, and Cooper's section leader would be none other than David Stirling. He and his colleagues would soon be detailed to train the new Commando units in Scotland,[12] and raids both training and operational burgeoned from mid-June 1940 onwards.

Chapter 7

Target:
Fortress Europe

Raiding Europe – The First Steps

While preparations for the Commandos went on, Major-General Dewing sought to organise a cross-Channel raid 'at the earliest possible moment', to test the concept's viability and boost morale on the home front. To this end, on 14 June, he turned to Clarke to rustle up a group of officers from the Independent Companies who could organise a scratch raiding force. Among those who answered Clarke's call were Major Ronnie Tod and one of Clarke's colleagues from his pre-war service with the Trans-Jordan Frontier Force, Major Arty Rice, Royal Suffolk Regiment.

Tod and Rice were tasked by Clarke with forming a new Independent Company and, in consultation with him, each hand-picked around a hundred volunteers. The unit was made up of some men from Nos. 6, 7 and 8 Independent Companies but mainly from No. 9. On the Isle of Wight, the new No. 11 Independent Company came under Tod's command. After only a fortnight's training at Southampton, and following Hitler's public declaration of 22 June – the day of France's surrender – that the British must be purged from the continent, a party of 200 (its size dictated by the number of boats and weapons available) set off to scout German defences and an airfield near Le Touquet, and to capture PoWs. The plans for the wryly named Operation Collar were drawn up by Clarke, assisted by Royal Navy Captain Garnon-Williams, who had set up his HQ on his yacht, *Melisarde*, on the River Hamble near Southampton, where vessels for the raid assembled.

Following a briefing from Royal Marines Colonel 'Jumbo' Lester, the raiding party embarked on 23 June from Dover, Folkestone and Newhaven in eight boats (including six RAF rescue craft) under the guidance of Lieutenant-Commander J. W. F. Milner-Gibson, Royal Navy. He had made nine landings in the previous three weeks to familiarise himself with the coast between Cap d'Alprech near Boulogne and Pointe du Hautbanc in the Berck Plage. The groups carried between them twenty Tommy guns (half of Britain's whole US-bought stock at that time), but as some craft proved defective, only nineteen officers and ninety-six other ranks were able to make their way to a rendezvous point ten miles from shore before making landfall.

Two parties beached but were spotted by the enemy and retreated, while another under Tod encountered a German cyclist patrol before exiting after an hour on occupied soil. Another party under Ronald Swayne, formerly of No. 9 Independent Company, landed four miles south of Le Touquet at Plage de Merlimont, where they shot two sentries and threw grenades in a building. It was the 'only . . . group [that] could lay any claim to success' and they had to swim for it when their boat drifted off (while Clarke, who was observing, was shot in the ear and lucky not to be killed). Still, they returned safely to Dover and Folkestone, and Collar 'proved that raids on the enemy coast were possible'. It also led to many newspaper headlines so that 'the word Commando was already an inspiration for many'. Six more raids were soon planned and MO9 stepped up its efforts to form ten Commando units, comprising a total of a hundred troops made up of regulars and reservists.[1]

Commando training

In the interim, in May 1940, a group of 'young officers who had served in the Scots Guards together in Norway' were likewise 'convinced that there was a need for raiders'. As Peter Kemp later recounted, Bill Stirling used his 'imagination and initiative' to organise a series of conferences in London, seconded by his Knife colleague, Brian Mayfield. They met Holland at MI(R), as well as 'a number of influential friends' that Bill had in Whitehall. He argued that the Independent Companies had demonstrated the possibilities of partisan warfare and 'had proved their usefulness'. However, there was 'no organised institution in this kind of warfare, no school or centre where troops could be trained in its principles'. Stirling pressed the case to adopt the theories outlined in Gubbins's guerilla warfare pamphlets, and he added that there was 'an untapped reservoir of officers and . . . men with the necessary qualifications and experience to act as instructors'.[2] His idea, as Kemp noted, was 'that six of us, reinforced by a few selected officers and NCOs should form the nucleus of a new training school' in Scotland, with the instructors released once the first training cadres had been through the school's regime. MI(R) approved Stirling's plan, as well as his appointment as Chief Instructor and Mayfield's as Commandant of the Irregular Warfare Training School (IWTS, also known as IWTC).[3]

The school's organisation was 'left to [a] . . . party who had served in the 5th Scots Guards' and to Lovat, who was tasked with requisitioning land. He acquired 200,000 acres of Cameron-Head Highland estates around Lochailort Castle near Inverailort, twenty-five miles west of Fort William, and not far from the Sound of Arisaig. Bill Stirling and his team were *in situ* by the end of May, and the first twenty-five student subalterns (including his brother, David) began arriving early in June for a four-week training course.[4]

Prior to the creation of 5th Scots Guards, Lovat had proposed an assault training course for his Scouts and had made himself chief instructor at their training camp on the Black Isle. Now, his cousin Bill gave 'Shimi' the task of developing 'special training' for the IWTS. According to David Sutherland, who attended a three-week course for No. 3 Commando that July, the regime 'was Lord Lovat's brainchild', though he had considerable help when devising it. As John Parker notes, the school became 'a home . . . for eccentrics' and, when it came to framing its syllabus, Lovat 'personally encouraged independent and unorthodox training'.[5] In particular, he drew on the experience of colleagues from Operation Knife, from which Lovat felt 'good lessons had been learnt'. He continued that 'those involved contributed something to a new technique', as well as offering 'the makings of a team'. One of them, Jim Gavin, took on demolitions training, while Lovat provided three ghillies from his estate to teach stalking and telescopically assisted sniping.

After graduating the course in June, David Stirling taught fieldcraft, while other fellow 5th Scots Guards who joined him were the battalion's CO, Colonel Coates, Freddy Chapman (Lovat's new second-in-command, and another fieldcraft instructor) and Mike Calvert, who had been sent there in May by MI(R). He had 'already been thinking deeply about the role irregular forces could play in war', especially in terms of behind the lines raiding against enemy communications. Indeed, he ran the school's demolitions courses up to mid-July, before returning to MI(R) to write a paper on 'the operations of small forces behind enemy lines, supplied and supported by air' (and then helping to set up the Auxiliary Units).

Calvert proposed small air-supplied units operating for weeks or months at a time, basing his views on 'what I'd learned in Norway and . . . Lochailort'. Further, the War Office provided the school with other officers, notably Captains E. A. Sykes and W. E. Fairbairn formerly of the Shanghai Police – who demonstrated unarmed combat and silent killing (and loaned their names to the standard Commando knife) – as well as Independent Company commander Hugh Stockwell and Laycock's in-law, Niven.[6]

The training programme took in concealment, survival and foraging, orienteering, infiltration techniques, intelligence-gathering patrols, ambushes, sabotage, protracted swims, forced marches, and night attacks, while Major Munn and two Guides with experience of irregular fighting on the North-West Frontier oversaw map-reading exercises. Later, boat movement and opposed amphibious landings were taught by Commander Geoffrey Congreve, Royal Navy, on the Firth of Clyde and at Dorlin and Mallaig.[7] Hence, David Stirling and his colleagues were well versed in Commando techniques from the summer of 1940 onwards, though none of the soldiers who embarked on the first official 'Commando' raid at Guernsey had yet passed through their doors.

Guernsey

Following Tod's No. 11 Independent Company raid, it was bolstered by 25 officers and 350 other ranks, in readiness for another attack ordered by Churchill on 2 July. Operation Ambassador was planned by the Directorate of Raiding Operations at the Combined Operations HQ. As Nos. 1 and 2 Commandos were allocated for parachuting – of which more later, though the lack of available aircraft reduced the scheme's scope at an early stage to No. 2 – it fell to forty men from 11 Independent Company under Tod and Captain Goodwin, Suffolk Regiment, to lead the mission. They would be joined by 100 men of H Troop, No. 3 Commando, led from 28 June by Major John F. Durnford-Slater, Royal Artillery, and based at Sherborne in Dorset. The raiders were assigned the task of hitting the German garrison of 469 all ranks at St Peter Port, Guernsey, on the night of 14–15 July.

By the end of June, No. 3 Commando (thirty-five officers and 500 men) had assembled at Plymouth and, in readiness for the cross-Channel hop, H Troop was shipped out – after prepping at the Royal Naval College, Dartmouth – by the destroyers HMS *Scimitar* and *Saladin*. Seven RAF rescue craft were used to ferry the raiders to shore on Guernsey, with No. 3 Commando making for the Jerbourg barracks via Telegraph Bay and Moulin Huet Bay. Tod's group was to land at Le Jaonnet Bay and head for Point de la Moye, providing a diversion for Ronald Swayne's group. Its target was the main occupation force at an inland airfield, where it hoped to destroy aircraft on the ground.

The Commandos' approach was cloaked by a diversionary fly-by courtesy of the RAF, but two of the launches developed engine trouble and the other craft landed off course due to a heavy swell. After Durnford-Slater's group waded ashore, the barracks was found to be empty and progress was halted by a German machine-gun post. The party withdrew, leaving behind four men who, it transpired, were weak swimmers (one of whom drowned). Even more ignominiously, Tod's party accidentally landed in the mists on Sark, due to a faulty ship's compass. Churchill fumed at the whole episode, calling it a 'silly fiasco' and 'disaster'. He decided that Commando raiding in the future would have to be reoriented to larger strikes and that all Commandos should be sent through the Inverailort training school.[8]

On 17 July, a political ally of Churchill's, Admiral Keyes, badgered him into making him Chief of Combined Operations. Churchill also asked the Secretary of State for War, Anthony Eden, to write a memo on current raiding plans taking in reconnaissance missions, sabotage, coastal guerilla raids and large scale combined operations. In the interim, on 19 July, Churchill handed responsibility for the nurturing of partisan raiding forces and sabotage in occupied Europe to SOE. On the same day, General Auchinleck (who would soon receive spurious reports of German paratroopers landing in Reading!) became GOC Southern Command. There, six Auxiliary Unit area commanders were appointed by Gubbins early in July.[9]

The Foreign Office's Section D had been planning non-military operations against the enemy since 1938 and, when war broke out, it had already set up arms dumps for potential British stay-behind forces to resist a Nazi invasion. But no such units had been created. On his return from Norway, Gubbins was assigned the job of forming such secret behind the lines groups. Charged with creating 'havoc and destruction among the enemy's supplies and communications' should the Germans invade, Gubbins asked the CINC Home Forces, General 'Tiny' Ironside, for assistance. On 2 July, Gubbins appointed Captain G. H. B. Betts (a veteran of the Burma Rebellion of 1931) as his GSO2, and they set about forming a staff of a dozen officers, 'largely . . . whom' Gubbins 'had known' from his recent service 'in Norway, France or Poland'. Each was allocated a coastal area, from Caithness to south Wales, and they were given 'vague instructions to form "cells" as best they could'.

Each officer was to organise groups of about thirty locals, operating in cells of five men each, using improvised explosive devices and incendiaries, as well as light weapons. Following a conference at London's Whitehall Place on Operations and Special Duties (such as intelligence-gathering), the local unit commanders (who were attached to the Intelligence Corps) co-ordinated their efforts with local division or corps HQs and set about recruiting 'gamekeeper or poacher' types who were deemed to be 'already trained in everything but explosives'. Gubbins pinpointed potential recruits as those who had been 'keen Boy Scouts and campers, wildfowlers, gamekeepers [or] hiking and mountaineering' enthusiasts. He told his patrol leaders to look for 'men who know the forests . . . woods, mines, old shafts, hills, moors, glens', as well as veterans of World War I. Other targets for recruitment were 'fishing and shooting ghillies, Verderers . . . farmers and farm labourers, tin and coal miners, market gardeners and fishermen . . . physicians and local council officials . . . blacksmiths, hoteliers and publicans'.[10]

Each unit was boosted by one or two men introduced by MI5 and, after a fortnight's training in night movement, rail demolitions, and weapons, patrolling got underway in Auchinleck's locale of Essex and Suffolk by the end of July. Some of the units were led by MI(R) and Independent Company officers who themselves 'had some knowledge of explosives and guerilla tactics', such as Mike Calvert. Later that summer, they did night operations, including a raid on the 3rd Division HQ of General Bernard Law Montgomery at Steyning, near Brighton, which startled and angered him when there was 'an explosion on his front lawn'. Betts also oversaw a training HQ at Coleshill, near Swindon, where 'a detachment of Lovat Scouts ... helped with the training' of patrols, not least in weapons handling, night movement and tactics. Another unit commander was Andrew Croft, a trans-Greenland Expedition member, Gubbins's Intelligence Officer in the Independent Companies, and an MI(R) staffer who would go on to serve with the SAS (plus the Commandos, LRDG and SOE).[11]

On 22 July, Eden reported his findings on unorthodox operations to Churchill and, thereafter, while still backing 'minor forays' based on their individual merits, Churchill modified the 'pin-prick' Commando strategy to one of large-scale Commando raids. Clarke and MO9 were instructed to redirect their efforts accordingly and Admiral Keyes drew up plans to this end. However, a lack of materiel to conduct such operations meant that, on 25 August, Churchill re-instructed Eden to plan once more for 'minor operations' in the coming year, 'all of which will depend on surprise landings of highly equipped mobile forces'. The PM wanted 10,000 men trained as 'small bands' capable of 'lightning action', and he underlined that they ought to work 'like packs of hounds' rather than as 'ponderous' forces weighed down by 'elaborate ... equipment'.[12] This equated with earlier edicts to his subordinates in mid-June, all of which would have a bearing on the SAS's story.

By Land, Sea – And Air

On 18 June, Churchill asked the War Cabinet and CINC Home Forces what they thought of 'Storm Troops? We have always', he noted, 'set our faces against this idea, but the Germans certainly gained in the last war by adopting it, and this time it has been a leading cause of their victory.' As a result, Churchill recommended that they form 'at least 20,000 Storm Troops or "Leopards" drawn from existing units, ready to spring at the throat of any small landings or descents' by German amphibious raiders or parachutists. He averred that they must be trained and equipped with the most up-to-date kit, including 'Tommy guns, grenades etc. [plus] motor cycles and armoured cars'. The Leopards would be composed of 'live wire' men in their twenties and, the premier added on 28 June, there should be a 'large number . . . of "Leopard" brigade-groups which can be directed swiftly, i.e. within four hours, to the point of lodgement'. Despite the reticence of some of his advisors, such as General Alan Brooke (then GOC Southern Command), Churchill pressed on with the scheme.[13]

Further, on 22 June, Churchill called for the creation of a force of 5,000 British paratroops to raid the continent and inflict damage on the Germans behind the lines. His support for the concept catalysed the RAF's extant plans for a paratroop training establishment, which had been under consideration since May. The RAF had experimented with parachuting after the First World War, a parachute manufactory was working at Letchworth, Hertfordshire, by 1926, and a parachutist training unit was set up at RAF Henlow, Bedfordshire, to teach bailing-out techniques to pilots. But no serious attempt to create a paratroop arm had been made.[14]

This state of affairs contrasted with other nations' armed services during the inter-war years, the Italians creating a parachute corps in 1927, and the Red Army conducting a combat drop against Basmachi tribesmen that year. In 1928, the US Army Air Corps held demonstration freefalls, and a visiting Red Army team reported favourably on these. In 1929, the Soviets repulsed an Afghan incursion into Tajikistan using paratroops and then established their own corps in 1931. Their example was followed by the Poles, Romanians, Hungarians and Germans, who prepared major airborne forces as a vanguard for their large-scale offensives in 1939–40.[15]

With the threat of German invasion looming over Britain in the summer of 1940, and in the light of 'confused reports' about the use of paratroops in the Low Countries (as well as the capture of German parachuting equipment), early that June the RAF stepped up its own preparations for an airborne force. Ringway Central Landing School, ten miles south of Manchester – commanded by Squadron Leader Louis Strange – set aside four Armstrong Whitley Mk 3 aircraft and twenty-eight parachutes in anticipation of orders to begin paratroop training. Strange also acquired permission to use Lord Egerton's Tatton Park Hall estate, five miles away, as a drop zone (and it became active on 10 July).

On 24 June, a peacetime glider pilot, Lieutenant-Colonel John F. Rock, Royal Engineers, 'was summoned to the War Office to be told that he would be ... establishing a parachutists' training school' at Ringway under conditions of total secrecy (which remained in force until that November). At a conference convened in the Admiralty by Lieutenant-General Bourne, the Central Landing School was instructed to prepare 5,000 parachutists. To this end, Rock was assigned nine instructors from the Army Physical Training Corps, led by Regimental Sergeant-Major Mansie (who would teach somersaulting and general PT), plus eight parachute-packers and five other instructors (including Lofty Humphries, later of 21 SAS), under RAF Henlow's Flight-Sergeant Bill Brereton. Other instructors attached soon after included stuntmen and members of Cobham's Air Circus.

The school received six Whitleys (and later Bristol Bombays) plus 1,000 parachutes (an equipment ceiling imposed by the Air Ministry), and all the school needed then was trainees. They arrived in the shape of C and D Troops of No. 2 Special Service Company – redesignated as No. 2 (Parachute) (Army) Commando – most of whom came from the Independent Companies. Five officers and sixty men – including Russian and Spanish Civil War veterans – mustered on 22 June at Cambrai Barracks on Perham Down, Wiltshire. They would be commanded by a former RAF officer, Lieutenant-Colonel C. I. A. Jackson, Royal Tank Regiment. Among those who volunteered for parachute training was Sergeant Reg Seekings, who would go on to be one of Stirling's original SAS recruits. He was rejected because he was seventeen stone (twenty-eight pounds too heavy to parachute), so he went on to No. 7 Commando and, later, Stirling's 3 Troop, No. 8 Commando. Hence, at least one SAS original was well aware of No. 2 Commando's parachute mission.[16] C Troop under Captain Bailey and D under Captain Park-Smith, Royal Marines, undertook ten days' training in map-reading and initiative tests, before travelling in late June and early July to lodgings at Gatley and Benchill, near Wythenshawe, Manchester. Soon after, they moved to Knutsford,

Cheshire, and paraded at the Sharston Hotel, where the now strengthened battalion was quartered as HQ, R, S and T Companies. They were divided into groups of six for training by instructors whose motto was 'knowledge dispels fear'. Among the trainees were the likes of Lieutenant Anthony Deane-Drummond, Royal Signals, who was selected because he had flown gliders before the war and made one peacetime parachute jump; and 5th Scots Guards Captain Martin Lindsay, a polar explorer. Additionally, Clarke – who had been in recent discussion with the Air Ministry about transport for all of the Commando units – went to Ringway 'with a colleague' to see No. 2 Commando on 18 July.

No. 2 had arrived there on 8 July to begin a programme of instruction that was due to last for up to a month. This would include 7–10 days' ground training focused on PT, infantry drills and lectures, plus 'strategy and policy in the use of parachute troops . . . in hostile raids . . . in areas to give support to revolutionists against the Nazi regime' and 'in cutting communications'. There would follow 7–10 days of more PT, parachute packing, aircraft disembarkation, map-reading and weapons training, then 7–10 days of ground/air instruction on air-drops, including films and drills. Finally, specialist tuition would be given in section movement and air operations.

Clarke observed the embryonic parachute unit's preparations, attending a planning conference with Strange and Rock on 19 July and taking to the air for a planned demonstration jump, which was cancelled due to strong winds.[17] Clarke's involvement in the parachute Commando project would have a telling bearing on the development of Stirling's SAS.

Four days after arriving at Ringway, the Commandos watched their parachute jumping instructors conduct a descent, and the Commandos followed their lead on 22 July. Their first fatality, on 25 July, was Driver Ralph Evans, RASC, when his 'chute failed to open during the school's 136th jump. As a result, Messrs Gregory and Quilter of the GQ Parachute Company were called on to set up a static line-operated rig for use with the 28-foot Irving X-Type parachutes supplied to the RAF. Despite sustaining other casualties with them, by September, the RAF had trained 290 Commando parachutists (who were awarded their wings after five jumps, including one at night), and there were 500 all ranks at the school. (A ceiling was imposed by the Air Ministry after it pursued its case with Churchill that 'the use of paratroops was a clumsy ... method of delivering men', as opposed to gliders. Indeed, 2,700 glider-borne troops were authorised by the Prime Minister as a result).[18]

Moreover, after Evans's death, while trial drops with dummies were carried out at Ringway (and one, on 26 July, was watched by Admiral Keyes), C and D Troops travelled with 5 Commando's Major Newman to Torcastle, near Fort William, thence Inverailort, for Commando training in August. As Sergeant Ernie Chinnery recalled, 'Lord Lovat took us out ... and taught us the art of stalking', using half a dozen of his instructors as quarry for No. 2 Commando. It is unclear precisely when David Stirling transferred from Inverailort to No. 8 Commando, but its officers were due to muster at the Duke of York's Barracks in Chelsea, London (the future 21 SAS HQ), before joining other ranks at Burnham-on-Crouch, Essex, in mid-September. Hence, it is most likely that Stirling would have known about the Parachute Commandos at Inverailort either by direct contact with them, or through the grapevine via his brother Bill or other instructors with whom he kept in touch, such as Lovat and Fleming. In time, Stirling's knowledge of parachuting came into play when he set up the SAS and, as Strawson knowingly notes with regard to the Commandos and paratroops, 'All these ideas ... inevitably contributed to David Stirling's own special adaptation of them.'[19]

After returning to Ringway between 30 August and 3 September, the Para Commandos staged mock attacks on the Home Guard stationed there, 'making use of ... unarmed combat' techniques taught at the IWTS, which 'resulted in the Home Guard suffering broken limbs!' C Troop then undertook explosives training at a nearby garrison, while two more parachute troops (the newly formed A and B) went to Inverailort, followed by further contingents through September.[20]

That October, the CINC India, General Robert Cassels, also sponsored the creation of a paratroop cadre 'to carry out experiments with the RAF and to provide a nucleus of trained parachutists from which a mixed brigade of British, Indian and Gurkha parachute troops could be formed'. On 2 December, he backed the creation of three paratroop battalions, but the War Office vetoed the scheme, citing a lack of available aircraft. Consequently, its commander-designate, Lieutenant-Colonel W. H. G. Gough, transferred to Ringway.[21]

Special Boats

As well as the airborne raiding forces training in the summer of 1940, one of David Stirling's future colleagues in No. 8 Commando, 'Jumbo' Courtney, experimented with small scale raiding by parties using boats. A game-hunter and experienced solo canoeist who had travelled much of the length of the River Nile, he proposed at the end of July to form a troop to use folbots to scout, raid and sabotage enemy shipping, fuel stocks and communications. Later, he outlined his ideas for Laycock, 'theorising that from his experience . . . a small force of men in canoes could carry out effective sabotage'.

Initially rebutted, Courtney made a dummy raid on the 13,000-ton RMS *Glengyle*, moored off Gourock in the Clyde, to illustrate the concept's viability. He took a gun cover from the ship and delivered it to a conference of senior Commando officers, including Admiral Keyes. Some officers 'showed a glimmer of interest' in Courtney's idea and, when he suggested another demonstration attack, Keyes consented. After successfully putting chalk marks on a ship's hull undetected, Keyes allowed Courtney to select a dozen men for three months' training with eight folbots at Corrie on the east of Arran. They would be attached to No. 8 Commando as its Folbot Troop and, in August, Courtney proposed that each commando should have a troop of thirty canoeists.

On 26 September, Courtney was seconded by the Directorate of Combined Operations for a raid on the Dutch coast, but it was abandoned on 17 October due to bad weather (though six of the SBS's twenty officers and men were 'attached to No. 12 Commando during the first raid on the Lofoten Islands in November'). Courtney returned to No. 8, where David Stirling was among the new officers privy to his small unit raiding plans.[22]

No. 8 Commando

According to 8 Commando's War Diary, Laycock was appointed its commander by Clarke on 11 July. At Eastern Command HQ, Laycock was given a letter of authorisation (dated 26 June) and a list of volunteers. He was instructed to raise two Commandos, each comprising ten troops. Each troop would have one captain, two subalterns and forty-seven other ranks (increased after the Guernsey raid to four officers and sixty other ranks), plus thirty-six HQ staff, giving a total of 536 all ranks per Commando.

During 13–15 July, Laycock interviewed officers who would select his troop leaders. Laycock owned that 'I called on my friends, whom I could trust', and one, Evelyn Waugh, received a letter on 22 August informing him that Laycock 'had a post for' him (which he assumed on 7 November). On 4 August, two officers and two NCOs travelled to Lochailort to train in the techniques that David Stirling and his companions would bring to No. 8 Commando. On 8 August, No. 1 Troop, under Captain Lord Sudeley, assembled at Burnham-on-Crouch, followed on 12 August by No. 4 Troop, under Daly (who would later take over No. 3 Troop). Other recruits to No. 8 Commando who would go on to the early SAS included Jim Blakeney and Ernest 'Bob' Lilley, Coldstream Guards, who joined at the behest of Lord Jellicoe, who led escape and evasion training and exercises at Burnham.[23]

On 12 August, Laycock issued training instructions to his troop leaders, noting their responsibility for the 'development of a special technique', which he anticipated might be 'difficult'. He added that normal drill would have to continue too, as experience showed that 'irregular units very soon deteriorate into a second rate rabble unless due attention is paid' to it. However, he underlined that 'drill is merely a means to an end and . . . the movement of men in formed bodies or in regular formation will NEVER be employed by personnel of No. 8 Commando'.

Elaborating on the 'special technique', Laycock explained that it entailed 'the acquirement [sic], improvement and perfection of various characteristics in the individual', notably physical fitness, mental awareness and offensive spirit. He required 'the instinct of the hunter . . . the lightning destructive and ruthless methods of the gangster . . . absolute self-reliance . . . a knowledge of various tricks, ruses and devices [and] above all, the ability to move and act at night fearlessly and noiselessly', in order to attain 'a difficult and hazardous objective'. Laycock underlined that raiders had to retain the initiative, whether operating as 'sub-units, or even as a [whole] Commando' – all ideas assimilated by David Stirling and his circle.

Trust between officers and men was critical, Laycock added, and while he urged each troop to 'prove itself superior' to others, he cautioned against 'petty jealousies' between gunners, guards, light infantry, household cavalry, riflemen and sappers. As for planning, 'Secrecy must become a fetish', he averred. Individual Commando training incorporated the use of the rifle, pistol, light and heavy machine guns, grenades, 3-inch mortars, smoke, rockets, incendiaries, bangalore torpedoes, knives and numerous enemy weapons. There would also be boxing, jujitsu, swimming, boatwork, climbing, map-reading, aerial photo interpretation, path-finding, observation missions, camouflaging, scouting, sniping, signals, unarmed combat, wire-cutting, demolitions, incendiarism, sabotage, cooking, first aid, prisoner care, and 'thuggery', most of which would be taught at night.

There would also be collective training at sub/section, troop and commando level on 'working by night and laying up by day', street fighting 'including the storming of hotels, HQs and billets', woodland fighting, 'patrols and forays', combined operations with the RAF and Navy, and 'operations from aeroplanes'. Further instruction would follow on the sabotage of motor transport, docks, arms dumps, power-houses, factories, telephone lines, wireless stations, railway installations, aerodromes, water supplies, locks and dams, plus the 'laying of booby traps and delayed action mines'.[24]

On 16 August, four more officers and three NCOs went to Inverailort, while individual and troop training (including a mock raid) began at Burnham on 20 August. On the 22nd, Laycock attended a meeting at the War Office and was informed that, four days later, there would be discussions about a reorganisation of 'irregular formations', including the Commandos and remaining Independent Company personnel (most of whom were due to gather in No. 1 Commando). On 27 August, Laycock's second-in-command, Major W. S. Curtis, visited No. 3 Commando to observe their beach-landing training, while, on the following day, men from No. 8 were called out when a bomb dropped a mile from their camp during an air raid. Their war diary records that 'a rubber boat, a bottle of schnapps and a cushion fell from one German bomber!' Next day, No. 8 received instructions to be ready to repel 'enemy parachute troops' with rifle fire 'at long ranges', should there be any landings.

On 10 September, the delayed War Office meeting on the restructuring of irregular formations took place, with Laycock and No. 3 Commando's CO, Durnford-Slater, among those attending. It was 'stated that the general policy . . . was that the Commandos were to be reorganised into Special Companies, about 250-strong, which were to be grouped four companies to a battalion', though, in practice, each Commando formed companies of 500, with two per battalion. The War Office added that 'Companies [were] to retain their individuality and independence of action', while No. 2 Commando 'continued its parachute training at Ringway undisturbed by the reorganisation'. The Special Service battalions (SSB) would be part of a Special Service brigade led by Brigadier J. C. Haydon. As the autumn proceeded and with the immediate threat of a Nazi invasion receding with the RAF's continuing successes in the Battle of Britain, Keyes pondered a raid on either the Azores or, by 30 October, Churchill's preferred option, the strategic Mediterranean island of Pantelleria, between Sicily and Tunisia (Operation Workshop).[25]

Keyes and the Assistant CIGS, Major-General L. Carr, visited No. 8 Commando and observed individual training on 13 September. The next day, two more of No. 8's officers and three NCOs went to Lochailort for 'special training' and, on 18 September, an exercise was held by the Commando in which men from 46th Highland Brigade played the 'enemy'. They commended the Commandos' 'unorthodox methods' and, six days later, the 'irregulars' were pitted successfully against a local garrison.

On 4 October, the War Office enacted its reorganisation plan and the Commandos came under the auspices of the Special Service brigade. A planning conference on 5 October decided to send some of the Commandos for 'a period of intensive training' in amphibious warfare, while No. 8 received orders to be ready to move at twelve hours' notice. On 10 October, No. 8 – along with Durnford-Slater's No. 3, now grouped together as No. 4 Special Service Battalion, under Laycock – was ordered to embark for the new Combined Training Centre (CTC) at Inverary,[26] which had been established on 21 August at Keyes's behest by an advance naval party under Commander

Marsden-Smedley. The Combined Operations School was commanded from 1 September by Vice-Admiral T. J. Hughes-Hallett, Royal Navy, who, along with some Army staff, was ensconced in the Argyll Arms pub.[27]

On 12 October, No. 8 Commando entrained from Burnham to Gourock under Daly, travelling thence aboard the MV *Ulster Monarch* to Inverary, where No. 3 Commando also arrived. A fortnight later, No. 8's war diary notes that a 'specimen pair of special rope-soled boots for landing operations' was received. 'Unfortunately, the boots are size SIX and both for the same foot!' Still, on the next day, the 'basic routine of marching and weapon instruction' was replaced by 'training to get ashore from landing craft using live ammunition'. Up to the end of the month, this was done on the shores of Loch Fyne, some way from No. 1 Independent Company's former base at the Achnacarry Training Centre (near Lochs Arkaig and Lochy). One participant in the Dieppe raid of 1942 commented on that debacle, 'Jesus Christ . . . this is nearly as bad as Achnacarry!'

On 29 October, No. 8 returned to Gourock aboard the *Glengyle*. They moved on to the Ayrshire coast at Largs the following day, disembarking after a period of bad weather for a train journey to a nearby barracks on the 31st. There they did individual training on the ranges, while Laycock spoke on 13 November of their reorganisation in readiness for 'special operations . . . which . . . have already been detailed'. A combined Commando force of 100 officers and 1,500 other ranks would be deployed to the Middle East for raids on the islands of Rhodes (Operation Cordite) and the Dodecanese, in order to establish a base in the eastern Mediterranean. On 21 November, Laycock was instructed by the War Office to be ready to depart by 13 December.

In the interim, on 18 November, Brigadier Haydon ordered company, inter-company and inter-battalion exercises, night, compass and intelligence work, map-reading, air photography interpretation, signals, wireless use, demolitions, road blocks, scouting, climbing, wiring, unarmed combat and weapons training, and the study of the history of combined operations, using lectures and booklets, including the official history of the Gallipoli campaign, Admiral Keyes's memoir of both it and the Zeebrugge raid of 1918, and W. G. Bradley's *Wolfox* (MacMillan). From 25 November, the brigade HQ oversaw the preparations of Laycock's composite 'Layforce', comprising 'the three most highly trained Commandos ... 7th, 8th and 11th Scottish (under Lieutenant-Colonel Dick Pedder)'. They would be supplemented by Captain Mike Kealy's A Troop, No. 3 Commando – three officers and sixty-two other ranks who had had mountain and landing craft training at Inverary and Loch Fyne in September – and Courtney's SBS.

At this juncture, David Stirling and Jock Lewes – members of 'the "smart set"', along with the likes of Ran Churchill and Evelyn Waugh, who, between dining out in Glasgow, made use of the Largs Marine Hotel, where 'uniforms were rarely worn' – pursued a shared passion for climbing on Goat Fell on the island of Arran. Stirling instructed Carol Mather and others, and while Lewes later owned, 'I hardly knew David' then, their acquaintance would become crucial to the SAS.

Further, Stirling reflected on this period that, 'at the back of my mind ... there was always a nagging doubt' about moving about on exercise 'like thundering herds of cattle ... in unwieldy groups of twenty or more'. To him, 'it seemed wrong' to lose the element of surprise and, while the Commandos had a 'critical spirit' in which 'no tactic was sound just because the book said so ... any ideas I had', Stirling noted, 'were pushed to the back of my mind.'

Following another move via Fairlie to Brodick on Arran, night landings were staged between 15 and 31 December. Laycock was briefed by the War Office's Colonel Graveley on Operation Workshop, and Nos. 3 and 8 Commandos staged a dress rehearsal beach assault on the night of 15 December. It was observed by the Vice CIGS, who was less than impressed by the Commandos' late arrival, caused by Sutherland oversleeping![28]

One of No. 8 Commando's troops, No. 5, was trained by Ran Churchill, ensuring that the PM was kept abreast of its actions, 'Special forces [having] become the in-thing as far as Winston ... was concerned'. Indeed, as Jellicoe later recalled, 'It meant that [the] views' of Randolph's associates 'were received at a very high level', which could well have benefited Stirling in mid-1941.[29]

Further beach landing exercises were followed by a week's leave for Nos. 7, 8 and 11 Commandos. On their return on 21 January

Stirling and Lovat set about playing pranks on the brigade's staff officer, Waugh, including writing letters to him purporting to be secret agents! Some Commandos also raided each others' HQs, and the 11th executed a 'carefully planned raid on an aerodrome'. It involved the distraction of sentries by two soldiers dressed as women, while others cut the perimeter fence and infiltrated the base for a simulated attack on the officers' mess with Mills bombs. Then, on 29 January, Layforce transferred to the 1,600-berth *Glenroy*.[30]

After a short stop at Brodick, they and a contingent of the Royal Marines' Mobile Naval Base Defence boarded the *Glengyle* and *Glenearn*. They received an official send-off from Arran on 31 January from Admiral Keyes, and Mather and Stirling shared a *Glengyle* cabin. Among their fellow passengers were Spanish Civil War veteran and future SAS original Dave Kershaw and Stirling's platoon sergeant, Bond. Accompanied by HMS *Kenya* and four escort destroyers, the flotilla was joined on 1 February by SS *Georgie*, before being buffetted by force 7 gales that resulted in 'some sickness'. The convoy rendezvoused with three County Class cruisers including HMS *Devonshire* on 7 February, and was joined by HMS *Forester* and HMS *Faulkner* two days later. They stopped off at Freetown, Sierra Leone, on 10 February and set off the next day. Major Daly, who had assumed command of No. 8, carried out inspections of its ten troops, plus signals and folbot sections, between the 13th and 17th, and on the 16th, all officers were told to study *Combined Operations 1940* and *Notes on Demolition and Sabotage*.[31]

The First 'Special Air Service' Raid

In addition to this doctrinal learning, Layforce was offered an instructive demonstration of heterodox soldiering in action in mid-February 1941. In early February, a contingent of Britain's own paratroopers had landed on Malta as a staging post for an airborne raid on Italy. It was to be conducted by No. 2 Commando, Special Service Brigade, or as it was redesignated from 21 November 1940 (with effect from 4 December, following a demonstration air drop in Wiltshire) the 11th Special (Air) Service Battalion. Prior to this, the unit had received an influx of volunteers and divided into parachute and gliding wings (the latter forming the core of the future Glider Pilot

Regiment) and some soldiers 'were getting so bored with development work ... that they were requesting transfers'. But on 3 December 1940, the battalion made a simulated raid on a village on Salisbury Plain, with thirty-two men parachuting from two Armstrong-Whitworth Whitleys for a group of VIP observers including the CINC Home Forces. The dignitaries gathered at Old Sarum before the exercise and 11th SAS Sergeant Arthur Lamley, RASC, later recounted that the 'brass hats ... fired all sorts of questions at us', before making for the drop zone. The exercise involved Auchinleck's Southern Command troops acting as German defenders of the Salisbury and Marlborough 'deserts,' emulating North Africa. The garrison troops were placed in large numbers at Marlborough, Hungerford and Pewsey, while others guarded key communications. The role of the 11th SAS was to drop in two groups of sixteen, as an exemplar for a future drop of ten troops.[32]

One group comprising two eight-man sub-sections (who represented A, B, C, D and E Troops) would attempt to capture the 'heavily defended' village of Shrewton, a few miles away from the DZ. The other pair of sub-sections (representing F, G, H, J and K Troops) under 11th SAS's second-in-command, Major Trevor Allan Gordon 'Tag' Pritchard, Royal Welch Fusiliers, would land east of Pewsey 'with the objective of capturing the [five] main crossings over the canal [using] speed and surprise'. Major Peter Cleasby-Thompson's men were designated as B's assault troop with Brens and heavy weapons. They were required to move 'with all speed under cover' from their DZ to 'carr[y] out a surprise attack' and seize Shrewton's bridges and church using 'guerilla tactics'. The original plan also called for D group to carry out diversions, with E in reserve. In the event, Cleasby-Thompson's force advanced swiftly on Shrewton and, in a scene reminiscent of the movie *The Eagle Has Landed*, seized command vehicles at gunpoint. The observation party of war correspondents and top brass 'cheered as the men ran for the village', Auchinleck doubtless being impressed by this display, knowing from his own father's experience of the Indian Mutiny of 1857 that surprise is vital for success (that rebellion having 'started with an attack on a church parade, since ... troops would not be' armed).[33]

The 11th SAS's parachute demonstration was one of the last big events during Auchinleck's tenure at Southern Command, the CINC having been informed early in November 1940 by Anthony Eden that he would be CINC India-designate from 21 November. The Auk was congratulated by Home Forces HQ on 11 December, before being replaced by General Harold Alexander and departing for the Raj with his chief staff officer, Ritchie, on 27 December 1940.[34] The 11th SAS's impressive trial parachute assault more than likely had a bearing on Auchinleck's thinking about paratroop operations when Stirling championed them in the following summer.

After the Salisbury Plain demonstration – and in line with the Air Ministry's recommendation to Churchill in September 1940 to undertake an experimental airborne raid with parachutists – it was clear to the authorities that the paratroops were ready for a grander effort. By 17 December, '22 teams of eight' men were fully trained at Ringway, the CIGS witnessing a 126-man air drop there four days before. Soon afterwards, Lieutenant Tony Deane-Drummond was directed by the Chiefs and the Directorate of Combined Operations to prepare in the strictest secrecy for a raiding mission on southern Europe.

The 11th SAS's CO, Lieutenant-Colonel Jackson, requested volunteers for a 'deep penetration' raid – Operation Colossus – which was 'to contribute to a wider plan to attempt . . . to disrupt the flow of supplies to Mussolini's . . . armies . . . in North Africa'. Of 11th SAS's 350 personnel, seven officers and thirty-one men were assigned by 2 January 1941 to X Troop – primarily based on their demolitions expertise – while Lieutenant-Colonel Rock and his staff pondered how the force 'should carry their weapons, if at all' during their descent. 'At this stage . . . it was considered enough just to get the men down in one piece . . . equipment would . . . follow'. Indeed, as John Parker notes, 'It was an ambitious first raid that had more to do with testing the effectiveness of such operations than the safe return of the men.'[35]

Its ostensible objective was to hit water supplies in southern Italy, notably the British-built, 93-mile Acquedotto Pugliese pipe and Tragino Aqueduct – the biggest in the world – at Monte Vulture, near Calitiri and Salverno. It delivered water to the key Italian ports of Taranto, Bari and Brindisi, as well as nearly 300 towns and villages. Training at Tatton Park 'on the basis of individual hit-and-run

Commando raids' was stepped up by Rock in January 1941, Operation Dragon on the 5th–8th also being for the benefit of observers including the CINC Home Forces. The exercise was designed to demonstrate 'how troops may be transported by air and [make] surprise pinpoint landings . . . at pre-determined places by parachutists and gliders'. On 6 January, two officers and fourteen men emplaned at White Waltham airfield and eight men dropped from a Whitley over a factory near Aldershot.[36]

Training at Tatton did not go without hitches and Sergeant Dennis was killed when he descended into the lake there. Then, on 1 February, the Knutsford Fire Brigade was called out to cut down parachutists from trees during a dress rehearsal for the Tragino raid. Undaunted, the 11th SAS practised mountain walking and survival techniques, and placed 800 pounds of explosive on Tatton Park's bridge in simulated demolitions. On 3 February, Pritchard and X Troop, 11th SAS, left RAF Mildenhall, Suffolk, in six Whitleys of No. 91 Squadron. At the aerodrome, they received a send-off from Admiral Keyes, who spoke of their 'important job' in attempting to 'learn what British paratroops can do', which he regarded as a 'very vital role' for the future.[37]

X Troop flew to Malta, where thirty-two other ranks and six officers, including Deane-Drummond, who had arrived there with an advance party in January, prepared to air-drop from two Whitleys on 10 February. That day, Pritchard briefed his men that 'the job on which you are now embarking is an experiment to see what you can do'. When they made their night-time jump, the parachutists landed off target due to a force 8 gale, but Pritchard pressed on with his party, including sappers under Captain Gerry F. K. Daly. Using a thousand pounds of explosive, Second-Lieutenant George A. Patterson and Sergeant Drury, both of the Royal Engineers, blew up part of the Tragino aqueduct, before making a sixty-mile overland march for a rendezvous with the submarine HMS *Triumph* off the River Sele, on the night of 15 February.[38]

The troop's three raiding parties, led by Pritchard, Captain C. G. Lea, Lancashire Fusiliers, and Second-Lieutenant G. Jowett, Highland Light Infantry, were all captured (with one fatality) before reaching the submarine, but many of the raiders subsequently escaped. 'After this heartening success, an expansion of airborne forces was ordered', resulting by 15 September 1941 in the creation of the 1st Parachute Regiment under Lieutenant-Colonel Richard N. 'Windy' Gale (this, in turn, absorbed the 11th SAS, by then led by Major Eric Ernest 'Dracula' Down).

The rest of X Troop's colleagues (some of whom made further demonstration drops, including one by 'Hinstock Force' at Baginton, twelve miles west of Birmingham, on 21 May, and, a few days later, another near Bray, Windsor, which was witnessed by King George VI and 'many senior officers') learned about their exploits from 'the newspaper reports' that covered their action in 'a short, guarded' way. According to 1943's *Combined Operations,* 'Their feat created a sensation in Italy,' including government statements about the incident and coverage on Radio Roma. And while the aqueduct was repaired within a month, 'The raid presented a new threat to the whole of Italy [and caused] a re-examination by the Italians of all important targets . . . [with] arrangements made to guard them as necessary.'[39]

Further, Sally Dugan asserts in *Commando* that Operation Colossus 'inspired many thousands of British soldiers to volunteer for parachute training'. In this regard, it is worth noting – though the fact has been overlooked by other historians – that, while Layforce was making for Cape Horn in South Africa, the ship's *Glengyle News* reported 'the exploits of British parachutists', who Mussolini informed 'the British HQ . . . had been rounded up'. The *News* added that, 'It is believed that some of the parachutists have made their escape', and their venture (also headlined in the likes of *The Times* on 15 February, *The War* of 28 February and *War Illustrated* of 14 March) was very likely a hot topic of conversation among those aboard the *Glengyle,* who included Stirling, Lewes and their colleagues.[40]

Rounding the Cape by 19 February, Laycock's force made Durban on the 21st and, soon after, illness struck. By the 27th, an 'outbreak of diarrhoea . . . reached its peak, with 240 cases'. The cruiser HMS *Glasgow* appeared on the 28th to replace *Devonshire,* which departed on 2 March, before a brief escort by HMS *Kandahar* and HMS *Flamingo.* After skirting Aden, they reached Port Suez on 7 March. Three days later, the troops prepared to leave for Kabrit camp on the shore of the Great Bitter Lake, at a junction with the Suez Canal, while the officers received a pep talk from Major-General J. F. Evetts (a pre-war supporter of the SNS, with whom Laycock had been in discussion on 8 February). Evetts informed them that, after 'a month's hard training', they would undertake a raid 'at an early opportunity . . . [and] he stressed the hazardous nature of possible operations'.

On 11 March, the Special Service soldiers disembarked via landing craft at Ferara Wharf, Geneifa. No. 8 Commando marched two miles under Captain Lord Sudeley (Daly being ill in hospital) and set up camp on 12 March. At that point, Laycock went to Cairo to talk further with Evetts, hoping to assure a place in upcoming special operations being planned by Middle East HQ.[41]

Chapter 8

Striking Back:
The Middle East

Raiding the Middle East

Prior to the arrival of No. 8 Commando and its associates in the Middle East on 11 March 1941, special operations were well under way there. By May 1940, the British position was threatened more than ever by the Italo-German Axis and Middle East Land Forces' GSI(R) drew up plans for guerilla operations, sabotage and subversion in anticipation of action by Mussolini. He declared war on 10 June, following the Germans' successes in western Europe, and Wavell 'faced . . . the prospect of operations on a diversity of fronts' across three and a half million square miles. This included Aden, Iraq, Cyprus, Egypt, Palestine, Somaliland, Sudan, Trans-Jordan and the Persian Gulf, which, *in toto*, he 'regarded . . . as the key to victory'.[1]

Consequently, Wavell built on the example of Allenby's deceptions of 1918, planning decoy forces and movements, fake radio traffic and other tricks to divert enemy resources. He 'considered the possibility of organising insurgency within neighbouring countries' and made enquiries about acquiring Wingate for this. After working with him in Palestine, Wavell later reflected, 'I carried away in a corner of my mind an impression of a notable character who might be valuable as a leader of an unorthodox enterprise in war.' Thus, on 18 September, Wingate was ordered to Cairo, where he arrived in October and wrote a paper for Colonel Adrian Simpson of GSI(R) about a large force of air-supplied, motorised desert raiders. Although his proposal was not acted on due to other developments (*detailed below*), Wingate's report was studied in 'minute detail' at Middle East HQ and sparked 'substantial interest' among the regional top brass in behind the lines raiding.[2]

Another heterodox soldier who hoped to influence the impending desert conflict by conducting raids was Captain Ralph Alger Bagnold. Like most officers, he was well aware of the unique nature of desert warfare, as delineated at the turn of the century in the semi-official book by Major-General Charles E. Callwell, *Small Wars*. A fixture in every officers' mess, it outlined that the desert demanded 'irregular warfare [which] must generally be carried out on a method totally different from the stereotyped system'. This was taken to heart by Lawrence and others during the First World War, and Bagnold's 'interest was already stirred by Lawrence's role' then.[3]

Bagnold was aware too of the desert reconnaissance Light Car Patrols (LCP) of 1914–18 – he had been transferred to Egypt after earlier service as a sapper in France. The LCPs inspired his desert motor expeditions when he was posted as a signals officer to Cairo in 1925. Along with fellow explorers from the Royal Tank Corps, Royal Engineers and Royal Corps of Signals, Bagnold ventured deep into the deserts of Sinai, Palestine and Trans-Jordan. From 1926, their Model-T Ford cars journeyed over a thousand miles a trip and, in 1929, they took on the Great Sand Sea of western Egypt. Prior to his transfer to the North-West Frontier that November, Bagnold and five companions in three Model-A Fords undertook a Royal Geographical Society-backed trek. In October 1930, one of their expeditions traversed 4,000 miles of the Great Sand Sea, winning plaudits from *The Times*. An admiring Italian Army officer in neighbouring Libya, Captain Lorrenzini, arranged to meet Bagnold and pointed out that the unguarded Sand Sea flank could be vulnerable to raids during wartime, leaving the (first) Aswan Dam and Sudanese railways open to interdiction. Bagnold realised this was 'not quite as outlandish as it might have seemed [and] Lorrenzini's conversation would stay with Bagnold over the years'.[4]

In 1935, Bagnold's account of his expeditions of 1924–32, *Libyan Sands*, was published (and Wavell, who arrived in Egypt on 20 July 1939 to take over as CINC, had read it). After travelling to China and retiring from the Army, Bagnold was recommissioned in September 1939. That November, he wrote a three-page memo for the GOC British Troops Egypt, Lieutenant-General Henry Wilson, suggesting small motor patrols to scout Kufra, but his proposal for long range patrolling

(LRP) was not taken up. However, with the Italians threatening Egypt, Bagnold sent his memo to 7th Armoured Division's Major-General Percy 'Hobo' Hobart, a 'man of imagination' with a 'far-seeing' mind. With his backing, it went to Middle East HQ. However, once there, it was deemed to be provocative, not to mention impractical, and it was rejected by Hobart's successor in January 1940.

Fortuitously, that June, Bagnold returned to Egypt en route to Kenya, when his troopship was damaged and stopped for repairs at Port Said. He travelled by train to Cairo and arrived there on 9 June, making for his old watering hole, Shepheards. His arrival was reported by the *Egyptian Gazette* and noted by Wavell. In the interim, Bagnold contacted Wavell's chief of staff, Brigadier Arthur Smith, with a view to meeting the CINC. On 19 June, Bagnold gave his LRP memo to Smith and asked if he could present his ideas to 'the Chief'. Wavell agreed to meet him on the 23rd and, when he read the memo, he 'grinned at the scheme', as he was already nurturing a 'policy of harrying the enemy'.[5]

On 17 March, Wavell had highlighted the need for 'light mobile . . . offensive patrolling' to hit 'the enemy's supply', in co-operation with the RAF. The 4th Regiment, Royal Horse Artillery, created motorised infantry columns with artillery to 'harass the enemy . . . [and] support the armoured cars' operating behind the lines. The 11th Hussars from 7th Armoured Division also did a truck-borne 'special desert recce' to Siwa Oasis, which 'established . . . that the direct route . . . was [the] only [one] feasible for small, light raiding parties'. Wavell then implemented plans for 'small lightly equipped mechanized detachments . . . to take the offensive'.[6]

Indeed, following Churchill's 'prodding', on 12 April, the CIGS, Dill, urged Wavell to be prepared to conduct 'desert patrols' to interdict enemy forces and 'destroy . . . supply and petrol convoys'. It was, he noted, 'a time when great daring is needed and great losses accepted'.[7] Hence, it became the 'task of the 11th Hussars . . . to harass and puzzle the Italian advance' with their armoured cars and to surprise them behind the lines, as they did at Forts Capuzzo and Maddalena soon after Italy declared war on 10 June. 'Raids and ambushes were successfully carried out', with over eighty Italian vehicles destroyed and 900 PoWs taken, while Brigadier W. H. E.

Gott's Support Group pursued 'active patrolling' and 'harassed . . . and inflicted a steady drain of casualties'.[8]

When he met Wavell at Middle East HQ on 23 June, Bagnold noted that the Italians could be building up forces around the strategically vital Kufra aquifer, garrison and airfield. Some 300 miles from Jalo, it was, along with the airstrip at Uweinat, 'a source of worry for Wavell', as it was a potential stepping stone to Sudan and Abyssinia. Bagnold proposed a reconnaissance to ascertain enemy dispositions and Wavell asked what he would do if no Italian build-up could be discerned, hoping to elicit from him the 'task which Wavell had intended for it all along – to attack and harass' the enemy. Bagnold suggested that some 'old fashioned "piracy" could be done' and, given that Wavell 'believed' – according to recollections by his ADC, Fergusson – 'that a small body of men far behind enemy lines can exert an influence on operations out of all proportion to their numbers', Wavell backed Bagnold's scheme.[9]

Wavell consistently prized 'boldness and daring, together with surprise in attack', having upon his arrival in Cairo declared that the desert 'should provide opportunities for more mobile and unorthodox warfare'. He was well versed in this, having, in 1927–8, while stationed at the 3rd Division in Aldershot, had a 'close association with the birth and early trials of the first mechanized formation . . . the Experimental Armoured Force'. Its work coloured his views 'on the conduct of armoured battles in the Western Desert', with its emphasis on 'mobility, fire-power and armour'. One visitor to the unit was the then Chancellor of the Exchequer, Winston Churchill, and, by the early 1930s, Wavell had 'made the acquaintance and earned the respect of a number of "unorthodox" military thinkers [including] Lawrence, J. F. C. Fuller and B. H. Liddell Hart'. By 1935, 'under their influence, Wavell developed an early interest in . . . "the motor guerilla". He believed that small forces of . . . highly mobile raiders might . . . infiltrate and strike at enemy LoCs', as Lawrence had done.

Further, as commander of the 6th (Experimental) Infantry Brigade, 2nd Division, from July 1930, Wavell 'introduced . . . imaginative and unorthodox methods' of training. He 'stressed the need for surprise movements and outflanking', plus offensive air support. One of his exercises in 1932 was 'the Round-up of Rebels . . . designed to train his brigade to deal with the Commando type of resistance, who preferred fighting in woods or towns to . . . "normal" ground'. Other manoeuvres involved using lorries for simulated island landings and incursions. To his peers, 'His tactics were always . . . unconventional and unexpected.' Indeed, Wavell spoke of wanting infantrymen to emulate the 'poacher, gunman and cat burglar' and to have a 'dash of the Elizabethan pirate, the Chicago gangster and the Frontier tribesman'. He 'began to incorporate calculated deception into his operational plans' and underlined 'the need for modernising minds' in the military establishment, which was wedded to 'orthodox soldiering'. To this end, he ensured that he 'knew practically every man in the Brigade' and underlined 'the value of the personal touch' as a way of encouraging initiative and innovation among his subordinates.[10] Hence, he 'always had time for the young . . . officer (or NCO) – providing that he was active and zestful, and the more unorthodox in his outlook, the better. One such was Harry Fox-Davies.'

In 1935, Lieutenant Fox-Davies, Durham Light Infantry, wrote a memo 'pointing out the importance of guerilla troops . . . basing his argument on the . . . principle that a handful of men striking at the . . . heart of the enemy's communications can do . . . lasting damage out of all proportion to their numbers'. His own CO dismissed his views, but Fox-Davies knew of Wavell's open-mindedness and 'decided . . . here was someone who would understand' him. He approached Fergusson 'in some distress' and asked him to 'shove' the memo 'under Wavell's nose'. Fergusson did so on 1 October and, the following day, Wavell responded to the paper about 'the scientific use of guerilla troops in future wars . . . As usual [Wavell also] mentally pigeon-holed the idea' for potential future use.

Fox-Davies emphasised the 'value of surprise' in hitting enemy 'supplies . . . wires' and commanders in their HQs, using 'well trained guerilla troops'. Wavell concurred, noting, 'I agree with very much of what you say. We are too orthodox. We do not pay sufficient attention to . . . surprise [and] we neglect [different] means of obtaining information.' However, Wavell was less sure about the idea of organising soldiers to fight behind the lines as 'trained guerilla[s]' in civilian garb. He observed, 'Where guerilla war has had most effect (Spaniards in the Peninsula, Boers in South Africa, Feisal's Arabs), practically the whole population has been involved [in] a national uprising.' Wavell added that guerilla war in Europe would be trickier because of civil opposition, language barriers and the prospect of reprisals against the population, like those meted out by Prussia in 1870–1 on the French *francs-tireurs*. Moreover, Wavell thought that men as adventurous as those Fox-Davies envisaged were a 'rarity', and he concluded that 'psychologically, I don't think the "trained guerilla" is possible'. However, he continued, 'I don't mean that you shouldn't make every effort to train men to be capable of carrying out enterprises behind the enemy's lines', but they should do so 'as soldiers in uniform'. He added that 'guerilla warfare . . . is well worth reading and thinking about', having himself already absorbed Sun Tsu's millennia-old treatise, *The Art of War*. In 1936, during another major exercise, Wavell sent for Fox-Davies and, 'without any previous warning to formation commanders, bade him carry out a raid on the rear of his opponents', much to their bewilderment and consternation.[11]

Later that year, one fortnight in September, Wavell was invited to return to Russia to observe its experimental exercises in Minsk. 'As one of the few Russian-speaking senior officers' in the Army, he 'was delighted to be nominated as head of mission'. He observed a parachute display by some 2,500 Soviet paratroops and 'returned considerably impressed'. Indeed, he wrote about 'the use of parachute troops' for the Black Watch's journal, *The Red Hackle*, although his article was not published because the War Office thought that it contained sensitive information. Still, it is clear that Wavell was 'much intrigued by his first sight of this very novel method' of troop delivery and he 'sought to develop the idea in the British Army', not least through the Army Co-operation Squadron at RAF Farnborough. While he felt that 'paratroops would not materially affect the trend of operations' as a whole, significantly for the future SAS, he felt that 'even the threat of their use would be likely to neutralise a large number of troops who might have to be detailed to defend back areas'.[12]

Given that Wavell's 'fertile brain was always . . . receptive of new tactical ideas', when Bagnold approached him in June 1940, despite an 'incredulous GHQ staff', Wavell sent Bagnold to Mersa Matruh camp to raise a special force for 'long range patrols'. This would operate under Wavell's direct control, under the auspices of the DMI.[13] Bagnold was given *carte blanche* to over-ride 'prevailing caution and suspicion at GHQ' and create LRPs by August. He set up three, each comprising two officers and twenty-eight men, plus an HQ, with forty vehicles. To assist him, he called on his pre-war travel companions Robert Harding-Newman; Captain Edward C. Mitford, Royal Tank Regiment; a Shepheards resident, Major Guy Prendergast, RTR/Sudan Defence Force; the Palestine-based archaeologist W. B. Kennedy Shaw (another admirer of *Seven Pillars of Wisdom*); and Tanganyika-based Royal Artilleryman Captain Pat Clayton.

Bagnold's volunteers included a contingent of Kiwis provided by Major-General Bernard 'Tiny' Freyberg, their previous loss of equipment at sea having rendered them missionless. Bagnold had wanted Australians with desert know-how, but with none available, the New Zealand Expeditionary Force sufficed. They gathered at Abbassia Barracks and acquired nineteen 1½-ton Chevrolet and ¾-ton Ford trucks from the Army, plus eleven Marmon-Harrington civilian cars and others from Cairo motor dealers. By mid-August, many were equipped with a 2-pounder anti-tank gun, Bofors anti-aircraft and Lewis machine guns, and stocked with enough special rations and equipment (including *chappal* sandals from the North-West Frontier) for at least two weeks' patrolling over 1,500 miles. Concealed supply dumps were positioned at strategic points in the desert with food, water, ammunition and fuel. After several reconnaissances of the Uweinat and Kufra garrison and airfields (the latter the strategic lynchpin of southern Libya), the patrols prepared to make for the Big Cairn in the Great Sand Sea.

R Patrol was led by Kiwi Lieutenant Don G. Steele, W by Captain Mitford and T by Captain Clayton, who embarked first from Cairo on 5 September with a personal send-off from Wavell, Bagnold later noting that the general 'loved little enterprises of this kind'. T Patrol was followed by R, also making for Siwa, and W, heading for Ain Dalla at the eastern edge of the Sand Sea with Bagnold himself. On 13 September – the day that the Italian commander in Libya, Marshal Rodolfo 'The Butcher' Graziani, sent elements of his forces under General Mario Berti (from a total of 250,000 men in the Tenth and

Fifth Armies, based in Cyrenaica and Tripolitania, who were arrayed against 86,000 men of the British Western Desert Force) sixty miles over the border to Sidi Barrani and Sollum – the LRPs headed into Libya. They set up a base at Big Cairn and Clayton patrolled around Tekro, while Mitford moved to Kufra and Steele to Siwa. On 20 September, Mitford destroyed Italian lorries and captured mail, fuel and prisoners at Landing Ground No. 7. On his arrival back in Cairo after 'a bloodless battle,' the LRPs' 'reputation . . . was made', and, 'Rumours spread through the bars and messes that the unit had raided General Graziani's HQ.'

Returning from the field on 1 October, having demonstrated the feasibility of LRPs, Bagnold was congratulated by Wavell and the LRPs were redesignated as the Long Range Desert Group. Bagnold later recounted that, 'The staff in Cairo decided that the role . . . should now be a more offensive one [and] Wavell gave us a free hand to stir up trouble in any part of Libya we liked, with the objective of drawing off as much enemy transport and troops as possible [in order] to defend their remote garrisons'. The LRDG made a 'very favourable impression . . . with those in Cairo – some of whom had been sceptical'.[14]

Early in October, Mitford headed for Gebel Uweinat and the garrisons at Ain Zwaya and Ain Dua, which he hit on 31 October. Clayton went 500 miles north to Aujila garrison 'to keep the enemy guessing'. He mined a road and hit six vehicles before returning to Cairo a week later, after a 2,000-mile trip. Steele hit Kufra airfield, destroying a Savoia S-79 bomber and fuel dumps, in the process convincing Wavell that the LRDG's strength 'should be doubled', while Colonel D. Hunt of GHQ Intelligence marked their value for intelligence-gathering.

That December, 'a Guards [G] patrol was raised, half Coldstream and half [2nd] Scots, under [Captain] Michael D. D. Crichton-Stuart'. He noted that the unit 'was still on the secret list' and 'none of us had ever heard of it'. However, 'like any other desert addict', he had read the works of Lawrence and Bagnold (as well as Doughty's *Arabia Deserta*). A Yeomanry (Y) patrol under P. J. D. 'Pat' McCraith of the Palestine-based 1st Cavalry Division followed. Bagnold planned for G Patrol to raid the 200-man Murzuk garrison and airfield in southern Libya, 500 miles south of Tripoli, in tandem with Colonel d'Ornano's

Free French, who had arrived from Fort Lamy in Chad. He wanted a major 'hit and run affair [to] make the Italians waste petrol, transport and aircraft in chasing' them.

By 20 December, Major-General Richard N. 'Dick' O'Connor's forces had pushed the Italians out of Egypt, and the LRDG moved from Cairo to Ain Dalla on 29 December, carrying seventy-six all ranks in twenty-four vehicles (among them Shaw as Intelligence Officer, and an HQ truck with, *inter alia*, Scots Guard and future SAS man 'Jock' Easton). They followed the Faiyum road to the Great Sand Sea and, after camping at the Kalansho fringe, on 5 January 1941 (the day that Bardia was captured by O'Connor, followed closely by Tobruk and Derna), they reached Wav-el-Kebir in Fezzan, 250 miles east of Murzuk and a thousand miles from Cairo. After Clayton linked up with d'Ornano's Free French (under Colonel Leclerc's overall direction), Shaw undertook a reconnaissance and, on 8 January, the combined force headed for the Italians' outposts at Murzuk. On 11 January, T Patrol, led by Lieutenant Bruce Ballantyne, and G under Sergeant Henson (with Crichton-Stuart co-ordinating), assaulted Murzuk's Hon airfield and fort. Clayton *et al* took thirty PoWs at the aerodrome and hit three Ghibli spotter planes, before attacking Traghen fort, skirmishing at Umm el Araneb, and arriving at Zouar in Chad, on 19 January.

A week later, T and G departed with 400 men under Leclerc from his base at Faya for Ouianga Kebir, thence Tekro. On 31 January, Clayton, with forty-four men in eleven vehicles, scouted the Gebel Sherif, south of Kufra. They were spotted by seven Italian trucks of the Italian Auto-Saharan Company, backed by three aircraft. In a firefight, three of T Patrol's trucks were hit and Clayton was taken prisoner. Ballantyne took part of his patrol to Kufra (and, by 9 February, had returned to Cairo), while the Kufra bomber squadron airfield and garrison of 1,200 were raided by Leclerc on 7 February, before he hit Sarra ten days later. The Italians surrendered Kufra on 1 March and, by then, the LRDG was back at Shepheards, preparing Training Notes outlining their principal objective as 'long range ground recce patrols' with the flexibility to be 'used offensively if required'.[15]

The LRDG's successes had 'propaganda value' and were publicised in spite of 'a nervous censor', forming as they did a colourful part of

Wavell's overall gains, O'Connor having advanced 500 miles from Sollum to El Agheila by 7 February, taking 130,000 PoWs and clearing Cyrenaica, including Tobruk. Consequently, on 12 February, a new Axis commander arrived in Tripoli to stem the tide – Rommel. It was a development noted not only in theatre, but by General Auchinleck, who kept one eye on the Middle East from India, having discussed Iraq and Persia with Wavell in February.

When David Lloyd Owen – a future LRDG member – spoke to Wavell about the Group at that juncture, the CINC 'spoke of it as something in which he took a very special interest'. Wishing to extend the scope of current raiding, Wavell had proposed action at Benghazi in January 1941 and 'discussed the possibility of a raid' with O'Connor.[16] Additionally, in the previous month, George Pollock, head of SOE's SO2 (Operations) branch in Cairo (among whose number was Great War desert veteran Colonel Will Stirling, who had been recruited earlier in the year) flew to SOE HQ in London. Pollock did so 'at Wavell's suggestion to discuss ... ways and means of intensifying [SOE's] work in the Balkans' with the head of SOE, the Minister of Economic Warfare, Hugh Dalton, illustrating Wavell's keen interest in its activities.

SO2 Cairo had already sent 'small parties of ... students [for] paramilitary training [to] Lochailort' and, by 1941, groups of three or four were attending the 'parachute course at Ringway', while SOE London was assisting the training of the Auxiliary Units, which from November 1940 were commanded by Gubbins. Among those offering them advice were Indian Army officers such as Bill Beyts of the 6th Rajputana Rifles, while Intelligence officers taught guerilla warfare, sabotage and patrolling designed to 'harass enemy communications and rear areas with ambushes, demolitions and acts of terrorism'. SIS's Section D provided tuition in the use of time-pencil fuses, and all this training was overseen by erstwhile MI(R) Commando instructor Peter Fleming. At the end of 1940, 'he was sent [by Gubbins] to Cairo with instructions to ferret out likely' candidates who could act as 'saboteurs, and set up a training school ... [to] teach ... them what to do', initially with a view to carrying out raids on Sardinia and Sicily.

On Fleming's arrival in Cairo, Wavell was 'much taken with' Lovat's and the Stirlings' acquaintance, and he was soon tasked by Pollock with raising a force of Italian PoWs for behind the lines operations against Graziani's Tenth Army – a scheme that was the brainchild of SOE's propaganda expert, Colonel C. M. J. Thornhill, a lifelong friend of Wavell and 'character of GHQ'. In fact, Thornhill was 'an amiable, indiscreet man who was often to be found propping up the bar in Shepheards', the Turf Club, or the Continental Hotel -- his fixed abode, with its own dance floor, cabaret of belly-dancers and acrobats, plus a blonde American compère called Betty. He was 'more often than not occupied in loud voiced argument . . . while dispensing cocktails and whiskies to his wide circle of friends', including his then-assistant (and both future biographer of sometime Continental resident Orde Wingate, and SAS soldier), Christopher Sykes. Pollock charged Fleming with organising twelve operatives – most of whom were Fleming's friends – for special duties under the codename Yak Mission.

Early in 1941, the Yak team was 'dispatched . . . to the Commando training school at Lochailort and . . . given a crash course in assassination and the use of explosives'. Fairbairn and Sykes offered a three-day course in close-quarter combat, as well as lectures on booby-traps and poisoning, and the mission was assigned two Tommy guns – 'the first ones seen in the Middle East'. Among those involved with Fleming was Bill Stirling, but despite their scouring Egypt in search of recruits, no Italian PoWs could be persuaded to volunteer. At this point, only 'a handful of senior officers in staff circles in Cairo knew anything about SOE', and Wavell's chief of staff, Smith, 'complained that GHQ was not being kept informed' of its activities. Indeed, most SOE personnel reportedly spent much of their time dining 'at Shepheards, [and] laughed and drank immoderately at parties'. Consequently, Bill Stirling felt that 'the organisation was getting out of control'. Nonetheless, the Stirling brothers' associate, Fleming, would be called on to carry out further special duties by the CINC in due course, and his association with the Stirlings would continue.[17]

Commandos in the Middle East

As well as LRPs, in July 1940, Middle East HQ was ordered by the War Office to prepare its own Commandos. Initially, Wavell had been sceptical about them, worrying that they would be 'taking [the best] men from . . . units'. But he identified a 'great scope for Combined Operations' and, on 26 September, Lieutenant-General Wilson instructed the 2nd Battalion, Highland Light Infantry, 'to train about a hundred men to raid . . . the coast between Matruh and Sidi Barani [*sic*], should the Italians press on to Matruh'. On 27 September, the unit planned officer recce missions, followed a week later by exercises involving a 'landing from boats', accompanied by sappers. The plan envisaged the deployment of three platoons, one holding the beach while the others carried out the raid, as well as laying anti-tank mines and roadside booby-traps. They were also meant to take PoWs, before retreating to the boats. The operation was delayed for some weeks but, on 1 November, Colonel J. E. Benson of the Western Desert Force noted that 2nd HLI had formed a 'self-contained' reconnaissance party of two officers and six other ranks in three vehicles to 'recce . . . the west coast of Matruh' on 5 November.[18]

In the interim, Colonel MacLeod of the ISTDC was directed to establish a Combined Training Centre at Kabrit and No. 50 Commando was raised from 570 volunteers recruited in-theatre. In September, Wavell authorised a Palestine-raised No. 51 Commando of 650 all ranks, which was created by mid-October. No. 50 set sail on HMS *Decoy* and HMS *Hereward* on 29–30 October, to hit the Bomba seaplane base. However, the raid was called off at the last minute when its transports were diverted by news of the Italian invasion of Greece on 28 October. (Among those on the ground with a British military mission there was Wavell's 'old friend' Colonel Will Stirling of SOE, who proposed paralysing Italian communications by fomenting revolt in Albania. He requested the delivery of 15,000 rifles by smuggling or parachute drops, to which Wavell acceded, though the 'suggestion was received with horror' at Cabinet level and over-ruled.)

At this point, the Cairo HQ Intelligence Branch's GSI(R) – which became G(Raiding), or G(R) – was charged with overseeing LRPs, the Middle East Commandos and irregular formations in East Africa. In November, a third, 400-strong Commando, No. 52, started a six-week training course like that at Inverailort (albeit half its length) at the Middle East Commando Training Centre, Geneifa, before No. 52 carried out Wavell's instructions to raid Eritrea from Sudan.[19]

Operating from Tuklein near the Ethiopian border, the Commando entered the fight on 24 December, albeit mainly in a conventional infantry capacity. Still, deep penetration operations were done by Colonel Daniel Arthur Sandford's 101 Force, led by Major Tuckey, these having been sanctioned by Wavell in September. He also made Wingate Commander, British and Ethiopian Forces, his composite 'Gideon Force' including British teams comprising an officer and five NCOs who were there to assist local guerilla bands of 80–200 men. On arrival in Khartoum on 6 November, Wingate co-ordinated his plans with G(R)'s Captain Dodds-Parker, before returning to Cairo at Wavell's request to lecture on 2 December on 'patriot rebellion and his plans for a guerilla campaign'. These plans were implemented soon afterwards and, by 19 February 1941, Wingate was travelling by camel to Safartak, his 'object . . . to cut the communications of the Italian army in Gojjam with Addis Ababa and to contain them' before hitting the 'great Strada Imperiale' road to Asmara. Communications between Gondar and both Dessie and Debarech were then targeted and, early in March, Wingate's forces conducted 'harassing' night operations in groups of ten or twenty, using 'guerilla tactics' and feints at Burye and Dambacha, followed by an attack on Mankusa fort, near Debra Marcos. Gideon Force – including G(R)'s Major Simonds, with whom Wingate had served in Palestine in 1937 – caused 'havoc' and proved 'an essay in deception', hitting Abina fort before carrying out several small actions and night raids between 19 and 24 March, as well as making an attack on Agibar on 18 May (when Wingate was again recalled to Cairo by Wavell). By the time that he returned, 'Wingate was . . . a legend in the Gojjam', demonstrating that the Italians were vulnerable to raids.[20]

During its time in East Africa, No. 52 Commando did small unit patrolling and interdicted Italian communications, as well as carrying out raids and skirmishes. No. 51 – which was due to hit Sidi Barrani and Buq Buq in Libya with forty men in December 1940, but was foiled by high seas and bad weather – joined No. 52 at Gedaref on 10 February 1941. There, the Commandos did patrols and ambushes around Keren, and two companies penetrated the Italian rear and attempted an ambush on the Gondar–Metemma road. It proved unsuccessful, however, 'the main lesson [being] that two companies were too large a force' for such an operation.[21]

As for No. 50 Commando – which had gone to Crete at the end of November 1940 – Churchill and the Chiefs of Staff agreed to it scouting and raiding both the Dodecanese island of Kasos, and Castelorizzo, off the Turkish coast east of Rhodes. This would be a prelude to bigger Commando operations by Layforce that were being planned (although Wavell's December 1940 proposal that Commandos seize an island using a disguised merchant ship was shelved). After a stillborn probing from caiques on 16–17 January 1941 (Operation Blunt), on 23–24 February, No. 50 Commando set out in 'Mandible Force' from Heraklion to Castelorizzo, as part of Admiral Cunningham's Operation Abstention.

On 25 February, 200 Commando soldiers set off to hit the Castelorizzo shore from HMS *Decoy* and *Hereward* (escorted by HMS *Gloucester* and *Bonaventure*) at Niphtis Point, while a detachment of twenty-five Royal Marines under Lieutenant Stacpoole disembarked from HMS *Ladybird*. However, just fifty Commandos landed at first, eight of the ten boats drifting in the swell and only Commander Nicholl and Captain M. G. Borwick making land. A firefight broke out at Mount Vicla fort, where Captain K. E. Harmon led ten men against a hundred defenders and took it despite 'determined resistance'. Sergeant C. Harrington made an outstanding contribution by clearing the north-east of Castelorizzo town single-handed, while Major S. M. Rose rallied 'fighting patrols' on 26–27 February. However, the arrival of reinforcements from Cyprus was delayed and No. 50 was obliged by the landing of superior Italian forces to depart 'tired out and exhausted' after four days of enemy aircraft fire and the loss of twenty-six casualties and several PoWs.

One of those accompanying the force was the SIS's Jack Hanson, who described the operation as a shining example of 'confusion, incompetence, ineptitude and mess'. Churchill was angered by the 'fiasco' and General Evetts noted that, in future, beach defences must be breached swiftly. He proposed 'experiments . . . with infantry tanks in wire-cutting and mine exploding' and, until then, no more Commando raids would be approved. SOE's John Pendlebury proposed attacks on the Dodecanese from Crete, but their 'capture . . . was . . . postponed until [Layforce] with specially adapted ships, arrived in the Middle East'.[22]

In November 1940, all Special Service troops had been placed under the Combined Operations Directorate, and MO(9) became redundant. Hence, on 13 November, Wavell requested the transfer of his 'old friend and former colleague', Dudley Clarke, from MO(9) to Middle East HQ, 'to join [his] personal staff . . . as Intelligence Officer for Special Duties'. Clarke arrived in Cairo on 18 December and immediately updated Wavell on the Commando 'units training in Scotland'. While there is some debate among historians about whether Wavell specifically 'sent for them' at this time, they did figure in the planning of Operation Workshop – the raid on Pantelleria (though it and Operation Brisk, focusing on the Azores, were eventually cancelled by the Chiefs of Staff.)

While awaiting Layforce's arrival, Wavell also expanded the scope of his offensive activities. He later observed that, 'I . . . always believed in doing everything possible in war to mystify and mislead one's opponent . . . with the use of multiple bluffs.' He saw that, 'This was work for which . . . Clarke's originality [and] ingenuity qualified him admirably.'[23] Thus, Clarke was tasked with overseeing GHQ deception plans 'under the codename Galveston'. He 'was put in charge of A [Airborne] Force' and directed 'to organise by every means available the deception of the German High Command'. Working 'out of a brothel in the Kasr-el-Nil area of Cairo', Clarke (also known as 'Colonel Croft-Constable') and his colleagues – including Major V. H. Jones, 14th/20th Hussars, who was 'an expert in visual deception', and Captain Mark Ogilvie-Grant, Scots Guards – carried 'out the orders of the Chiefs' on strategic deception, first drawing up a cover plan for Operation Compass – Wavell's planned assault on the Italians at Sidi Barrani.

Within days of arriving in Cairo, Clarke studied a recently acquired Italian officer's diary. It revealed the Italians' fears of airborne landings behind the lines and, given that, 'One of the first rules of deception is to play on real fears', Clarke decided to devise a notional airborne force as a 'deterrent to enemy attack and an aid to deception in the offensive'. On 30 December, GHQ noted that, 'The Air Section suggests that some use might be made of dummy parachutes . . . to make the Italians believe we are using parachutists in the Western Desert at the present time, when Italian nerves are jumpy.' The GHQ

Intelligence section averred that the Italians would 'likely . . . be taken in by dummies' and Clarke decided to concoct 'cover plan Abeam, which the CINC was anxious should be kept to as small a circle as possible'.

Implemented from 11 January 1941, Abeam was 'the first [theatre] Order of Battle deception plan', part of which was to 'give the impression that the [fictional] 1st SAS Brigade [had] arrived in Egypt from England on 30 December'. It was supposedly composed of one parachute and two glider battalions that were busy training in secret at the Bayir Wells camp, south of Amman in Trans-Jordan. The name '1st Special Air Service Brigade' was chosen by Clarke in the light of the existing airborne Commando formation – formerly 2nd Commando, now retitled 11th SAS – which was preparing for its own raid on Italy to help relieve pressure on the Allies in North Africa in February 1941.

Clarke subsequently noted that Wavell had no airborne troops and there was 'little prospect of any becoming available for a very long time. We thought that if we could make [the enemy] believe we had airborne troops in reserve, it would not only add to our own strength, but would make him dissipate some of his [to protect] LoCs, rear areas and airfields against possible airborne attack.' A Force's scheme included the planting of false information in diplomatic channels to create the impression of a Middle East SAS Brigade. It was said to have 500 paratroops in ten platoons (A–K Detachments), equipped with carbines and grenades, as well as 'special containers' housing Bren guns, anti-tank mines, demolition charges and 2-inch mortars. The A Force story had it that the SAS had been formed at Perham Down in June 1940 and trained at Ringway until September, before moving to Whitchurch. On arrival in the Middle East, the phantom SAS force purportedly entrained from Suez to Lydda, before moving to a yeomanry camp at Latrun in Palestine, thence to Amman and El Qatrani, where the brigade mustered before camping under the Arab Legion's guard at Bayir Wells.

A Force also put out the fable that the SAS planned to move to Crete, ready for 'a swoop on Graziani's HQ'. Indeed, on 2 February 1941, the *Parade* newspaper published photos of 'Abyssinian parachutists training with British units', though the pictures taken at

RAF Heliopolis in Egypt actually portrayed a grinning 'local laundryman' dressed up as a paratrooper (*see illustration on p. 140*)![24]

On 4 February, Clarke arranged with Group Captain Paynton of RAF HQ Middle East that all RAF stations in the theatre be 'issued secret instructions . . . to report leaks of information re [the] presence of British parachutists or gliders', and 'deliberate whispers' to this effect were 'started in the RAF'. Additionally, the SIS's 'D Office' disseminated the story in Palestine and Iraq, while documents were planted in Palestine and Egypt, as well as on a Japanese consular official travelling to Turkey. A request was made too for two soldiers to 'act with guarded indiscretion' in Cairo.

Meanwhile, A Force staged phantom troop movements and exercises, deployed decoy and dummy lorries, tanks, artillery and roads, and utilised RAF pyrotechnics. One member of A Force, Jasper Maskelyne, was a 'brilliant stage magician' (and Clarke himself had an uncle in the Magic Circle). Maskelyne experimented with searchlights and mirrors to confuse enemy aircraft, and when the LRDG undertook its raids 'early in 1941', Clarke offered Bagnold assistance from RAF Hudsons dropping diversionary flares, fireworks and 'dummy paratroops'. Indeed, as part of their first operation, A Force provided the LRDG at Sidi Barrani with 'hundreds of [dummy] figures dropping down under parachutes'.

Following this 'triumph, Wavell pressed for an energetic use of long-distance deception and the active use of deception plans'. He and Clarke 'decided to create a notional army and to make it fight'. By 28 March, Clarke's staff had become Advanced HQ A Force, part of the 'notional Brigade of the "SAS" . . . allegedly based in Trans-Jordan'.[25]

Cue Layforce

When Layforce arrived at Geneifa, Nos. 50 and 52 Commandos had been amalgamated under 52's Lieutenant-Colonel George A. D. Young. 'Within two days of their arrival, the [UK] Commandos were visited and inspected by . . . Wavell' and Dill (then visiting Egypt), who 'knew all about them' and was a 'most staunch supporter'. Wavell likewise 'approved their departures from . . . normal' soldiering. Laycock's Commandos were officially renamed for a short period. Lieutenant-Colonel J. B. Colvin's No. 7 became A Battalion, Special

Service Brigade; No. 8, under Daly, who had resumed command on 23 March, was B Battalion; Lieutenant-Colonel Pedder's No. 11 was C Battalion; and Lieutenant-Colonel Young's 50/52 became D Battalion, based at Camp 53. On 16 March, Laycock attended a conference at Kabrit, followed by another in Cairo on the 20th. He returned to Kabrit on the 22nd, by which time routine training was underway.[26]

Within a week of their arrival, the SBS was 'teamed ... at the instigation of the staff at GHQME' with Narvik veteran Lieutenant-Commander Nigel Clogstoun-Wilmott, Royal Navy. Intelligence was needed for Operation Cordite – the raid on Rhodes – and GHQ 'determined to develop a force skilled in beach recce and Commando operations'. Clogstoun-Wilmott proposed at a conference in Cairo on 1 April that the SBS (including new recruits from Ran Churchill's troop) should scout the island and map its beaches, and 'Laycock agreed'. Soon after, Clogstoun-Wilmott went ashore and mapped the area around Hotel des Roses, followed by Rhodes town on the next night.

In addition, GHQ planned to 'make use of the imaginary "SAS Brigade" as part of the cover plan for "Cordite"', by placing dummy gliders on Cretan aerodromes and spreading a rumour that the SAS Brigade was preparing to take Scarpanto. However, on 3 April, Cordite was postponed when the Germans took Benghazi. Still, Courtney continued to plan raids from HMS *Medway*, 1st Submarine Flotilla, in Alexandria, and his second-in command, Lieutenant Robert 'Tug' Wilson, Royal Artillery, tried to mine ships in Derna and Benghazi on 24 April. However, he and Marine 'Wally' Hughes were prevented from deploying limpet mines from their folbot by choppy seas.[27]

Meantime, on 30 March, Wavell received instructions from the Chiefs of Staff to implement 'Plan A-R' (Anti-Rommel), to divert his forces by deception. 'Wavell instructed Clarke ... to simulate preparations for an attack on Axis LoCs between Tripoli and El Agheila', involving a 'notional amphibious attack mounted by a Commando force under ... Laycock', along with a flanking attack by the imaginary 10th Armoured Division, and an airborne assault by the non-existent 1st SAS Brigade. Clarke's plans were complete by 4 April and approved two days later by Wavell, and rumours were spread across Cyrenaica of impending attack.[28]

Robert Rogers, who founded his Rangers special force during the Seven Years War, inspiring key SAS men in 1941.

Lawrence of Arabia's operations in 1917–18 showed the potential for Middle East special forces in 1940–1. *Tank Museum Bovington*

General Allenby, who pioneered Middle East deception in World War I, providing lessons for Wavell and Clarke. *W. A. Jones Collection*

Left and below: Light Car Patrols in the Middle East during World War I, progenitors of the LRDG and SAS. The desert terrain often posed difficulties. *W. A. Jones Collection*

Above: Roger Keyes as a young officer. Keyes led the Zeebrugge raid in 1918 and was Chief of Combined Operations in 1940–1. *W. A. Jones Collection*

Right: Winston Churchill, champion of special forces, including the Commandos and the SAS. *W. A. Jones Collection*

Mike Calvert (*third left*) is among those briefed by Orde Wingate (*standing wearing pith helmet*) during the Chindit operations in Burma. *Imperial War Museum (IWM) MH 7883*

Above: Commando instructors at Lochailort in 1941. The staff included Stirling's cousin, Lord Lovat.
Liddell Hart Centre (LHC)

Left: Lochailort, where Commandos including David Stirling trained in 1940. *LHC*

Above: A Fairbairn Sykes Commando knife, standard kit for the SAS in 1941.

Right: White's Club in Piccadilly, London, where Stirling signed up for the Commandos.

Left: Going ashore from landing craft during Commando training at Lochailort. *LHC*

Generals Auchinleck (*left*) and Wavell, CINCs Middle East in 1941 when the SAS was formed.
IWM E5448

J. C. F. Holland (*front, far right*), co-founder of SOE, at Rorkee College between the two world wars.
Photograph reproduced with the kind permission of the Royal Engineers Museum and Library

Above: Group Captain Michael Devlin at RAF Helwan in May 1941 when SAS deception measures were in place there. *Jim Devlin*

Right: Ralph Bagnold, founder of the LRDG, which worked with the SAS from 1941. *Photograph reproduced with the kind permission of the Royal Engineers Museum and Library*

E Force was based at Jalo fort in August 1941 and assisted both LRDG and SAS patrols later that year.
Company Sergeant-Major Ronnie Gamble

Above: General Freyberg as a junior officer in World War I. He commanded troops in Crete in 1941 and faced German paratroopers.
W. A. Jones Collection

Left: Dudley Clarke, co-founder of the Commandos and SAS.
W. A. Jones Collection

RMS *Glengyle*, which transported Stirling and his colleagues to Egypt early in 1941. *Francine Bailey*

Alexandria port, where the SAS is alleged to have acquired parachutes for its first jumps in June 1941.
W. A. Jones Collection

Shepheards Hotel, Cairo, where Stirling and other key players in the SAS story resided in 1941.
W. A. Jones Collection

Cairo military hospital. David Stirling wrote his memo on the SAS here in June 1941 while recovering from his parachute accident. *W. A. Jones Collection*

Above right: RAF Kabrit. The SAS's camp was adjacent to it in 1941. *Sergeant Peter Verney*

Right: RAF Heliopolis, which the SAS raided for equipment in 1941. *Company Sergeant-Major Ronnie Gamble*

Left: General Neil Ritchie, to whom Stirling presented his SAS memo in July 1941. *Major A. N. B. Ritchie*

A Bristol Bombay, like those used by Stirling's men in 1941, part of an A Force deception scheme featuring Abyssinian paratroops (*pictured*) – actually Egyptian laundrymen. *PRO Kew*

An E Force lorry at the Great Sand Sea fringe, an LRDG/SAS patrol area in 1941.
Company Sergeant-Major Ronnie Gamble

Above: RAF Helwan, the site of another SAS deception scheme in June 1941. *Geoffrey & Mike Grierson*

Right: A Luftwaffe aerial photo of Derna port, an SAS target in 1941. *Phil Verbana*

Siwa Oasis in 1941. The LRDG patrolled from a base here in support of the SAS.
Company Sergeant-Major Ronnie Gamble

Sergeant Curry at Jalo fort from which the LRDG operated in support of the SAS in 1941.
Company Sergeant-Major Ronnie Gamble

A desert landing ground south of Tobruk in 1941, an area targeted by the SAS in November and December. *Sergeant Keith Hansen.*

An SAS patrol in Cairo in 1942. *LHC*

David Stirling, founding father of the SAS, in 1941. *IWM E21340*

Over and above such ruses, on 7 April, Layforce received orders to move, with A Battalion bussed to Ismailia and thence the *Glengyle*, B and C to the *Glenroy* and *Glenearn* at Ferara, and D by train to Alexandria. A, B and C moved on 8 April and the *Glen* ships rallied at Port Said the next day. Laycock's advance HQ was in place aboard the *Glengyle* by 10 April and, after conferring with his superiors in Cairo, on 11 April, Laycock received orders for a 'recce . . . of [the] coastline in [the] Western Desert'. The brigade was informed that it should 'prepare to operate in raiding parties of 200', and B and D Battalions went by rail to Alexandria, then Sidi Bishr. 'Selected men of 8 Commando, including [future SAS originals Jim] Almonds and' martial arts exponent Sergeant Lilley were transferred to the destroyer, HMS *Decoy*, and lowered in small boats to 'practise . . . silent rowing', so as to be able to move 'ashore . . . get round the German lines and cut their supply and communications lines'.[29]

The Commandos in the Middle East looked set to emulate the success of their brethren in the UK, who in March had made for the Lofoten Islands off Norway as part of Operation Claymore.

The Lofoten Raid

On 21 February, 500-plus men of Durnford-Slater's No. 3 and Lovat's No. 4 Commando, under Brigadier Haydon, embarked from Gourock on the landing ships RMS *Queen Emma* and *Princess Beatrix* – commanded by Commodores J. Brunton and C. A. Kershaw – to hit the Lofoten archipelago. The convoy under Captain C. Caslon made Scapa Flow in the Orkneys by 1 March and, on the following day, refuelled off Skaalefjörd on the Faroe Islands with five escort destroyers, HMS *Somali*, *Bedouin*, *Tartar*, *Eskimo* and *Legion*, and their heavy covering force, HMS *Nelson*, *King George V*, *Nigeria* and *Dido* now on the scene. The flotilla reached the Lofotens – 900 miles north of the UK, west of Narvik, and north of Bodo – at dawn on 4 March. With navigation assistance from the submarine HMS *Sunfish*, the assault force of twelve landing craft, with thirty-five men in each (including fifty Norwegians in all), landed with the intention of hitting the ports of Henningsvaer, Svolvaer, Stamsund and Brettesnes.

The Commandos were accompanied by War Office Intelligence officers and Royal Engineers, who undertook demolitions at eighteen industrial sites and seven other targets, including factories producing herring and cod liver fish oils used in the Germans' explosives industry. Due to faulty intelligence, No. 3 landed far from any opposition forces, but eleven ships were sunk and scout parties took 225 German PoWs, while Lovat met one German column. He subsequently noted that, 'Although there had been no fighting, any action was better than no raid at all [and at the] top level, Lofoten was hailed as a considerable success [which] put British Commandos firmly on the world map.'[30]

The Invasion of Greece

Before the Rhodes raid could build on this success, however, the Germans invaded Greece and Yugoslavia on 6 April, scuppering Operation Cordite. Following the recent example set in Skopje, and in 'rehearsal for the full-scale attack . . . upon Crete' in May, on 26 April, the 'airspace over Corinth' in Greece was 'filled with . . . troop-carrying planes . . . disgorging hundreds of paratroops'. Two battalions of Germany's 2nd Paratroop Regiment – 800 men – dropped in twenty minutes from sticks of three planes over the Corinth Canal. One observer, Lieutenant Tyson, Royal Engineers, noted that they 'landed unarmed [but] descending parachutists form an extremely difficult target owing to the way they oscillate in the air'. He added that they 'immediately set about collecting their weapons (a small sub-machine gun) and then gathered into groups of about 12–20 men'. They made for the Corinth bridge, but it was blown up by Captain J. Phillips, Devonshire Regiment.[31]

A further report for Middle East HQ about the German paratroop raid, by Lieutenant-Colonel W. L. Leggatt, was 'given the widest possible circulation'. He noted (not entirely accurately) that between 1,200 and 2,000 parachutists dropped over the Canal from 200 feet out of Junkers 52s, about thirty men jumping out of each aircraft and landing over an area of 200–300 yards. They soon gathered their weapons from 6 ft x 1 ft steel containers dropped by the third aircraft of each stick and formed patrols of six men. They were 'able to produce intensive machine-gun fire within about two minutes', ensuring that defenders were unable to 'shoot up parachutists at leisure'.[32]

This German invasion prompted Wavell to send Fleming's Yak Mission to Greece, the SOE-backed unit having spent February and March working on plans for sabotage in Yugoslavia that now came to naught. But Fleming had made 'useful contact . . . with A Force' and 'picked up many ideas' from Clarke and, when Fleming asked Wavell to deploy Yak 'to organise resistance along the German lines of communication [he] immediately granted his request'. Their focus was on 'harassing the German advance in the Monastir Gap' and they hit railways as the Allied forces retreated south to the coast, including two at Larissa, as well as points on the coastal road. But while Fleming's 'small party . . . did what it could to harass the German advance . . . and managed to carry out a number of important demolitions', GHQ was disappointed with the results. 'Wavell, previously a supporter, joined in . . . the recriminations' and sent 'a private wire . . . to Dill saying that special operations in the Middle East was a "racket".' British reinforcements, including thousands of men and vehicles aboard Layforce ships, then went to Greece, while Fleming transferred to A Force, where he spent 'a few weeks' . . . profitable time'. Wavell used Security Intelligence Middle East MI6 double agents in North Africa to 'convey to the enemy the impression that' his 'forces in the Western Desert had been seriously weakened by sending reinforcements to Greece'.[33] But while the Greek collapse by 21 April meant that the Allies had to retreat – with Layforce's landing craft 'suffering considerable damage' in the process – new plans were soon afoot for further diversionary operations, and Laycock continued to press for his men to be involved in them.[34]

Chapter 9

Bardia or Bust

With shipping diverted by the Greek invasion, Wavell addressed the SBS and confessed that he now 'didn't know why they were there'. John Parker adds that there was 'a curious reluctance to use Layforce on the kind of operations for which the men had been raised' and, when a BEF was sent to Greece, 'to Laycock's dismay and fury he was kept behind in Egypt'. However, after Rommel had reoccupied Cyrenaica (except Tobruk, held by 25,000 Allied troops led by General Leslie Morshead's 9th Australian Division) in March–April 1941, 'Laycock was eager to prove the worth of his untried units.' With their morale dipping due to inactivity, he 'arranged for them to be exempted from' plans for a new theatre 'reserve force' in favour of 'sorties along the coast with the intention of harassing the enemy'.[1]

On 12 April, a planned coastal reconnaissance was cancelled due to poor weather, but C Battalion's troop leaders were 'told of [a] possible raid in [the] near future [and] Laycock was determined to go ahead', believing that, 'The very future of Commando operations in the desert seemed to depend upon the success of this raid.' He knew there were 'many dissenting voices amongst the army commanders who attended the planning conference on board HMS *Warspite*' on 14 April. But, as C Battalion undertook landing craft drills off Alexandria that afternoon,[2] Winston Churchill circulated his 'The War in the Mediterranean' memo. It ordered that, 'German lines of communication across the Mediterranean and from Tripoli to Agheila must be subject to incessant harassment and interdiction', and he urged Wavell to regain the 'ascendancy over the enemy and destroy his small raiding parties, instead of our being harassed and hunted'.[3]

On 15 April, Colonel Hope of GHQ Middle East 'brought orders for immediate raids on Bardia and on the coast road near Bomba. It was decided A and C Battalions [would go] to Bardia, and 150 men of

[Daly's] B Battalion to Bomba.' Five troops of A Battalion would assault Bardia harbour, raid the barracks and set up road blocks, while three troops held the beach. C Battalion would implement 'Project B' and make for the Sollum–Sidi Barrani highway east of Tobruk to attack motor transport, take prisoners and hit stores to the west. Similar action would be taken by B Battalion, which transferred to HMS *Decoy* under Sudeley. Major Napier of C Battalion told his troop leaders, 'remember your night attack drill. Stick in your parties and think of the other parties. Go in as a team.' Among them were future SAS men, eighteen-year-old Lieutenant Eoin McGonigal, Royal Ulster Rifles, an erstwhile Commando instructor on Arran, and Lieutenant Bill Fraser, Gordon Highlanders; as well as Scots Greys' officer, Arab Rebellion veteran and son of the Director of Combined Operations, Major Geoffrey Keyes.

On 15 April, C Battalion received instructions for its three-hour raid and, next day, the *Glengyle* and *Glenearn* made out to sea. However, they were held up by a heavy swell in Bardia Bay and Courtney reported that his folbots could not launch from their submarine. As a result, the operation was scratched, though a planning conference on 18 April 'announced the desire of GHQME that [the] Bardia raid should take place at the earliest opportunity'. Hence, on the night of 19–20 April – coincidentally both Hitler's birthday and the moment that David and Bill Stirling's brother in the 2nd Scots Guards, Lieutenant Hugh J. Stirling, was 'killed on patrol' at Sidi Barrani – the raid finally got off the ground.[4]

The day after, Almonds, Riley and Kershaw met David Stirling at the Cairo racetrack and they took the train to Almariya camp near Alexandria (to which B and C Battalions returned on 22 April). There, rumour had it that the raid 'had been a success', though that was not how Laycock saw it. The *Glengyle* had taken the Commandos, accompanied by the cruiser HMS *Coventry* and three Australian destroyers, HMAS *Stuart*, *Voyager* and *Waterhen*, to their target. However, an advance reconnaissance party from Courtney's SBS (officially designated 1st Special Boat Service Brigade on its transfer to Alexandria on 13 April) arrived late, after their conveyance, the submarine, HMS *Triumph*, was strafed by British aircraft and lost its navigation light. Courtney's own folbot was wrecked in the swell as he tried to cast off from the submarine, while the *Glengyle*'s landing craft were delayed by mechanical faults with their davits. When the raiders, under Lieutenant-Colonel Felix Colvin, finally landed, faulty intelligence saw them in an area devoid of opposition assets.

No. 1 Detachment of fifty men was meant to hold the beach while No. 2 (twice No. 1's size) set up road-blocks. No. 3 (also a hundred men) would carry out a harbour assault and No. 4 (fifty men) attack vehicles and take prisoners. A second beach was assigned to No. 5 (seventy men), who were to attack vehicles, while a third beach was targeted by No. 6 (seventy specialists in bridge/highway demolitions). No. 7 (thirty-five men) was to meant take out AA guns on a fourth beach.

In practice, three of the raiding groups destroyed a bridge and some lorries, and one attacked the harbour (with Waugh, Keyes and Seekings in tow). Corporal Baxford and Sapper Angus of Captain Jocelyn Nichols's detachment blew up four naval guns on D Beach, but one officer was killed by friendly fire, and five others, plus sixty-five other ranks, were captured on the wrong exit beach. The Ministry of Information asserted that the raid 'was a considerable strategic success ... Alarmed by it, the enemy diverted the greater part of a German armoured brigade from Sollum [to Bardia].' But, in its immediate aftermath, 'the raid was ... a disappointment' to Laycock, who had hoped unequivocally to 'prove the effectiveness of the Commandos'. He was 'justifiably very annoyed' and 'ill-content with this performance', though he noted that 'many valuable lessons were learned'.[5] Indeed, Waugh 'wrote a short memo' arguing that night-time favoured the defender and that, 'Only the smallest parties should be used in night operations.'

Some days later, Laycock gave a 'lecture ... on the faults of the raid', but 1943's *Combined Operations* argues that, 'The expedition ... appeared to show that considerable advantage could be gained by following a programme of small-scale raids on the enemy's lines of communications ... along or near the coast.' A Middle East HQ meeting of 20 April in fact recommended reorganising the Commandos into their own Middle East Commando HQ, with at least one new unit.[6] However, Wavell's attention had been diverted by events in Greece and Rommel's counter-offensive, which saw the

Allies retreat back to the Egyptian border and the LRDG take up a mainly defensive posture at its forward bases in Kufra and Siwa, only G and Y patrols skirmishing from the latter before being relieved in July 1941.[7]

On 26 April, Wavell directed C Battalion to head for Cyprus to bolster its defences, securing it while the Australian 7th Division planned an offensive against Vichy French forces in Syria. Churchill had ordered this in the light of both Rashid Ali's pro-German revolt of 1 April against Britain's presence in Iraq, and the decision of Vichy's General Dentz to allow German air bases in Syria. Concurrently, news came in that the Germans were about to invade Crete (Operation Mercury). Wavell had received Ultra electronic intelligence intercepts in March that German airborne forces were moving under General Süssman to Plovdiv in Bulgaria and, on 19 April, the CINC warned the Greek government-in-exile on Crete that a German airborne assault was possible. (Italian paratroopers from the Libyan Division had already landed on Cephalonia.) However, while the Joint Intelligence Committee warned of impending action on 27 April, Wavell and the Chiefs believed that they had time to build up reserves to prevent it. On 28 April, they even stated that it could be a German deception.[8]

Still, despite their uncertainty and the postponement of Operation Cordite, on 14 April, Middle East HQ decided to go ahead with A Force's deception plan for Crete, 'as the presence of gliders may well be taken [by the enemy] as a threat to Cyrenaica as well as the Dodecanese'. Hence, 'an advance party of the SAS Brigade' under Major V. H. Jones arrived in Crete on 16 April, prior to a group 'seventy strong' with one officer who were due to land on 28 April to 'play an important part in [the] deception plan which the CINC ha[d] in mind'. By then, however, Wavell faced the prospect of Crete being assaulted and the SAS deception was cancelled on 22 April. Jones's party was recalled by Middle East HQ's Brigadier Whiteley and a glider force of 30–50 dummy planes and four light trucks armed with Brens remained in Egypt.[9]

Paras to the Fore

While we cannot be certain that Stirling, Lewes and other pioneers were aware of either the 11th SAS operation in Italy, or the German paratroop drop on Corinth on 26 April (though Stirling probably was), Lewes's biographer asserts that, 'In April 1941 [he] requested the permission of Robert Laycock to create his own small parachuting force to operate behind enemy lines.' Lewes and his colleagues certainly knew of the air assault on Crete on 20 May by General Student of Fliegerkorps XI. His invasion plan included an initial landing by 6,000 men (six paratroop battalions and one glider-borne battalion) from 7. Fleigerdivision on Crete. Their speed impressed Churchill so much that it convinced him 'there was an important role for paratroops'. Indeed, on 26 April – the day of the Corinth action – the PM had attended a parachute and glider demonstration near Bury St Edmunds featuring six Whitleys dropping thirty-two men (from a total of 800 fully trained UK paratroops).[10] Soon after, he urged the Chiefs of Staff to press ahead with plans for 5,000 paratroops and, among the top brass, 'There was a feeling of urgency about the training of British paratroops because of the Germans' success.' At the end of May, the Chiefs presented a joint RAF–Army memo proposing a new parachute brigade based around 11th SAS, comprising four battalions and an airborne troop of sappers, as well as a similar unit for the Middle East.

This provided a receptive environment in which those seeking to champion the paratroop cause there could press their case. By then, Auchinleck was also assessing the scope for airborne troops in India and, although no parachutes were available in the Raj before mid-1941, the Viceroy, Marquess Linlithgow, noted that plans were being made in Delhi for an airborne unit 'on a very small scale'. Indeed, in late May the Ringway staff were informed that 'a similar school was to be formed in India', and that 'the CO and a nucleus staff [would be] provided by Ringway'. Its deputy CO, Squadron Leader Jack Benham, Auxiliary Air Force, was pencilled in for this position, but when he took over from Strange at Ringway, Group Captain Maurice Newnham was offered the Indian post on 9 July.[11]

Meantime, Dudley Clarke pursued his paratroop deception plans with Wavell's support. On 4 April, Clarke had seconded Lance-Bombardier R. L. Smith and Gunner M. H. Gurmin of the Staffordshire Yeomanry 'for special escort duty'. This was a 'highly secret duty personally explained to [their] CO' three weeks before their secondment. Smith and Gurmin were tasked with travelling on 13 April to Alexandria, thence Cairo two days later, to carry out an A Force scheme. On 11 April, Clarke directed his purported SAS men to adopt the guise of Lance-Corporal Smith and Trooper Gurmin of the Royal Artillery (a regimental cover, incidentally, that was apparently used by the SAS during the Greek Civil War of 1945-9, as detailed in *SAS: The First Secret Wars*).

The yeomen 'gunners' were attached for the purposes of the ruse to '1st SAS Battalion (Parachutists)' and were instructed to 'keep this up throughout ... [their] stay'. They were each given a dossier containing 'the story of [their] ... movements etc. over the last few months', and Clarke told them 'you must learn this thoroughly in order to keep up the [pretence]'. The scenario had them 'serving in England last summer with a battery of artillery when volunteers for parachute work were called for after Dunkirk. [They] were sent to the Central Landing School, Ringway Aerodrome' that June, and gained their wings after jumping from Whitley aircraft – just as the 11th SAS had done. Clarke's dossier claimed the men had served with a Commando and, in September, 'It was turned into the 1st SAS Battalion' under Lieutenant-Colonel Jackson. Along with imaginary 2nd and 3rd SAS (Glider) Battalions, this comprised an SAS Brigade. It reportedly left the UK in November, arriving at Suez on 30 December. From there, the phantom formation was said to have gone by train to Latrun camp near Ramaleh, before moving by lorry to Amman, then flying to Bayir Wells. Training had purportedly gone on until recently, with the SAS arriving in Cairo on 5 April. As Clarke pointed out to his plants, this was 'information that you'd normally keep very secret', but he told them to 'let a word or two out if you get the opportunity'.

As instructed, the pair of SAS frauds wandered about Cairo, where they 'attracted a considerable amount of attention'. They visited the Sharia El Dine cabaret and were queried by 'a member of the Royal Tank Corps' about their uniforms. On the following day, they visited the city's Services Club and an 'RAF man asked a few questions'. Two days later, the pair 'attracted an enormous amount of attention in Port Said', an infantry sergeant-major and staff sergeant in particular being 'very interested' by their guise. After their return on 20 April, Clarke noted that the pair had 'done a really useful piece of work which has done much to help along a . . . plan in which the CINC has personally interested himself'.

Indeed, by the end of the year, Clarke could note that, 'The presence of parachute units in the Middle East was widely believed by the troops' on both sides, as well as 'the local inhabitants'. By 20 April, Clarke was also putting out the story that the imaginary SAS brigade had 'completed training and [wa]s in the process of movement via Egypt to Crete, where it is well placed for action against either Libyan LoCs or [the] Dodecanese'. Two days later, Major Jones's A Force advance party to Crete was recalled, but before Clarke went at Wavell's behest to Turkey on 26 April, he set up A Force's Advanced HQ at 6 Sharia Kasr-el-Nil. By 8 May, it comprised two officers and ten other ranks.[12]

Additionally, on 25 April, Lieutenant J. M. Robertson, Argyll and Sutherland Highlanders, was directed to 'operate dummy gliders' being placed at the 'disused' Helwan Aerodrome, near Cairo, in co-operation with its CO, Wing Commander Rees. On 26 April, Robertson received orders from Air Vice-Marshal Wigglesworth (Senior Air Staff Officer to the AOC, Air Chief Marshal Arthur Longmore) to have K Detachment SAS (one of ten purported parties, comprising fifty-seven sappers under Sergeant-Major Jerram, Royal Engineers) based at Helwan by 10 May. Jerram had seventeen aircraft *in situ* two days later, while Robertson went 'by special train' with twenty men 'complete with camp equipment' to Fuka airbase, south-east of Mersa Matruh, and fifty miles from Bagoush. There, they disguised sixteen gliders as bombers by 17 May.

On the 25th, Clarke noted that there was 'considerable activity' at Helwan and that, as the airfield was observed by enemy informers, 'I should very much like to give the watchers something definite to report. After discussing the matter with Wing Commander Rees, I think that the best thing we could do would be to arrange some dummy parachute dropping.' Clarke elaborated that 'one or more aircraft from Heliopolis should fly over Helwan' and, for a period of three days over a week or so, 'drop parachutes with dummies attached over the aerodrome. Wing Commander Rees will recover these, pack the parachutes and return them to Heliopolis'. In the second week of June, 'the RAF flew over Helwan three [times] to drop dummy parachutists', observed by the local inhabitants, as Clarke had hoped.[13]

In the interim, Laycock was seeking work for Layforce and attended a conference at Alexandria on 28 April. There, 'It was decided that any troops of Layforce available at Sidi Bishr should take part in [the] defence of Alexandria against possible raids by light mobile forces.' On the following day, he attended a meeting on 'HMS *Warspite* to discuss future raiding policy on [the] N. African coast', and a decision was taken to despatch half of B Battalion to Tobruk – to which the Germans had laid siege on 12 April – 'for immediate raiding action in [the] west' on German communications. An advance party under Lieutenant Alston made its way there for a three-week stay, before returning to Mersa Matruh, not having been committed to battle. The planned despatch of 100 men under Sudeley 'to land behind the enemy's left rear', eighteen miles east of Tobruk, was also thwarted by Rommel's offensive.

Concurrently, the other half of B Battalion prepared to move from Kabrit to Mersa Matruh 'to rehearse raids on beaches' should the Allies be forced to withdraw. On 30 April, Laycock met with the GOC Desert Force 'to discuss [the] co-ordination' of raids with other operations and, on 2 May, 250 all ranks of B Battalion were 'ordered [to] embark' on the destroyer HMS *Aphis*, 'early [on] 3 May for Tobruck [sic]', ready for a raid on the Gazala airfield west of it. On 6 May, Laycock contacted Wavell's chief of staff, Arthur Smith, and admitted that his 'situation [wa]s now becoming desperate'. He noted that he had 'continually volunteered for daring action which has been continually promised' but not effected. He added that his men's one-year Special Service commitment would expire soon, so they needed to be committed quickly to the fight. He owned that the recent Bardia raid 'was not very skilfully executed', but he was 'convinced that there is tremendous scope for our activities against enemy LoCs where, if we are lucky, we might create considerable havoc'. He continued that 'all ranks share this view', concluding, 'I most earnestly entreat that employment be found for us soon, if only in the form of small but infrequent raids carried out by say ... 50 to 100 men.' He later reflected that, 'It appeared obvious' after the Bardia raid 'relieved the pressure in that area [that] considerable advantage would accrue to us through many small scale raids on the LoC[s] in the Western Desert, which would keep the enemy continually apprehensive as to the security of his communications.' If such tasks could not be found for Layforce, Laycock feared its disbandment.[14]

Smith responded to Laycock's plea on 6 May, noting that Wavell 'very much regrets that the Special Service Brigade has so far had a very disappointing time through no fault of their own', and he assured Laycock that Wavell was 'personally interested in their well-being'. However, he begged patience, for 'the time will come when we shall be able to take the offensive'. In the interim, B Battalion kept itself busy with day and night patrols on the salt lakes and training with rifles and Bren guns at the adjacent RAF camp, while D did a simulated night raid on an enemy aerodrome and a railway via small boats. On 11 May, Laycock conferred with GHQ before visiting Desert Force HQ on the 12th for a conference the next day. On the 14th, he and Waugh made their way with an advance party to Mersa Matruh aboard HMS *Aphis* and the rest of B Battalion made ready to follow on 16 May. On the 17th – the day that a contingent from D Battalion faced German paratroops on Crete – Waugh drove from Cairo to Mersa Matruh with Peter Fleming, where, on the 18th, he 'demonstrate[d] types of bomb and boobytrap', including time-pencils, for 'a poor audience'.[15]

By that time, according to Waugh, GHQ's Lieutenant-Colonel Maurice Hope had 'devised a series of minor operations against enemy LoCs on the coast of Cyrenaica'. On 20 May, eleven officers and ninety-nine men set off on the *Aphis* to 'mount a raid' on a German airfield on the 'islet of Ain el Gazala', twenty-five miles west of Tobruk. However, they were attacked by Junkers 87 Stukas both on the 21st and during a second attempt on the 27th. Rough seas prevented further forays, so the operation was cancelled, as was the move by the rest of B Battalion to Mersa Matruh. This dismayed Laycock, who had gone to G(R) on 21 May to discuss more raids from the *Aphis*.[16]

On the 22nd, while Auchinleck met Wavell to co-ordinate forces deployed to Iraq from India, Laycock discussed with G(R) 'the conversion of up to two Battalions [of the] Special Service Brigade into four Long Range Desert Groups', each initially equipped with four trucks, as well as the potential 'suitability of the personnel of Layforce for conversion to an LRDG' force by September. Following its successes, Wavell wanted to expand Bagnold's force. Using Layforce personnel was 'put forward by G(R) and agreed to in principle by the CINC' (though the LRDG's own preference was for reinforcements from New Zealand or South African motorised units). As ever, Laycock 'stressed the adaptability of SS personnel', adding that, 'Most men would continue for a further period . . . if they knew that the Battalions were going to be used for special operations of the type for which they have been trained.' He also ensured that B Battalion was 'exempted from' plans for the theatre reserve 'and kept on Special Service'. But a final decision about the remainder of Layforce rested with Wavell and, when Laycock headed back to Mersa Matruh on 23 May, the matter was still in abeyance.[17]

Laycock and Waugh then sailed on HMS *Abdiel* for Sidi Bishr, near Alexandria, where they set about re-establishing a brigade HQ. They also prepared to despatch C Battalion on 3 June as part of a build-up for the proposed incursion into Syria, and to deter a German invasion of Cyprus. Indeed, on 13 June, at the behest of the CINC Mediterranean Fleet, Admiral Cunningham, Waugh prepared a 'Pencil Party' (equipped with pencil time-fuses) of twelve men from A Battalion to 'lie up in the neighbourhood of the aerodrome' at Nicosia and 'sabotage enemy aircraft . . . at night', before making their 'escape as best they could'. In the event, the party was not deployed to Cyprus, but 800 men of A and D Battalions were sent from Alexandria to fight under Laycock in Crete, arriving there on 24 May.[18]

The Germans had reinforced the island with 16,000 troops (12,000 landing from 750 gliders over the Heraklion, Rethymno, Galatas and Maleme airfields). General Freyberg's garrison was in trouble, 'small bodies of paratroops not only establishing themselves astride all roads but securing many tactical features', a fact that may have affected Wavell's thinking about the potential worth of paratroop operations. On 23 May, the *Glenroy* set off with HMS *Coventry* and two escorts but, after failing to land at Sphakia due to bad weather, the Commandos returned to Port Said. After the *Glenroy* was hit by Stukas, they landed on Crete from HMS *Abdiel* on the night of 24 May. They took up a defensive position in which they were dive-bombed, before conducting outflanking night moves on 26–27 May. The Commandos faced heavy fighting around Maleme and, by the 28th, the battle was all but lost. They covered the retreat of remaining Allied forces from Heraklion to Suda Bay, and Laycock ordered 'a few light counter-attacks [by] fighting patrols of seven or eight men', before the Allied withdrawal from Babali Hani to the coast. In the process, Layforce lost most of its strength as PoWs or wounded, and only twenty-three officers and 156 other ranks were evacuated on 31 May.[19]

'When Col. Laycock returned to Egypt on 1 June 1941, after the evacuation of Crete, he was told that it had been decided to disband the Special Service Brigade . . . on the grounds that it could not be kept up to establishment.' Indeed, according to Waugh, while Laycock was on Crete 'at the end of May', B Battalion's CO, Daly, 'went out of his mind, rushed to Cairo, saw . . . Wavell and, on his return, told his men that those without [units] were to go to infantry base depots'. However, there would be an 'exemption' in the shape of 'a small force which he proposed to make into a long-range desert patrol', apparently taking up Middle East HQ's proposal to expand the LRDG.[20] This did not actually come to pass, but B Battalion's senior officers were clearly determined to retain some of their personnel on Special Service in whatever capacity.

Chapter 10

Searching for a Role

On 31 May – the day on which the Chiefs of Staff responded to Churchill's badgering after Crete to form parachute brigades in the UK and India (the latter for use in the Middle East) – Wavell declared that Layforce was no longer viable. Alan Hoe notes that regarding the reasons for his conclusion, 'the history books are unclear', though he surmises that it stemmed firstly from German advances preventing more raids, secondly because shipping could not be spared for the Commandos and finally that they were under strength after Crete.[1] Laycock himself noted that it was 'solely because it was impossible to keep ... up to strength'. Hence, GHQ offered Daly's B Battalion the option of joining either a force bound for No. 204 Military Mission to China, which required ten officers, twenty warrant officers and a hundred other ranks, or the LRDG.[2] Clearly, Stirling and others were aware of Bagnold's unit, which was currently mainly confined to base by the Axis offensive, awaiting relief by the Sudan Defence Force. However, it appears from existing records – Tony Kemp noting that there is 'little paperwork [on] the early period in North Africa', because Middle East HQ 'burned the bulk of its records' in 1942 – that Stirling and others sought another form of employment, with an experimental parachute unit organised in Kabrit under Lewes.[3]

Lewes's biographer asserts that, 'In May 1941 [Jock Lewes] received the news of the invasion of Crete with a mixture of dismay and great interest ... If German paratroopers had succeeded in Crete, then Jock was convinced he could make it work with a small scale operation against Axis air bases and installations in the desert.' Reportedly, 'Laycock permitted Jock to detach' a small 'band of cut-throats' from Layforce 'in May' and engage in the 'training of his parachutists' thereafter. If so, then Lewes must have discussed the endeavour with Laycock before Layforce's future was considered at GHQ staff conferences on 22–23 May (prior to Laycock's departure for Crete). Laycock must have been content for one of his subordinates to pursue a project that could offer Layforce a foothold on which to continue in some form. Stirling adds that, 'In June of 1941 . . . Lewes applied and got permission to detach a section . . . and to train it on the lines required to enable it to cover an operation which he . . . planned.'[4]

To carry out the enterprise, however, Lewes needed both equipment and assistance from those who knew how to parachute, as well as volunteers for the experiment. Lewes later noted that he was given 'complete freedom to train and use [the volunteers] as I think best', which he admitted he had 'longed for all my soldier days'. But crucially, he added that he was currently 'preoccupied . . . with a special task *allotted to me*' (emphasis added). This is a critical point that has been overlooked by historians, for it clearly indicates that the impetus for the experiment was *not* from Lewes.

Waugh added that, at this point, 'various officers volunteered for individual recce and demolitions and for parachute work'. To this end, 'a few Commandos, like Carol Mather and George Jellicoe, were trying to make . . . small raids on German airfields' after they returned from the aborted Tobruk raid at the end of May. Mather and Jellicoe 'conceived the idea of a two-man raid from Tobruk' via a landing craft, and Mather recalled that, 'We argued that two people could achieve just as much confusion behind enemy lines as could the ponderous presence of a gunboat with a cargo of 100 troops.'[5] Such two-man raids were the stock in trade of B Battalion's SBS, which was planning such a raid by Courtney and Company Sergeant-Major Barnes on Mersa Brega on 7 June, using a folbot deployed from the submarine HMS *Taku* (though in the event the operation was aborted).[6]

Mather's and Jellicoe's proposed raid was authorised by the Tobruk garrison commander, the 'perceptive' Australian General Morshead and, early in June, the pair linked up with the 18th (King Edward's Own) Indian Cavalry Regiment, tagging along on its reconnaissance patrols, before participating in three night landings from a small boat as one of a pair of two-man raiding teams. Navigational problems prevented them undertaking demolitions, however, and a planned co-ordinated raid on the El Adem and Gazala airfields with Captain 'Jock' Haselden of G(R) was likewise abandoned on 15 June in the light of the heavy defences.[7] Still, Mather's and Jellicoe's two-man efforts could have inspired their B Battalion colleagues such as Lewes and Stirling to try out similar raids, given the opportunity, although this was currently very limited.

Only Courtney's SBS was then active from Alexandria and, from 12 June, Lazaretto Creek in Valetta harbour, Malta, as part of 'Shrimp' Simpson's 10th Submarine Flotilla. Following 1 SBS's beach reconnaissances, sabotage, special agent insertions and rescue of troops from Crete, on 22 June, Captain Wilson and Lieutenant Scofield set off for Sicily aboard the submarine, HMS *Urge*. On 29 June, they struck a railway tunnel between Taormina and Catania using time-delay bombs, as well as wrecking five trains and three bridges.[8]

As for the LRDG, it was being reorganised by Eighth Army into two squadrons: A, comprising G, Y and the new H Patrol, based at Siwa under Mitford; and B, consisting of R, S and T, at Kufra. Hindered by a lack of fuel, they were restricted to daily reconnaissances around the Gebel Akhdar and transporting intelligence agents, including one to Gambut on 10–11 June, though G was busy on the 21st identifying desert landing grounds prior to its relief in July.[9]

With Layforce needing a share of any such action if it was to avoid disbandment, 'individual . . . recce . . . and parachute' missions were apparently 'allotted' by Laycock after talks at GHQ. Indeed, as mentioned, Waugh noted that Lieutenant-Colonel Hope and HQ staff officers 'devised a series of minor operations against enemy LoCs [with] names from theatrical farces, Rookery, Nook, Walls' and Cuckoo. B Battalion's would-be raiders were directed to ambush enemy transport, contaminate their water supplies and 'destroy . . . aircraft on the ground'. However, poor weather and the fragility of the Navy's Eureka boats confounded their efforts.[10]

Additionally, although he only had four men at his disposal by 5 May, Lewes may have expressed an interest in parachuting to Laycock either late in April or, in the light of Crete, around 21 May. (It and the Corinth operation were also known to Stirling, as he admitted to Stevens).[11] The chance to try parachuting out was most likely presented to Lewes by Laycock before 23 May, when Churchill was pushing for more paratroops and Wavell was facing the prospect that his and Clarke's own deception scheme to use the 1st SAS had been derailed by the invasion of Crete. Consequently, it appears that they sought to supplement the dummy parachute drops scheduled at Helwan aerodrome for the second week of June and the other measures in place at El Fuka with an additional experiment there involving real paratroops.

Wavell, who was both a long-standing exponent of airborne operations and personally interested in the retention of at least part of the Special Service brigade, apparently sought to kill two birds with one stone. He could boost A Force's deception effort with trial parachuting by Layforce personnel at Fuka, thereby also offering some of them a chance of alternate future employment.

BBC Radio 4's *Of One Company* posited that Lewes 'intercepted fifty parachutes for a General Wavell initiative', but did not elaborate on what this was. But the general's involvement in Lewes's 'allotted' task would explain how the lieutenant was so readily able to secure both scarce equipment (according to Stirling's recollection, twelve parachutes from Port Said), and the facilities to use them. This is a far more credible version of events than that summarised by John Parker, wherein Lewes 'just happened to be around' as the parachutes literally 'fell off the back of a lorry', following – also according to Stirling – 'a complete muck up by the shipping people'. Or indeed, as Hoe and Morris put it, because Lewes simply saw parachuting as 'a way of making life a little more interesting during the ... resting up phase before the next major offensive'.[12]

While the UK TV History Channel's 2004 *Great SAS Missions* asserted that Lewes conducted 'an unofficial parachute jump', it is much more likely that Wavell sanctioned it. Wavell was well aware both of Churchill's edicts on paratroops and the initiative to this end in India, which, backed by Auchinleck on 15 May, involved 750 infantrymen volunteering for what would become the 151st British Parachute Battalion (and, on its transfer to the Middle East, 156 Para). The two generals were in regular touch and Wavell would have known from his own HQ staff about the trans-shipment of parachutes to India. He would have been able to arrange for their diversion to Fuka, facilitating Lewes's trial paratroop-cum-deception drops, which, Lewes noted, would be 'a means to a very proximate end', namely, A Force's ongoing strategic deception.

Searching for a Role

One of those in Lewes's small party of novice parachutists – 'two or three friends', Stirling subsequently recalled – who travelled to Fuka, was Irish Guardsman Private Joseph Michael 'Mick' D'Arcy, who reportedly wrote a memo about their efforts during May 1941. However, while D'Arcy's memoir is headed 'May 1941', it notes that Lewes '*and his party* first went to an RAF HQ located somewhere near Fuka' (emphasis added). This formal, third-person account indicates that D'Arcy was subsequently dictating his recollections for an official written report that formed part of a dossier on the 'History of "L" Detachment SAS Brigade and 1st SAS Regiment', collated by Captain B. P. Schott, King's African Rifles, in July 1942. D'Arcy was likely recalling the events of a year or so before and, while he doubtless remembered when he was first drafted into the parachute experiment – May 1941 – the trial jumps were actually done in the second week of June, along with the dummy drops at RAF Helwan.

Among the soldiers who D'Arcy noted was present at Fuka was Stirling. By all accounts, in the previous weeks he had been 'forced into inactivity broken only by day and night exercises which had no particular point except to "keep the men busy"'. Hence, he spent much of his time in the fleshpots of Cairo, using his brother Peter's flat as a base. Additionally, 'the lack of success of the 8 Commando operations preyed heavily on Stirling's mind', not least as he had been on 'one or two abortive but very exciting operations'. He identified the loss of surprise as the key to their failure and, as Stirling recounted for his biographer, 'Something along those lines had been disturbing me since the pre-Layforce training days.' As Hoe notes, Stirling 'never dropped ideas completely, just put them into a separate mental compartment to be rekindled'. In the light of 8 Commando's failed seaborne raids, Stirling concluded that the Germans had to be attacked in their flanks, where they least expected it. He averred during his recollections that, 'I had these thoughts loosely in mind when I met Jock' for 'the parachute' experiment.[13]

According to some accounts (not least Stirling's own), Lewes bumped into Stirling in Cairo and 'invited' him to join his parachute experiment. But Lewes's biographer notes that Stirling 'persuade[d] Lewes to take him along' after Jock told him that he had taken delivery of a batch of parachutes. Lewes later reflected that Stirling 'appreciated the long-term value of my experiment more accurately than I and wanted to be in on it to exploit its novelty'. But if Stirling demonstrated perspicacity about the potential of parachuting, he also had cause to join in for the less prosaic reason that he had missed a number of parades due to nights out on the town, using the Cairo American Hospital's beds to shake off his hangovers before returning to camp with a doctor's note for 'pyrexia of unknown origin'! He had also had to visit hospital with a slashed eyeball after cutting it on a thorn bush during a night exercise and, while he was there, 'His superiors reviewed his service record [which] did not make impressive reading.' (Mather adds that Stirling once floored an Egyptian taxi horse with a punch during a dispute over a fare!) Hence, when Stirling heard of Lewes's scheme, he had a solid practical reason to try to join the enterprise, as well as pursuing his own thoughts about devising a means of 'undetected approach right on to the target'. (Randolph Churchill's biographer asserts that Stirling was also 'partly inspired' by events in Crete.) Thus, Stirling 'talked Lewes into letting him become part of the experiment', though Jock later noted that he felt Stirling was 'interfering with *my task*' (emphasis added), reinforcing the fact that Lewes had been assigned this special job. Indeed, Lewes bemoaned that Stirling came 'in on it in the last days when all the arrangements were made', Lewes having been busy 'for weeks' over-seeing preparations – far from the spur of the moment whim to break the monotony of camp life as per the accepted version of events.[14]

D'Arcy asserted that Lewes had 'been frustrated in his plans for a seaborne operation', so 'decided to try it by parachute'.[15] But while the Guardsman patently knew in outline the strategic background to the experiment, he would not have known the place that Lewes's 'allotted task' had in Clarke's secret A Force plans. These currently included the positioning of 'half of "K" Detachment, 1 SAS Brigade, with about thirty gliders, hastily converted to dummy bombers . . . at Fuka and El Daba from 16 May to 20 September, to help in displaying extra strength for the then much-depleted Desert Air Force.' Clarke informed the War Office on 15 June that 1st SAS was 'now located at aerodromes in Egypt, especially Helwan, where gliders are likely to be identified and parachute dropping practise can be seen by the public'.[16]

Lewes would have been made aware of the SAS contingent at Fuka, and D'Arcy went on that Lewes 'discussed the details [of his task] with an RAF officer, who, although none of the party had jumped before, was most helpful'. Indeed, 'none of the ORs had even been in a plane before'. The RAF's willingness readily to assist Lewes underscores the fact that his task was allotted to him by a higher authority, as such novices would not have been afforded much co-operation had they simply turned up at an RAF base with a consignment of half-inched parachutes and asked to make some jumps for a jolly! Further, D'Arcy recalled that the RAF officer 'showed us the parachutes we were to use [and] from the log books, we saw that the periodical examination' of them by RAF personnel 'had been omitted'.[17] This reference to log books clearly shows that the RAF possessed documentation about the parachutes being used by Lewes. If he had received no authorisation to use this kit – reportedly originally destined for India – objections would surely have been raised.

Lewes's biographer recounts that Jock had drawn up tactical plans for three operations, contingent on the success of the trial jumps. Thus, despite the lack of any recent inspection of the parachutes, Lewes put faith in the RAF's packers and 'decided that they were OK'. He wanted to proceed come what may in order to press the case for a Layforce paratroop unit. As regards Lewes's operational plans, D'Arcy adds that 'Lt. Stirling and [Scots Guards Sergeant Jim] Storie were hoping to do a job in Syria'.[18]

Their proposed *modus operandi* of a two-man job mirrored concurrent 'individual . . . work' done by the likes of Courtney and Mather, who returned to Alexandria to learn that Daly's second-in-command, 'Bones' Sudeley, had been leading patrols around the Tobruk perimeter with a contingent of eight officers and ninety-six other ranks. However, by 22 June, it was reported that, 'All ranks have lost heart through disappointment and inaction', and only one officer and twenty other ranks 'wish to remain with Layforce'. Sudeley returned to Alexandria 'in a poor state of nerves and got hopelessly drunk', and Daly 'ordered the entire party to return . . . to base to set about raising a new force which he himself was going to lead'.[19]

In the interim, 'the remaining officers [in Alexandria] held a council of war in the Cecil Hotel' and 'it was felt that another attempt should be made on Tobruk', led by Captain Dunne. However, Mather queried plans for raids with 'large numbers', and these were stymied when Layforce received its disbandment orders early in July.[20]

Prior to that, the Syria operation was to open with an invasion of Lebanon by 7th Australian Division, backed by 'X Force' – Layforce's C Battalion under Major Keyes. On 6 June, the Australians advanced from northern Palestine into Lebanon, making for Beirut and thence Damascus. However, the Australians were held by the French 22nd Algerian Tirailleur Brigade at the Litani River and so, on the night of 6–7 June, twenty-seven officers and 456 other ranks of the Commandos were deployed from Haifa by RMS *Glengyle*. Accompanied by HMS *Ibex* and HMS *Hotspur*, they scouted the coast before landing at night in three detachments on 8 June and making for the Kafa Bada bridge.

The Commandos faced heavy fighting and the leader of one group on the central front, Lieutenant-Colonel R. H. H. 'Dick' Pedder, was killed. Captain George R. M. H. More's group advanced on the French left, only to require assistance from Keyes, who had landed in the wrong area to the south. Captain More advanced on a French gun position before Keyes took over and captured the redoubt. However, C Battalion sustained 123 casualties prior to its relief by the 25th Australian Infantry Brigade and was then withdrawn to Cyprus and later Alexandria.[21]

Lewes probably seized on the upcoming Syria operation (along with two other unspecified aerial drops) as a means of demonstrating the viability of tactical parachute insertion for behind the lines raids as an adjunct to strategic operations. Indeed, Stirling wrote in 1942 that his own plan for the SAS 'was largely based on Jock's ideas and was merely an application of them on a unit basis'.[22] Hence, Lewes's thinking about raids and their potential application to his paratroop blueprint demands consideration.

Lewes's Raiders

Lewes's biographer notes that Jock 'admired Eastern philosophies and ideas', although it is unclear if he had read Sun Tsu. Nonetheless, the Australia-raised Welsh Guardsman had experimented with explosives as a schoolboy and he and his brother had 'a conspicuous interest in all things military'. Jock had enrolled in the cadet corps at King's

School in Sydney in 1932 and he reportedly knew the *Field Service Regulations* better than his times tables! He and fellow cadet Owen Dibbs 'discussed the idea of . . . lightly armed, superlatively trained intruders behind enemy lines', and they organised their fellow cadets into small raiding parties and carried out night raids. These 'confirmed in Jock's mind the value of surprise attacks', which were a facet of some of the texts in *The Bible* – required reading for the young Lewes.

By 1934, Lewes was considering seeking a commission in the Indian Army, recently active on a large scale in the North-West Frontier against Pathan guerillas. But he 'calculated that [a world] war was inevitable and that experience in other fields' would prove useful to him when the conflagration came. Hence, he set about travelling internationally, before enlisting in the Oxford University Training Corps at the end of 1938. As war loomed, he signed up with the Welsh Guards and, by February 1940, he was on a patrol course at the Small Arms School in Hythe, Kent. He next went on a programme run by Bill Stirling at Bisley and excelled there, becoming the Welsh Guards' Weapons Training officer at Roman Way Camp, Colchester. Lewes drew up his own patrol curriculum and, when he arrived in North Africa, he took the initiative in drilling his men in desert marches. Moreover, Jellicoe has noted that, 'Like David Stirling, Jock had come to believe soon after his arrival in the Middle East . . . that success in raiding operations behind enemy lines would lie with highly trained, small and select forces rather than with larger' Commandos of hundreds of men. He believed this to be the case 'after taking part in or witnessing a number of unsuccessful operations by Layforce'.[23]

However, it was not just recent experience that told in Lewes's ruminations over the future of Middle East raiding. Lewes was conversant with the unorthodox operations of a British soldier during the Seven Years' War of 1756–63, between the British and French empires. Major Robert Rogers was a Massachusetts-born British Army officer who set up a 'small unit of Scouts and raiders' to confront the French and Native American forces. In the first half of 1941, when considering current raiding tactics, Lewes is said to have 'raised the subject' of Rogers's exploits 'with small teams' fighting behind the lines, which he noted was *not* a 'new concept'. Indeed, by early 1941, notes on Rogers were being circulated among Commando instructors in Scotland who were until recently colleagues of Stirling and Lewes. Lewes's biographer cautions that it is unclear whether Jock knew details about Rogers's operations,[24] but he was hardly likely to have cited them as an example if he was unfamiliar with their nature or outcome. Hence, a brief resumé of what Rogers did is in order.

Rogers's Rangers

From his teens, Robert Rogers had witnessed Indian hit-and-run raids on local communities and garrisons and, in 1754, he served in a militia defending against their attacks. In 1755, he joined a band of volunteers who were trying to resist encircling moves by French forces and, by that August, he was in charge of his own column of a hundred men. In September, they slipped into French territory and undertook reconnaissance work and guerilla raids against the enemy. Indeed, Rogers produced standing orders for his troops which, by and large, still hold good as essentials to success in guerilla operations. In summary, these covered the following: the need to have weapons ready for action at all times; economy of force; stealthy, fast and carefully protected and concealed movement; the acquisition of accurate information on which to base offensive action; anti-ambush drills; path-finding; planned retreat; the deployment of camp sentries; the conduct of dawn assaults; offensive ambushing; and close-quarter action. Rogers and his men pioneered some of the key techniques of the sophisticated guerilla fighter and special operations practitioner. As one authority has noted, 'The principles governing their deploy-ment have served as an inspiration for such operations ever since', and their example certainly made a lasting impression on Lewes.

Following Rogers's band's successes during the autumn of 1755, he became 'a camp hero' and, that November, he formed his own 95-strong company known as 'Rogers's Rangers'. 'During the winter of 1755–56, Rogers carried out a series of scouts and raids upon the enemy which laid the basis for his later ranging tactics.' He emphasised fieldcraft and 'aggressiveness' and carried out very small unit recces with two or three companions prior to deploying a larger offensive party at night and laying up near a target ready for an early morning assault the next day. 'Rogers's coolly executed expeditions excited unprecedented [press] notices' and 'even the military shared the excitement' of the 'sole British successes' of the period.

By March 1756, Rogers's forces had grown and he had at least one company always on active duty, reconnoitring the enemy, gathering intelligence on their movements and setting out to 'destroy their . . . Magazines and Settlements', intercept their patrols and cause 'continual alarm'. His rangers moved 'silently, threading through green forests or slipping in birch bark canoes over autumn-tinted waters . . . crunching on snow shoes', or slipping into enemy territory to carry out ambushes from the undergrowth.

By August 1756, Rogers had broken new ground and extended the duration of some of his ranger patrols to over a month. By the new year, his companies regularly went out on patrol with a two-week ration and undertook larger engagements as the opportunity arose. In February 1757, two more companies of rangers (a sobriquet adopted by the SAS in the post-war years, as outlined in *SAS: The First Secret Wars*) were formed. Their eight- or ten-man patrols operated in single file with point and flank protection and used silent signalling and counter-ambush drills. They moved with relative impunity, alternating routes and retaining maximum vigilance. 'Without formal training, Rogers had . . . compressed . . . backwoods fighting experiences into a simple exposition of small unit tactics . . . based on mobility, security and surprise.'

By November 1757, the 'Independent Company' of rangers was made an established part of the Army order of battle. It came under the direct authority of the CINC, General William Shirley (setting a precedent for command that would be duplicated by Stirling) and, by late 1757, new ranger recruits were required to have experience of 'hunting, tracking and long marches'. Presaging the formation of the Commandos by nearly 200 years, the British military establishment had accepted the principles and value of a special raiding force.

Following further ambushes and reconnaissances-in-force (with groups of up to 300 men), in January 1758, five more ranger companies were formed by the British authorities. However, that March, with the French causing uproar around Crown Point on Lake Champlain, it was decided that that area would 'have to be taken and a garrison installed'. Hence, a large scale reconnaissance was ordered and it was argued that 'the men best equipped' for this dangerous mission 'were the Rangers, whose methods were not dissimilar to those of the Indians'.

In March 1758, a combined force of 180 men under Rogers reconnoitred French positions at Ticonderoga, stealthily approaching the locale on snow shoes. There, Rogers deployed a counter-ambush reconnaissance party and sent a sixteen-man group under Lieutenant Phillips on a night-time advance to the French lines. Also undertaking silent marches and laying up prior to their attacks, two sections under Rogers and Captain Buckley laid an ambush for a French–Amerindian platoon of ninety-six men, killing forty, before retreating with fifty losses of their own. This incident illustrated that larger-scale engagements could be less advantageous to his forces than smaller raids. Indeed, by this stage in the war, the raiders were misused more and more by the the CINC, who deployed them as an adjunct to large-scale operations, such as that at Louisbourg, where four companies of rangers totalling 600 men were committed to the fight.

Other raiding units acted as a vanguard for General Wolfe at Quebec, landing from boats for the attack. Still, smaller operations also continued and, even when faced with odds of seven to one, Rogers's soldiers were able to fight successfully and take flight, notching up several 'daring achievements' in the course of their duties. Only when the units' role was reoriented wholly to larger operations by the high command from March 1759 were there greater tribulations for Rogers – notably at Fort Caillon. Even so, his forces tried to 'split into small parties' after skirmishes and, by the time of the French capitulation in the region in September 1760, Rogers had proven the worth of his rangers. Although the scarcity of Rogers's published *Journal* means that it is unlikely to have been read by Lewes,[25] at least the thrust of Rogers's exploits and achievements were known to him.

Lewes's Paras

When D'Arcy reminisced about the first parachute jump by Lewes, the Irish Guardsman was referring to events in the second week of June 1941. On their third day at Fuka, Lewes's party conducted their first experimental parachute drop, resulting in a back injury to Stirling that

170

led to his hospitalisation on – according to a War Office report sent to Stirling's family – 15 June, just as Wavell launched his Operation Battleaxe counter-offensive against Rommel. If that date is correct, then Lewes and his party arrived at Fuka on 13 June and did their first flight the 'next day' (while Laycock was in Cairo on 12 June 'to discuss [the] future role and organisation of Layforce').

D'Arcy reported that they flew over the airfield in a mail-delivery Vickers Valentia and 'threw out a dummy made from sandbags and tent poles'. This went 'OK' and was followed on the plane's landing by a ten-foot ground-based jump from it. On 'the following afternoon' – 15 June – after another practice flight, they decided to jump at dusk and 'were told to jump in pairs' by the accompanying RAF officer.

Lewes and his Welsh Guards batman, Private Roy Davies, went first, followed by Stirling and D'Arcy. Davies was reportedly 'a little shaken' on landing, while Stirling descended too quickly. He was expecting a freefall lasting about five seconds during their 2,000-foot jump, but 'some ten seconds later he knew something was wrong'. He saw that 'a large section of his canopy was flapping, [having] caught on the tail-plane . . . then ripped'. He landed heavily, 'injured his spine and lost his sight for about an hour'. On landing, D'Arcy was 'a little shaken and [sustained] a few scratches'. He was followed without incident by Sergeant Storie, while Welsh Guardsman Evans reportedly missed his chance to freefall due to 'the approaching darkness'.

The incapacitated Stirling was taken to the Scottish Military Hospital in Cairo, this time with a trauma more serious than the self-inflicted ones of the previous weeks. Despite the setback, on the morning of 16 June, Lewes decided to try again and a dummy package was followed out of the aircraft by Evans, who 'hurt his ankle' on landing. D'Arcy and Davies were next, before Lewes, 'trying to avoid some oil barrels rather badly damaged his spine' as he hit terra firma. Storie 'landed OK', but when reporting on the progress of the experiment to Middle East HQ (again indicating its involvement in the scheme), Lewes was obliged to detail their mishaps. After some rumination, Jock's planned operations were cancelled by GHQ, 'chiefly because the parties were too badly shaken by the practice jumps'. Lewes's biographer disputes this, arguing that they should have been given more time to prove themselves. He contends that

Lewes's operations were shelved because, as Stirling later stated, there was a 'lack of decision at the top' over whether to go ahead with Lewes's plans.[26] However, the reason for HQ's hesitation is more likely to have been because Wavell, the trial's sponsor, while loathe to pull the plug on it, had not been given a clear demonstration of the viability of desert parachuting. Lewes's paras could not be considered ready for deployment as part of Wavell's overall strategic plans and, in any case, the Battleaxe offensive was faltering by 19 June. Two days later, despite the fall of Damascus to the Allied advance, Wavell was telegrammed by Churchill that he would be relieved of his post by Auchinleck. Thus, the Auk left India on 27 June and arrived in Cairo on 30 June.[27]

Despite this downturn in the fortunes of both Lewes and Wavell, it appears that A Force was still able to benefit from the parachute experiment's misfortunes. By 28 June, Lieutenant-Colonel R. J. Mansell (GSI) had 'new material for use' in the ongoing deception plans. In line with Clarke's edicts that ruses should, if possible, have some basis in fact – to make them more convincing to enemy informers – Mansell referred to 'a British parachutist [speaking] through the railings of Agusa hospital on 29 June' about a parachute jump on 11 June 'at Helwan'. The purported para was said to be 'recovering from a broken ankle' and to have revealed that, 'The new parachutes specially produced for the East are still not very satisfactory and one of his battalion was killed the same week.' By 4 July, Clarke was able to report to the War Office that, 'There is a very fair chance that we have ... succeeded in establishing the fact that airborne troops are available in this Command', which was the intent from the 'beginning of this year'.[28]

In the interim, on 2 July, Wavell handed command to Auchinleck, though they 'conferred for several days before Wavell left on 7 July'. Two days before, they were instructed by London to arrange for Layforce to return home and, on 6 July, Churchill pressed Auchinleck to 'have regard especially to the situation in Tobruk' and to take the initiative there.[29] Clearly, during this period Wavell had far more pressing issues to attend to than Lewes's inauspicious parachuting trial and, when Wavell was sidelined, the paras' enterprise was too.

Stirling to the Fore

In the interim, on 20 June, Stirling wrote home that he would 'probably apply to be returned to England, depending on how things [take] shape out here', implying that GHQ had yet to decide the fate of Middle East special forces (including Lewes's team). However, by the last week of June, Jock had been relieved of his 'special task' and Laycock was busy exhausting 'every means of getting' B Battalion into action. At the end of the month, the CO prepared to 'set off for home, with the full permission of Wavell, to report on the Combined Operations and Commando situation in the Middle East, in search of a formula which would reconcile the shortage of manpower with the ... desirability of keeping an amphibious striking force in being'.[30] En route, he would visit Geoff Keyes in Syria and inform him of the likely disbandment of Layforce. (As a result, Keyes wired his father, urging him to lobby Churchill, 'begging that he should ask for them to be sent back to' Britain). Accompanied to London by SOE's Peter Wilkinson, Laycock determined 'to complain about how his force had been used' to both the War Office and Churchill, who was also kept informed of developments by his son, Randolph.[31]

In the meantime, Lieutenant-Colonel Daly went back to Cairo to seek approval for B Battalion to conduct 'small raids as opportunity offered' near Tobruk. Permission was granted and Lewes was 'requested ... for [an] advance party'. On the night of 6 July, he was joined by Riley, Bond, Kershaw and Almonds, who left Alexandria aboard the Australian destroyer, HMAS *Vendetta*. The party of five officers and seventy other ranks was led by Major Kealy, Devonshire Regiment and 3 Commando, and included Sergeant Tommy 'Tubby' Langton, SBS.[32]

Two days before Lewes's departure, Stirling asked one of his hospital visitors, Waugh, to 'get Jock' to come along that evening – 2 July – because he had 'been doing some thinking and ... want[ed] his opinion'. Soon after speculating on 20 June that he might return to the UK, Stirling ruminated on Layforce's seaborne raids and concluded that 'the chances of taking' the Germans 'by surprise [were] exceedingly slim'. Further, raiders were vulnerable in the sea when retreating from a mission. After days 'looking at the maps of the coastal defences', Stirling noted that 'a phrase struck me forcibly; "Great Sand Sea" ... This was the one sea which the Hun was not watching', due to its supposed impenetrability (an analogy also drawn by Lawrence and Clarke). Stirling 'instinctively thought he was on to something [and] amassed a sheaf of jottings' on a possible desert raiding strategy.

By 22 June, when he was visited by Hermione Llewellyn, Countess Ranfurly (a one-time secretary to General 'Jumbo' Wilson who worked for SOE, resided at Shepheards and was an acquaintance of both the Stirlings and Wavell), and his brother Bill, David noted that he had 'a scheme to put to HQ', once he had got his 'legs to function again'. As J. V. Byrne notes, 'The two Stirling brothers would certainly have discussed matters at a time when David was formulating his ideas', and, by the time that David met Lewes on 2 July, he had formulated his concept of strategic behind the lines raids by small parties of paratroopers.[33]

Just as Stirling and Lewes were making their first trial jump in mid-June, another unorthodox soldier, Orde Wingate, arrived back at GHQ Cairo, having been ordered to return after disbanding Gideon Force on 1 June. After a week at the Continental, where he had a room next door to Thornhill, Wingate set about writing a report (which Thornhill read) on Gideon Force, completing it by 23 June. Wingate's 2,000-word essay on 'guerilla-force theory' referred to Lawrence and called for the creation of a guerilla brigade. He argued that with 'Long Range Penetration', 1,000 air-supported guerillas could tie down 100,000 enemy personnel and raise the prospect of rebellion in the enemy rear. Prior to presenting his paper to GHQ, Wingate discussed it with Dudley Clarke, 'a friend of Palestine days', who proposed revisions (which Wingate, ill with malaria, dismissed). Wavell was apprised of the paper's thrust and tone by 18 June and, while GHQ was 'pained' by Wingate's insubordinate comments about some senior officers being 'military apes', HQ staff studied his proposal for fresh behind the lines guerilla operations at just the time that Stirling was formulating his own ideas on the subject.[34] This inadvertently laid the ground for his presentation some weeks later, and the pair's common interests were duly noted by those concerned.

When Lewes met Stirling to discuss his ideas on 2 July, Lewes reportedly said, 'hold on, Dave', you want 'small teams . . . Roger's Rangers operated like that'. While Stirling averred in later years that, 'as a young man, I didn't read any military history at all' and that he was uninterested in 'most academic subjects, [he] except[ed] . . . history'. Indeed, Stirling must have been heartened by the precedent referred to by Lewes, involving as it did the American wars that so fascinated him. Moreover, historians have failed to highlight the fact that Stirling's raiding proposal differed from Lewes's own, for Jock added a reservation that, 'This is Africa – the distances are huge and the desert's not an easy place to operate.' This implies that Lewes envisaged short-duration tactical operations, as per Mather and Jellicoe's recent SBS-style endeavours. Stirling's key contribution was to develop the scope of such raids to a strategic level, using Wavell's favoured parachute deployment of parties 'some distance from the objective', before laying up overnight, hitting a target, then 'walk[ing] out . . . for part of the distance [before] we get someone to pick us up', such as the LRDG.[35]

Leroy Thompson asserts that the LRDG played no part in the formation of the SAS, but while Stirling subsequently professed to know 'precious little' about it initially, he *was* aware that 'there was this unit operating deep in the desert in an intelligence capacity'. Indeed, he confided to Gordon Stevens that, 'I knew about the LRDG by then' and what it had achieved to date. In fact, 'when I was laid up writing my paper, I talked to everyone who knew anything about the game [and] was visited by Michael Crichton-Stuart [of the LRDG].' However, Stuart opposed the idea of the LRDG being used as a taxi service for Stirling, implying that David had this in mind as an alternative to parachuting. Indeed, Stirling admitted that, 'When I first came out to Cairo I was hankering for the LRDG concept.' He also knew of the activities, if not the detailed plans, of SOE, for whom his brother Bill had been working (while staying at his brother Peter's flat), and the LRDG was busy ferrying special agents to targets.[36]

Lewes agreed that Stirling's raiding proposal was 'quite interesting' and had 'its merits'. However, he identified an Achilles heel in the amount of explosives that must be carried by raiders for their sabotage missions. Moreover, they would need someone 'to authorise all this' and, given that Middle East HQ had just shelved Lewes's 'special task', he did not 'hold out much hope' that Stirling would 'get very far'. Countess Ranfurly lamented Wavell's imminent departure, noting that, 'He is one of the very few senior soldiers who back young methods of war.' She added on 3 July that this was 'tough luck on David Stirling ... how they would have enjoyed each other'. Still, Lewes told David, 'If you [do] get anywhere ... talk to me again.'[37]

With Wavell due to depart for India, and his proposals for a guerilla brigade put on ice by GHQ, Wingate, stricken by malaria at the Continental, tried to commit suicide on 4 July and was taken to the 15th Scottish General Hospital. As Wingate's biographer Sykes notes, 'At that time [Stirling] was attempting to organise the ... SAS', and, as Stirling recounted to Sykes, 'It had been suggested ... in good faith, that he [Stirling] and Wingate might usefully combine, since they shared many ideas.' Although it is unclear who proposed this, Stirling told Stevens that 'Wingate made a blitz to take over me ... He wrote me a long letter ... inviting me to join up with him, or saying he'd like me to go under him in some capacity.' However, Stirling recognised that Wingate's 'technique of organising guerilla attacks was quite different to mine ... so I refused'. Stirling wanted to pursue his own plan and ensured that he even 'avoided meeting' Wingate, though he had the utmost 'respect' for him and, after hearing of his suicide bid, 'recognised a formidable man ... who could face ... death for his beliefs'.[38]

One officer who would have been well placed to propose their collaboration early in July and who was privy to both their plans was Dudley Clarke. The *Great SAS Missions* TV series noted that he was 'one of the few people Stirling trusted enough to discuss his idea' while in hospital. Further, Stirling recounted to Stevens that, after having the idea of using the LRDG dismissed, 'I built parachuting into the paper, not because it was an efficient means of arrival ... but ... because it provided a good opportunity of putting the idea to MEHQ', which had been involved in Lewes's effort. Stirling asserts that 'psychologically, the parachute was the ideal propaganda means of putting over the proposition of the role of the unit' that he now envisaged for small behind the lines strategic raids, as opposed to Wingate's large-scale guerilla raiding. Moreover, Stirling must have been told by Lewes that Middle East HQ had sponsored his parachute experiment, for Stirling admitted that 'I was anxious to get [the] full co-operation of . . . Dudley Clarke.' Stirling adds that he 'told him' of his scheme and owned that 'Clarke was a very great influence on me'. Hence, the two Shepheards residents must have become acquainted before Stirling drew up his 2 July memo, otherwise Stirling would have had no reason to discuss the idea of parachute raids with him in the first place. Their paths must have crossed when Stirling participated in Lewes's A-Force-sponsored paratroop trial and, when they discussed its revamp as a strategic rather than tactical unit, Clarke 'promised to give me all the help he could', Stirling noted, 'if I would use the name . . . the SAS'.[39]

Waugh observes that, on 7 July, orders came through that Layforce would be disbanded in August, on the return to Egypt of No. 11 Commando (scheduled for 7 August), while Laycock went to the UK to discuss its future. At that point, it comprised 150 all ranks in Captain Nichols's A Battalion, who would disperse to units in the Middle East, UK and Far East; 350 all ranks in Major Keyes's C Battalion, most of whom would be retained; a smaller number in D; and the rest of B, most of whom would be dispersed to infantry battalion centres for reassignment, the Coldstreams already having been returned to unit. Some Layforce officers had transferred to the Cheshire Yeomanry and other units in Britain, while Daly himself went 'half crazy' and 'chased a black waiter in the dark during an air raid!'

All told, 500 men were returned to unit in theatre; 60 went to the UK; 125 shipped out to the Far East (initially for training by Mike Calvert at the Bush Warfare School in Burma, before joining Mission 204 in China); another 41 joined a military mission to the USSR; and 11 were absorbed into the LRDG. This left around 300 all ranks, mostly from C Battalion, whose future had yet to be decided, but who wished to stay on for 'special deployment' by Middle East HQ. On 9 July, Auchinleck, who 'admired and cultivated imagination and daring', informed the War Office that he wished to retain the rump of Layforce, reversing previous plans for its disbandment.[40]

Mather notes that, by then, Stirling 'already had a nucleus' of volunteers for his proposed unit, drawn from those who had returned from Tobruk. He approached them 'before he went to GHQ' on his crutches 'to get support for his idea' from the new CINC. However, when Stirling outlined his plans at Shepheards, 'the Great Sloth' convinced few of his fellow officers to join him as, Mather admitted, 'We thought we knew David too well for it to work.' Indeed, Ran Churchill and Robin Campbell had hoped to undertake their own raid on the Gazala airfield in June, but it had been called off, and 'Stirling was the only one of the three who remained convinced that there was still a place for Commandos.'[41]

Undeterred, Stirling averred that, given the strategic nature of his proposed unit, it should be commanded by the theatre CINC, in order to prevent it 'becom[ing] involved in the tactical battle' (as per Rogers's Rangers). In order to achieve this, Stirling determined that, 'It had to be the highest authority that I approached with the idea.' Some historians aver that Stirling was 'not on social terms with anyone' at Grey Pillars, but others assert that he had 'contacts', notably Clarke and Ritchie (who had served with Wavell during the Great War). Lewes's biographer asserts that Ritchie 'was an acquaintance of Stirling's father, with whom he had shot grouse', and Stirling revealed to Gordon Stevens that he aimed to approach Ritchie through his colleague Arthur Smith, who shared his Scots Guards background. BBC Radio 4's *Of One Company* concluded that, 'We can never know how Stirling persuaded' his superiors to adopt his scheme, and it even suggested that, as Ritchie's office was on the third floor of the HQ, Stirling cannot have hobbled his way there, so that the fence-scaling episode is 'a legend, a myth'. Ex-SAS man Michael Asher goes further, declaring that Stirling was a 'mythologiser who told countless tall tales about the origin of the SAS [and] wove many of the creation myths surrounding its establishment'.[42] (The fact that A Force activities continued to be top secret after World War II, when deception became an integral part of the Cold War, might also explain the necessity of continued deception by those involved.)

Paddy Mayne's biographer agrees that, 'The birth of the SAS, like many creation stories, over time became rich in myths.' Be that as it may, Stirling *did* acquaint Ritchie and Auchinleck with his ideas soon after Wavell's departure, though his timing *was* fortunate. As Hoe notes, 'Auchinleck ... was already under pressure from Winston Churchill to make his presence felt.' Ritchie added that he and the Auk were 'looking at ways of tying up German manpower', and both had been involved in Delhi's planning for paratroops (like those of the 11th SAS, who had impressed the pair at Shrewton in December 1940). Indeed, 'Churchill was pressing Auchinleck to engage in any kind of guerilla attack . . . to divert German attention and supplies . . . from . . . Russia [and] Ritchie was aware of this'. Further, the Germans' newly deployed Messerschmitt 109F fighter was superior to the RAF's remaining Gloster Gladiators and few Hurricanes, and 'there was scant chance of destroying' the Me-109s 'in the air with the Western Desert Air Force's few overwhelmed fighters', making airfield sabotage a more attractive option than ever before.[43]

On 14 July, a memo on 'Volunteers for Special Service' listed those from B Battalion as: Lieutenant-Colonel D. R. Daly; Captains W. Sillar, M. R. Kealey and the Lord Milton; Lieutenants R. S. Churchill, C. W. Alston and A. D. Stirling; and 2nd Lieutenants M. Brown, J. S. Lewes, H. A. D. Buchanan, T. B. Langton and C. D. Mather. Moreover, a second memo of 14 July, by Geoff Keyes, noted that 'about ten' men of C Battalion wished to transfer 'to parachutists if possible', including Captain Glennie and Lieutenants McGonigal, Fraser and Ingles (who wished to enlist with the paras or the Army Air Co-operation Squadron). This implies that Stirling may have secured provisional permission to pursue his project by 14 July. Indeed, John Laffin asserts that Ritchie 'was so impressed that, on his own considerable authority, he told Stirling to make a start with his planning', and Stirling told Stevens that Ritchie's response was 'to get on with it'. Clarke's sponsorship may well explain Ritchie's swift support and the plan's rapid implementation. (A Battalion was also discussing 'short raids' on Bardia, the Italian coast and the Greek and Dodecanese islands on 15 July).[44]

By 16 July, Stirling had typed up his memo on the 'Case for the retention of a limited number of Special Service troops, for employment as parachutists'. Given that 'three days after his unconventional presentation at GHQ, Stirling was summoned to return' to discuss his proposal with Auchinleck, Ritchie and Smith, it seems that his first visit to Grey Pillars was on 13 July, followed by another on 16 July. Indeed, that evening – the day before Laycock departed for Britain to discuss the future of Layforce with the PM – Stirling discussed the scheme with his CO. He received 'Laycock's enthusiastic support' and they considered a list of potential personnel for the unit. Stirling proposed recruiting Lewes, while Laycock suggested one of 11 Commando's officers, who, according to *Great SAS Missions*, Stirling knew 'quite well' – Lieutenant Blair 'Paddy' Mayne (of whom more later).[45]

The Case For

Stirling's memo of 16 July argued that, given Layforce's likely disbandment, 'There remains no *ad hoc* organisation for raiding enemy LoCs, aerodromes, oil dumps and other enemy dispositions on which damage can be inflicted.' He argued that, in view of the German invasion of Russia, now was 'a time which seems especially propitious for these raids', with the Germans' attention diverted to the east. He noted that there had been a lack of action by Special Service troops in the Middle East because of insufficient air support. But he observed that 'Commandos have been able to make several damaging raids on enemy occupied territory' in Europe from the UK, indicating that Stirling had kept abreast of widely reported developments by other Commandos since leaving Britain earlier in the year.

Stirling 'suggest[ed] the immediate establishment of a parachute training centre' – a scheme similar to the one Auchinleck had been overseeing until recently in India. The lieutenant outlined that his parachute operations would be 'primarily of the strategical type'. He emphasised that 'the Germans have demonstrated with huge losses of personnel in Crete that the tactical landing of parachutists is not practicable except in the face of wholly unorganised opposition.' However, demonstrating his familiarity with paratroop operations elsewhere, he owned that the Germans' 'many successes, notably in Greece [demonstrated] the results to be gained by small strategical landings' during daylight. He focused on the 'landing on Northern Greece behind our lines to prevent the demolition of a key bridge' as a prime example of what could be achieved. He sought to develop the Germans' methods by undertaking 'the landing of small parties by night on a wide range of objectives . . . in Lybia [*sic*] and elsewhere'.

In preparing his memo, Stirling also approached 'Group Captain Guest of the Western Desert RAF HQ', who was involved in A Force deceptions, including K Detachment, SAS. Guest may well have been one of the RAF officers who loaned Lewes assistance at Fuka, and he gave Stirling his 'opinion that the project is sound. He strongly maintains', continued Stirling, 'that night landings by parachute are practicable and [could be] effective. Moreover, he confirms that personnel and aircraft are available for training and operations.' Stirling added that exfiltration might involve a submarine, so that the paras' missions would need to be 'on a scale to warrant the use of a submarine'.

With regard to training, Stirling elaborated several detailed technical points, indicating that he must have been aware of similar arrangements elsewhere, namely Ringway. He outlined that the programme would involve two phases. The first would see the creation of a small operations/instruction facility, from which 'already highly trained' SS troops could 'carry out small scale operations at night' within three weeks. Stirling added that these missions would be 'both useful in themselves and would give the RAF and us the essential experience and information on which to develop the training centre and increase the scope of its activities'. The second phase would be an expansion of the training so that 'the night landing of fifteen to twenty parties' simultaneously would be feasible. Stirling said that he had identified at least fifty men from No. 8 Commando who would be suited to the task by virtue of their 'initiative, power of improvisation and individual resource'. They were already 'thoroughly trained' in the use of Thompsons, grenades and 'elementary demolitions and the handling of explosives'. They would receive tutelage in parachute packing and operation; injury-avoidance PT; 'advanced training in demolitions and sabotage and the handling of explosives at night'; the identification and sabotage of enemy aircraft, tanks and armoured cars; training in the demolition of oil and petrol dumps, water sources and communications facilities; observations, wherein, often 'they will be required to lie up for some days before or after the tackling of their objectives'; and refresher Special Service training.

Stirling concluded that, 'Weather will not restrict their operations to the same extent [as] seaborne Special Service troops', that they offered a wider range of offensive possibilities, required less fore-warning to deploy, would be 'economical in manpower and require no covering troops', and could 'gain the maximum effect from surprise'.[46]

On 18 July, Auchinleck sought from the War Office 'approval for a . . . unit to operate in four-man sections, behind enemy lines with parachutes'. The HQ added that it proposed to retain a 'small proportion of Special Service personnel for special operations in enemy territory primarily by small parties and sabotage methods'. The proposed Special Service force would have a 'small HQ and two Troops', each of two sections, in turn comprising three sub-sections of an NCO and three other ranks, giving a total of around fifty raiders. They would be trained in 'landing and taking off by sea and also night dropping by parachute'.[47]

On 19 July, Churchill again urged Auchinleck to hit the Germans, as well as making SOE responsible for co-ordinating future partisan efforts. GHQ and Laycock were determined to retain an Army special forces capability in the light of SOE activities in Crete, and they won the support of the War Office in this regard. Daly, Stirling, Lewes, Langton, Milton, Kealey, Sudeley and others were due to return to the UK but Laycock arrived there on the 21st to 'plead for the Commandos in the Middle East to be kept in being' in some form. On 23 July, his lobbying paid off, Churchill recommending Layforce's reconstitution and directing Ismay and the Chiefs of Staff to make immediate arrangements for 'the Commandos . . . to be reconstituted as soon as possible'. The Prime Minister wanted them commanded by Admiral Sir Andrew Cunningham, who, from 1 August, would 'be charged with all Combined Operations [in the Mediterranean theatre]'. Laycock was ordered to return to Egypt to oversee the changes, as Cunningham's deputy. Intriguingly, Churchill stated that this was preferable to new units 'being formed by a committee of officers without much authority', indicating that he could well have been aware via Randolph of the efforts of Laycock, Stirling and others to this end.

Further, on 24 July, Churchill ordered Auchinleck to London to discuss the situation, and the CINC flew out on 26 July.[48]

By this point, despite the fact that Auchinleck noted with regard to 'irregular units' being raised in the Far East that, 'I've always been rather sceptical . . . of the value of . . . specialised small units', the general 'was quick to make use of' reports from A Squadron, LRDG, of its recent reconnaissances around Bir el Gseier 'for his autumn offensive'. Furthermore, Stirling 'was given permission . . . to raise' and train his 'parachute detachment' and plans to staff it were already in hand. While other historians have neglected the fact, the new unit was not authorised simply to undertake Special Service tasks as it saw fit. Rather, as Stirling subsequently related to Virginia Cowles, Auchinleck declared that it would form part of A Force's strategic deception plans from the outset, thereby backing the initiative begun under his predecessor, Wavell.[49]

Indeed, on 20 July, Group Captain Guest noted that he had informed Lieutenant J. M. Robertson of K Detachment, 1st SAS, that he believed 'the enemy has seen through our show', the Germans having failed to attack Fuka of late, presumably because they felt that there were no real targets of note there. Hence, he had recommended the shipment of dummy gliders to 'different landing grounds' and noted that, as the battle front was static in mid-July, 'There seemed to be prospects of other employment for K Detachment.' It moved to Cairo on 19 July and its gliders were shipped to Shallufa at the end of the month, then to Cairo later on that summer. On 27 July, a conference at the GHQ Training Branch was convened on the 'implementation in regard to the build up of the 1st SAS Brigade', to try to convince the Germans that there was an airborne brigade in Egypt. The imaginary formation was about to get a tangible boost to its ranks in the shape of Stirling's unit. Among those present at the meeting were Stirling, Clarke, Major P. A. Hobbs, Wing Commander Selway, and future SAS stalwart and Coldstream Guardsman, 2nd Lieutenant Ian G. Collins.[50]

Evidently having been briefed by his superiors at GHQ on the role that he would be expected to fulfill, Stirling informed the conference that 'the purpose of the Special Service unit' was two-fold: 'primarily to train for parachute schemes' and 'to be used later on any combined operation' required by GHQ. Clarke, however, was keen to disabuse Stirling of any notion that his unit would be free to operate at its own behest. He pointed out that it would be 'impossible to hide the formation of this Parachute unit', which, in turn, implied that it ought to be incorporated into A Force's deception plans. Even so, in time, Stirling clearly hoped to mark out a distinct strategic operational as well as deception role for his unit, and he urged that, from the start, his men should have a 'special badge [and] be looked on as a highly specialised force'. Not for the last time, Stirling had to demonstrate a willingness to be flexible in order for his special force to prosper.

Lieutenant-Colonel F. H. Butterfield of the adjutant-general's office at GHQ had informed Stirling that his initial recruitment should be made from the 120 remaining unassigned volunteers of Layforce who desired further Special Service. However, Stirling obtained permission to choose any Layforce personnel, and he 'had, with the full approval of the O.C. Scots Guards, very provisionally selected 21 other ranks from Layforce returned to Scots Guards and a further 18 other ranks from [the] Commando Depot and IBD [Infantry Brigade Depot]'.[51] Stirling added that, in order to 'get the best possible personnel, he wanted to recruit from some specially trained Layforce personnel at Tobruk . . . as the best officers had already accepted other positions'. Stirling was told by Colonel J. A. Baillon of Training Branch that he must recruit them 'in the proper way', while the unit also applied for a medical officer, a company sergeant-major and a quartermaster having already been selected by Stirling.

While Wing Commander Selway acknowledged that he had 'not been given any previous information about this new Special Service unit', he promised to 'report fully on the possible co-operation' that the RAF could afford it. Stirling emphasised that this was key to his future plans and, while Stevens notes that Stirling 'somehow . . . acquired a camp', in fact the RAF responded to his needs and offered him a Blenheim bomber base near the Kabrit Commando training school, south of Port Said.[52]

Given that the paras could be required 'to train for any combined operation scheme', the conference agreed that they should be furnished with Thompson and Bren guns (along with Webley pistols and German firearms), plus 'boots, knee pads, anklets, jock straps . . . crash helmets, overalls and containers'.[53] The RAF also had about 200 parachutes in stock, but further orders would have to await the arrival of a major instructor (doubtless from England, where the Parachute Training School had moved from Hendon to Ringway by July, under Wing Commander Maurice Newnham, who was 'instrumental in establishing RAF [rather than Army] control of parachute training'). Indeed, Clarke referred to the 11th SAS, noting that, 'From experience in England it was very important pilots and parachutists should be trained in aircraft that would be used on actual operations.' While numerous historians have asserted that the naming of the new Special Service unit was down to Stirling – and Steve Bull avers that 'the name picked out of the air . . . was "L" Detachment, 1st SAS Brigade' – in fact, it was Clarke's initiative, and far from mere happenstance. L was not adopted either for Layforce or Learner, as some have speculated, but because it was the next letter in the alphabet available for a new detachment of A Force's imaginary SAS formation. As Bull more accurately continues, 'L Detachment's title . . . was a deliberate deception . . . calculated to give any observant enemy the impression that the British had a complete airborne brigade in Egypt.' He adds that, 'In these details may lie the real formation of the SAS.' This is indeed the case, for GHQ hoped that Stirling's force 'might be a valuable distraction and propaganda tool for use against the enemy'. However, Bull's belief that, 'It was remarkable that . . . Stirling's apparently madcap schemes should have been accepted by . . . Auchinleck', overlooks the many factors described that assisted the creation of Stirling's 1st SAS.[54]

Indeed, A Force's own war diary for 1940–1 notes that Stirling's 'unit . . . took up the name of "1 SAS Brigade" both as a cover for itself and to assist the "Abeam" plan' (though, after the war, Laycock oddly referred to it as '7th SAS'). Stirling asserted in 1948 that he adopted the SAS title 'to humour' Clarke, and the BBC Radio 4 team presumed that Clarke must have been 'tickled' by Stirling's proposed parachute force, while Stirling told Stevens that Clarke was 'delighted'. But, as Stirling recounted to Cowles, when Auchinleck gave him permission to proceed with his plan, the general informed him at the outset that 'his force would be known as "L Detachment" of the SAS Brigade'. He outlined Clarke's latest strategic deception scheme to Stirling and told him that 'Whatever comes of your project . . . your presence will greatly relieve Clarke's burden.' Hence, Stirling's L Detachment had a dual operational and deception role from the start, with its first planned drop timed to coincide with Auchinleck's upcoming offensive in November. The newly promoted Captain Stirling set about organising his six officers and sixty other ranks (five troops of two sections, each with an officer/NCO and four men, plus HQ staff) to be ready for action by then.[55]

Chapter 11

The Originals

In August 1941, Wavell received detailed instructions about raising a force of 2,500 parachutists and a brigade of airborne troops in India. Auchinleck, who had overseen the enterprise before him, was himself summoned to London to explain his upcoming offensive plans. On 1 August, he met the Cabinet Defence Committee and outlined that 'continual pressure was being kept up on the enemy by light forces both in the Sollum area and Tobruk'. He discussed the position with Churchill on 2 August, by which time Wilson and Hughes of the SBS had set off (on 24 July) from HMS *Utmost* to derail a train on the southern Italian mainland at the Gulf of St Eufemia. (Sergeant Allan and Marine Miles also sank a merchant ship at Benghazi on 21 July, but they were captured before they could make it back to their submarine, HMS *Taku*).[1]

The LRDG was more active too, following its relief at Kufra by the Sudan Defence Force, with Lieutenant Jake Easonsmith hitting an Italian patrol near Gambut, and Lieutenant-Colonel Bagnold suggesting reconnaissance of the area between Bouerat el Hsun and El Agheila in Sirte. T Patrol parties under Captain L. B. Ballantyne and Lieutenant Ellingham set off for a two-week mission from 30 July, and Middle East HQ directed S Patrol under Holliman and Olivey to move to Jalo and Agedabia, with the aim of identifying 'water supplies and possible landing grounds' as 'part of the plan for the November offensive'. By 1 August, after handing over command of the LRDG (then numbering 230, and operating in patrols of half their previous size) to Major Prendergast, Bagnold had returned to Cairo to become Inspector of Desert Troops and to raise, train and oversee the operations of 'up to five formations similar to the LRDG in the Western Desert and Syria'.[2] One was a Long Range Intelligence Patrol suggested to GHQ by RAF Flight Officer Derek Rawnsley. He was permitted to operate in three trucks with Australian drivers, assisted by Lieutenant-Commander Wilmott, Royal Navy, and a Royal Engineers Survey Section demolitions officer, Lieutenant R. Leach. They trained for behind the lines raids on enemy depots and dumps until October, and carried out reconnaissance patrols and mapping for the impending major offensive, Operation Crusader, due to begin on 11 (postponed to 15, then 18) November.[3]

David Stirling was also preparing for Crusader, with GHQ hoping the SAS would hit airfields at Gazala and Tmimi, thereby relieving pressure on Malta from the enemy's aerial offensive. On 1 August, Lieutenant-General Arthur Smith of GHQ noted that 'Guardsmen of Special Service battalions . . . are available for a) parachute [and] b) folbot' activities and he directed that their 'training should be carried out' under the auspices of 22nd Guards Brigade. Additionally, Clarke 'helped [in] the organisation [of L Detachment] a great deal in the early days, not least by . . . get[ting] the word out that recruits were needed'. Stirling's biographer mentions Clarke's assistance as a matter 'of passing interest', but his involvement illustrates again that L Detachment was integral to his deception plans.[4]

At this stage, Stirling listed 'all the names he could remember from Layforce and the Scots Guards who he felt might be interested' in joining him and, with Laycock's backing, he made his brother Peter's flat his HQ. Stirling decided that the first person he should contact was Lewes, whom he rated 'critical' to the training of L Detachment. As Cowles notes, 'He had the sort of mind . . . needed to organise the training and to thrash out . . . problems.' Further, Lewes had been 'operating behind enemy lines [at Tobruk] and he would be of great help in picking the right men', not least those he had observed under fire.[5]

As part of the harassment operations done in July around Acroma and El Adem, near Tobruk, Lewes had participated in Mike Kealy's scheme for 'a well planned raid' with a force of three officers and forty men (including Sergeants Riley, Almonds and Lilley), on Italian lines near two hillocks known as 'Twin Pimples' (not 'Pineapples', as per some accounts). The hills overlooked the (Indian Army) 18th Cavalry's defensive sangars in the deep Wadi-es-Sehel, near the Derna road, a thousand yards from the Italians. General Morshead had already conceived of his positions 'as bases for offensive actions', and 'love and kisses' missions were undertaken as a matter of course, with two-man patrols or groups of six to ten men under an NCO moving two or three hundred yards from Allied lines 'to shoot up any prowling enemy patrols', carry out reconnaissance, hit 'supply parties' and gun positions, lay up for a day before night skirmishes and, in the case of the 43rd Australian Battalion, grab Axis PoWs.

'For some days before the [Twin Pimples] raid, [Commando] officers and men . . . went out with the Indians' of Colonel Prentice's 18th Indian Cavalry motor group on desert patrols, in order 'to become more familiar with the ground'. Apparently, 'they learnt much from their Indian comrades, whose skills in moving at night over ground' were deemed second to none. David Sutherland noted that, 'When it came to fieldcraft, movement and observation in desert conditions, they knew it all.' After several patrols and nocturnal excursions out of Ras el Madauar, on the night of 17 July, three Commando officers and two parties of fifteen men disembarked from HMS *Abdiel* at 1.00 a.m. They carried out a raid at 1:13 a.m., half equipped with rifles, half with Tommy guns, and all with grenades and sporting Indian-style rubber-soled shoes. Under the cover of diversionary raids and a barrage from the 18th Cavalry, they and half a dozen sappers of the 9th Australian Division moved in single file before splitting three ways to hit the Italians and their arms dumps. They inflicted over twenty fatalities for one in return, withdrawing after quarter of an hour.

Kealy was joined two days later by Sutherland, who observed that Lewes was 'a rare conceptual thinker'. According to one authority on Lewes, 'between March and July' he had already 'established himself as an unconventional officer' and 'he was given permission to take out ever more adventurous patrols by night with the aim, at first, of taking prisoners and eavesdropping'. By 25 July, Lewes could comment that the enemy's ground 'belongs to us by night', and 'we have been especially rough with him lately' (two officers and sixteen other ranks of the Rajputs killed twenty-seven Italians in a raid that night). Two days later, Lewes carried out his own successful PoW snatch thanks to 'good stalking', before moving further inland to rest up on 28 July.

Lewes and his colleagues moved to Pilastrino, two miles west of

Tobruk but back within the perimeter, the next day, and carried out a reconnaissance on 1 August for a raid the following night. The recce was aborted when Lewes's five-man party was spotted, and another on the 4th was abandoned when Lilley set off a mine. Lewes then led a larger party of two officers and fifteen men on a night patrol on 5 August, with the aim of cutting German communications. It too was halted by mines and they returned to Pilastrino to rest. It was reportedly 'about this time [that] David Stirling came to see Lewes to talk over his ideas', though he is said to have approached Lewes soon after meeting Ritchie, revealing that he was 'fairly sure that GHQ Cairo were about to give in to his request' to form a parachute unit. This dates Stirling's first attempt to convince Lewes to join him in mid-July, albeit that this was unsuccessful.

According to Lewes's biographer, Stirling then travelled 'several times to Tobruk [to try] to persuade Jock to join the new parachute unit', travelling on HMS *Aphis*. However, at each meeting in July and August, Lewes questioned Stirling's suitability for *his* task, and Stirling saw that Lewes wanted to be reassured that 'I was going to stay with it and also tackle . . . MEHQ'. Further, Stirling felt that Lewes was still 'not in full agreement with the small unit concept' of four- or five-man parties, Lewes believing that groups of ten or twelve were the optimum, as demonstrated in Tobruk. Indeed, in August, Lewes's 'later . . . patrols became more aggressive and left base with the intention of killing and harassing the enemy'. By the 20th, they had earned him a 'reputation', Sutherland noting that 'the detachment achieved much during the seven weeks on the perimeter', with Lewes 'far and away the most daring'. This proved a double-edged sword, as he was given 'the responsibility of the most important and difficult tasks'. That frustrated Lewes, who felt at the beck and call of others once again. However, as part of the reorganisation of the Commandos ordered by Churchill, Lewes and his team were relieved of their Tobruk commitment and, facing the fact that 'Layforce ha[d] finally disintegrated', Lewes agreed to join Stirling 'in a new venture'.[6]

On 25 August, Lewes went on HMS *Hastings* to Alexandria and stayed at the Cecil Hotel on 26 August, before making for Shepheards on the 31st. Stirling recalled for Stevens that Jock was hospitalised at this point and that, 'I went to see him there and got him cornered.'

On the following day, Lewes 'decided . . . he needed Stirling's help' and became part of L Detachment at Kabrit camp on 2 September. He was greeted two days later by the 'Tobruk Four' of Almonds, Blakeney, Riley and Lilley, who travelled there via HMS *Glasgow*, then by train through Ismailia and Geneifa. On 4 September, they were dropped off by a lorry at Kabrit and, that evening, were joined by Stirling's former platoon sergeant, Bond. The gathering at Geneifa was addressed in a tent by Stirling, who, despite being 'vague about what "L" Detachment was going to do', soon had a large number of volunteers from whom he was able to interview and select about fifty. They included most of Stirling's 3 Troop, No. 8 Commando (which had been absorbed by 2nd Scots Guards) under Jimmy Brough. Among them were Johnny Cooper; NCOs Rose, Bennett, Tait, Lilley, Cheyne, Du Vivier, Byrne, Brown and Seekings (who had 'always had an ambition to be a parachutist', having tried to join 2 Commando at Ringway); Spanish Civil War veterans like Dave Kershaw; and two officers (not four as in other accounts), Lieutenants Charles Bonnington (future father of climber Chris) and Thomas.[7]

Further, on 8 August, GHQ had contacted C Battalion, which had arrived from Cyprus at Almariya the day before. Middle East HQ requested that Stirling visit 'with a view to finding out if there are any volunteers for a Special Service unit, which he is forming. Captain Stirling will explain the purpose of this new unit.' By 12 August, with C Battalion in the throes of disbandment, 'officers and ORs wishing to volunteer for duty with . . . Stirling' were allowed to do so. On that day, Countess Ranfurly noted that Stirling had written to let her know that 'my parachute unit is now training' and, on 15 August, 2nd Lieutenant McGonigal was posted from C Battalion to the SAS, followed three days later by Lieutenant Fraser.

On 28 August, they were joined by twelve other ranks from C Battalion, including Company Sergeant-Major Yates (and, later, Sergeant Pat Riley). On that day, the SAS was incorporated into the order of battle, Auchinleck offering Stirling his assistance in its recruitment 'shortly after the Prime Minister's visit' to press the CINC to reorganise the Commandos and redouble their special operations.[8]

In fact, on 27 August, Wilson and Hughes of the SBS had already made a shore landing with Thompson machine-guns and explosives on the Gulf of Taranto in southern Italy. After a cliff climb, they sabotaged the spans of a railway bridge over the River Seracino. By this time, they had become a 'local legend among the submariners and navy in Malta and Alexandria', and they won equal acclaim in Cairo and London. (Three days later, two parties from No. 1 Commando also made short-lived landings at Hardelot and Merlimont near Boulogne on the French coast, while sixteen men of 12 Commando had hit Ambleteuse on 27 July.)[9]

On 1 September, C Battalion was formally disbanded and a new Middle East Commando established by Middle East HQ, drawing on Layforce's 300 or so personnel, bolstered by recruits from Inverailort. The revamped unit comprised an HQ Depot at the Combined Training Centre in Geneifa; the SAS Commando (Parachutists) of seventy all ranks (2 Troop); a General Service Commando comprising a reconstituted 11 Commando of seventy all ranks, under Keyes (3 Troop); 4 and 5 Troops, totalling 160 personnel, from the remnants of 51 Commando; and the Folbot Troop (6 Troop, the SBS) of thirty all ranks, attached to the Navy. On that day, L Detachment was constituted with 1 Troop and 2 Troop under, respectively, Lewes, and McGonigal's pal, the erstwhile OC 7 Troop, 11 Commando, Paddy Mayne.[10]

Numerous sources state that Mayne was at that time in military police custody for assaulting his battalion CO, Geoffrey Keyes. But despite a run-in with him, it appears that Mayne was in fact preparing to head for the Far East, before Stirling convinced him to join the SAS. While the detachment was steadily growing, Stirling confided to Countess Ranfurly that he had 'very little visible means of support (just three tents and a three-ton lorry). However, [he went on] we raid neighbouring units at night and return ... with tents and other movable goods.' These activities were organised by the quartermaster, Jerry Ward, and after Stirling addressed his new recruits on 4 September, they were authorised to carry out a night raid on a nearby Kiwi camp. A dozen men, including Lilley, Kershaw, Almonds and Riley, were despatched in the three-tonner to the New Zealanders' base to 'requisition' tents, beds, tables, chairs and other kit. They made four trips over six hours and took a haul including sixteen tents, a piano, wicker chairs and a bar![11]

On 5 September (the day on which Brigadier 'Dracula' Down took over command of the UK-based 1st Parachute Battalion – itself dormant due to a lack of available aircraft and shipping), Lewes 'outlined in great detail the programme he had in store' for his volunteers, and paratroop training began in earnest at Kabrit. This involved the construction of towers and scaffolding by mid-October, swings, wooden trolleys, and gym equipment, Lewes explaining that 'the end product [would be] to become independent in every way, operating either alone or in small groups'. Work began on several twenty- and forty-foot wooden towers, and the SAS's men were obliged to do Suez Canal crossings, demolitions of buildings, night marches (including, by 28 September, a thirty-miler), intelligence-gathering patrols and live-firing exercises.

Fraser taught map-reading, McGonigal weapons handling (including Axis firearms, such as the Italian Beretta pistol and German 'Schmeisser' sub-machine gun) and Mayne PT, while Bond was platoon sergeant and Lewes focused on medical matters, planning, timetables and organisation (as well as dissipating a threatened mutiny over erecting tents).[12]

As practical preparations were made, Stirling made 'endless trips to GHQ to arrange air co-operation' and stores, and to garner political support in Cairo, where sceptical middle-ranking officers dubbed the SAS the 'Short Range Desert Group', due to their proximity to the city's bars! He was assisted by 'Ian Collins of No. 8 Commando, who had agreed to act as his P[ersonal] A[ssistant] for a few weeks before returning to the Coldstream Guards in England'. Stirling visited both the GHQ DMO and, on 10 September, the CO of the LRDG, Colonel Prendergast. That evening, the SAS commander also met the LRDG's new G Patrol commander, Alastair Timpson, who recalled that Stirling and Prendergast had organised dinner at Shepheards, where the SAS CO recounted 'his plans to form a new parachute unit which he intended to use in the forthcoming offensive and would require LRDG co-operation'. Stirling then, despite some of his musings of later years, knew much about the LRDG's abilities from the outset and discussed its role in his upcoming parachute operation with its senior officers.

Stirling also sought assistance from Ringway, 'sending several urgent signals' there, demonstrating that, like Clarke, he was familiar with its role in paratroop training. However, the new Airborne Forces Establishment was undergoing reorganisation by the RAF at the time, Squadron Leader John Callastius Kilkenny taking charge of its syllabus and ground training. He likely felt that he had enough on his plate already, though Bob Bennett told Gordon Stevens that Ringway believed that the desert was unsuited *per se* to parachuting. Hence, Kilkenny failed to 'reply in detail' to Stirling's 'cables and co-operate with . . . the SAS', providing only 'cursory answers' to his questions about training. Consequently, in addition to using trolleys at the naval base HMS *Saunders*' training ground, Lewes had to work out himself how to perfect a technique of jumping, using speeding 15-cwt Bedford trucks to simulate airborne landings. He found that driving at up to 30 mph and then jumping simulated a parachute landing, though it resulted in several injuries to his comrades![13]

By 16 September, Laycock had returned to take charge of the new Middle East Commando, and Stirling's SBS associates carried out two abortive night raids on 22 September from HMS *Utmost* near Naples and on Sicily. At the start of October, the SBS had to argue with Combined Operations HQ, Alexandria, that their raids should continue, using new shorter-fused demolitions charges. (A few days later, Operation Chopper/Deep Cut also went ahead and 5 Troop, No. 1 Commando, under Lieutenant Scaramanga, went ashore at St Vaast, near Cherbourg, while a party under Captain Davies landed at Courseulles. The former party killed three before withdrawing, leading to a 'monthly raid' programme involving sections of Nos. 2, 5, 9 and 12 Commandos. Additionally, Operation Archery, a raid on 27 September on South Vaagso, Norway, resulted, along with the bombing of Herdla airfield, in spectacular newsreel footage, the liberation of a hundred Norwegians, and the diversion of a large number of Germans).[14]

On 25 September, Middle East HQ noted that 'Stirling's party . . . are training assiduously with their parachutes [including] intensive training in night operations [and] occasional flights in a Bristol Bombay bomber.' However, reportedly 'opinion in Cairo – except that of Auchinleck and Ritchie – was that' the SAS would fail. Indeed, 'staff officers . . . from the Army and RAF came down to Kabrit and expressed themselves astonished at what was going on [and] how

Stirling had sold his . . . idea.' By 6 October, practice jumping had extended beyond rail-mounted trolleys, platforms and lorries to aerial jumps, and had resulted in six casualties. Fortunately, 'Ritchie regarded "L Detachment" as his particular toy [and he] visited Kabrit on several occasions and frequently sent other high-ranking officers to watch the parachute jumping.' Plans were drawn up by 4 October for a synchronised raid by the SAS on their target airfields (and an official request made on that day 'demanded from [the] RAF' 125 parachutes), in tandem with Eighth Army HQ's plan for 110 men of 11 Commando to hit Rommel's Beda Littoria HQ. (Incidentally, on 29 September, Auchinleck had told the LRDG's commander, Bagnold, 'I am very impressed by the work done by your . . . patrols. Their latest . . . is a fine example of their skill and daring'.)[15]

In mid-October, one visiting RAF group captain derided the very idea that the SAS could hit German airfields behind the lines, and Stirling swiftly secured a £100 wager that the 'parashites' – as the SAS's critics called them – could infiltrate RAF Heliopolis, ninety miles from Kabrit. In the interim, on 17 October, Laycock informed the Auk that the SAS 'are already well advanced in their training and . . . when properly equipped will constitute a unit of considerable potential'. However, he asked that Stirling be loaned a 'really go-ahead squadron leader' to assist the preparations.

At that point, Stirling himself made a jump from a Bombay without incident, but, after landing, while he was observing the next jump 'to study movement in the air and landing patterns', two parachutists' canopies failed to open and they were killed. 'Stirling was considerably shaken' by the deaths of Joe Duffy and Ken Warburton, Seaforth Highlanders, and he cancelled the rest of the day's jumps. It transpired that the fatalities were caused by a faulty parachute linkage, something that Ringway had experienced some weeks before. Stirling subsequently complained bitterly that Ringway had not informed him, and only after the two fatalities did it send 'some training notes and general information, which arrived at the end of October after the completion of our parachute training course'.[16]

The first jump made after the SAS's fatalities was, according to Riley, made by Jock Lewes – not Stirling, as most accounts claim. He was next, and all three landed without incident. But the other major contribution made at this time by Lewes came in the field of demolitions.

On 18 October, the Eighth Army's General Staff wired GHQ that 'as regards Stirling's party, Eighth Army want as many as possible' (reinforcing the ongoing efforts of other raiders, such as the SBS, which set out to target Italian rail lines at Ancona that day, 'Tug' Wilson and Marine Hughes leaving aboard HMS *Truant* to hit a train on the main east coast line north from Brindisi between Ancolia and Senegallia on 27 October).

Lewes realised that if the SAS was to hit and run swiftly, they would need lighter explosives than the 5-pound charges available to them. MI5 was consulted and GHQ provided an Egyptian railwayman and a senior Royal Engineers officer, who argued that a lighter demolition was not feasible. Undaunted, over the next couple of weeks, Lewes undertook his own experiments (as Lawrence had done) and devised an incendiary 1-pound 'Lewes Bomb' from plastic explosive, engine oil and thermite. It became standard kit for the SAS and earned him the tag 'the wizard'.[17]

Meantime, Ringway's focus remained UK-based paratroops rather than the fledgling forces of the Middle East and India. On 20–22 October, the Manchester aerodrome played host to BBC and Gaumont newsreel teams who filmed the base's 'hectic November of 1941', as the RAF assumed exclusive responsibility for the preparation of the UK's paratroops (while press photos were taken on 24 October). Indeed, when the 50th Indian Parachute Brigade HQ was set up in Delhi under Brigadier W. G. H. Gough – who oversaw the formation of the 151st British, 152nd Indian and 153rd Gurkha Parachute Battalions, as well as the 411th Engineers Section – he, like Stirling, received little help from Ringway. Some of its instructors went to the new Airlanding School at Delhi's Willingdon Airport, including Flight Lieutenant 'Bill' Brereton, who had been 'one of the earliest pioneers of parachute jumping at Farnborough'. But, while the RAF/Army party of fourteen arrived with parachutes 'as part of their personal baggage', these were 'the entire stock' at the school and, 'for a long time these were the only parachutes they could lay their hands on'. Although one jump was made on 15 October, 'It was not possible to make much headway with training without an adequate supply of parachutes.' Yet,

'No immediate help was forthcoming [due to] the closure of the Mediterranean to Allied shipping'.[18]

The Middle East fared little better but, on 24 October, GHQ noted that seven Bombays from No. 216 Squadron, RAF, would be put at the SAS's disposal, allowing for ten raiders per plane. Additionally, Ringway 'sent . . . Captain Peter Warr, who greatly helped with the forthcoming operation', and he in fact 'joined the SAS' in due course.

Once Lewes had produced the means by which the SAS could rapidly destroy large numbers of planes, the next step was a dress rehearsal. At the end of October, Stirling took up his bet with RAF Heliopolis' CO. According to various accounts, 4–6 officers and 40–55 SAS men marched three days and four nights to the base and infiltrated it, putting stickers saying 'bomb' on planes parked about the aerodrome. Mayne's group alone affixed forty-five before heading for the Assabea barracks. The following morning, the SAS's hit-and-run raid was discovered, much to the ire (and admiration) of the RAF and GHQ Air Staff officers, and to the benefit of Stirling's coffers![19] He and his men had proved that they could hike a great distance to a target undetected by the enemy, hit it, and retreat in good order. The key element that had yet to be proven was parachute insertion, and they would soon have the chance to demonstrate its virtues, or otherwise, as a precursor to the impending operations against Rommel.

Chapter 12

The First Raids

As the SAS made their final preparations for their raids as part of Operation Crusader, their special force colleagues in the LRDG were already on the hoof. Holliman's S1 patrol engaged an enemy convoy on 7 November, and the rest of the Group had moved from Kufra to its new Siwa saltwater lake HQ by 10 November, ready for further action in five raiding groups from the 15th (while Easonsmith's R1 was attached to the SAS to pick them up after their raids).[1] On 13 November, Auchinleck visited the SAS at their training camp, where he was filmed for a newsreel, and he watched them do an incident-free 2,000-foot jump. Stirling recounted that the Auk 'was very enthusiastic about the unit, and so was General Ritchie', while Lewes added that the CINC 'values us' and had thanked the SAS's officers 'for a good unit whom he trusts'. Jock noted Stirling had 'established it without and . . . I have established it within . . . This unit cannot now die, as Layforce died.' However, there was a chance that such a fate could befall the SAS as they counted down to zero hour, as bad weather threatened to frustrate their planned 8,000-foot parachute jump.[2]

Despite 30-knot gales, however, other special forces soldiers were already committed to battle, including a group of six officers and fifty-three other ranks of the 11th (Scottish) Commando, whom Eighth Army HQ had designated for a strike on Rommel's HQ. Operation Copper Flipper featured Laycock and Geoff Keyes, who set off from Alexandria with their colleagues aboard the submarines HMS *Torbay* and *Talisman* on 10 November. Split into four detachments, they were to target Rommel's house at Beda Littoria, the Italian HQ at Cyrene, an Intelligence centre at Apollonia, and numerous communications targets. After landing on the coast from the *Torbay* via folbots on 14 November, the raiders linked up with three G(R) officers led by

Captain Haselden. Having been transported by the LRDG's T2 patrol under Captain Hunter, Haselden, in Arab dress, had carried out recces three days before with Lieutenant Ingles and Corporal Severn (SBS). Of those who disembarked from HMS *Talisman*, most capsized and only Laycock and seven other ranks made it ashore. Indeed, it took seven hours for the raiders to land, guided by two pairs of SBS soldiers (including Lieutenant Langton and Corporal Freebery), and only thirty-six of the fifty-nine who set out made it ashore (others like Sutherland scrambled back to the subs). After laying up for a day and forming two raiding parties, Keyes, Captain Campbell and seventeen other ranks stormed Rommel's HQ on 17 November, while Lieutenant Cook and six other ranks hit communications south of Cyrene, and Laycock and three companions secured a lay-up position, ready to gather any stragglers from the landings. Keyes was killed and most of the raiders failed to make it back, only twenty-two surviving and just Laycock and Sergeant Jack Terry returning to Eighth Army HQ, forty-one days later – just in time for Christmas – after an arduous desert march.[3]

Despite the prospect of gales that could wreck the SAS's mission, 'conflicting weather reports led Stirling to consult his officers'. Part of Stirling's pitch at GHQ on 16 July had been that the SAS would be less affected by adverse weather than Layforce, and with Laycock and his comrades taking the fight to the Axis, Seekings recalled that the SAS's officers felt immense pressure to go ahead, while all of its personnel were for it.[4] As a result, though GHQ felt that it was nigh on impossible to parachute in the prevailing conditions, the SAS leadership – mindful that a cancellation would also dent the men's morale – determined to press on with Operation Squatter (a wry codename doubtless chosen to reflect the uninvited presence of the SAS behind the enemy's lines). The 11th SAS had hit Tragino in similarly bad conditions and this might have had some bearing as well.

On 16 November, five detachments (twelve-man parties made up of three sub-sections of four men), led by Stirling, McGonigal, Lewes, Mayne and Bonnington, took off in No. 216 Squadron's Bristol Bombays from Bagoush for a drop zone twelve miles from their three target airfields at Gazala and another two at Tmimi. However, after a ninety-minute flight over the Gulf of Bomba, the expected Bomber Command guidance flares were obscured by clouds and the planes hit a storm (later assessed as the worst rain in thirty years, with winds in the desert hitting 90 mph), obliging them to drop to 500 feet. Soon afterwards, Bonnington's aircraft, flown by 'Charlie' West, had to drop even lower before putting down, where a skirmish with Italian forces (with one PoW) was followed by a hurried take-off. Italian air defence fire then forced West to crash-land, sustaining one fatality (his co-pilot).

Meanwhile, McGonigal's plane went missing and was not seen again, its occupants presumed dead or captured. Stirling's stick landed at 25 mph, and all of them sustained injuries in the tempest, while one man went missing. After two hours scurrying about in the maelstrom, they met up but were unable to find the canisters containing their detonators, effectively ending their sabotage mission. Mayne's group was also scattered to the winds, sustained two casualties, and recovered only a few containers, to find that most of their fuses were damp in any case. Lewes had been nicked by ack-ack fire, but Stirling and Sergeant Tait scouted north, while the remainder of the stragglers, led by Mayne and Sergeant Yates, made for the Trig al Abd, thirty miles south of the coast. They then marched the forty miles to their rendezvous at Rotunda Segnale and were picked up by the LRDG, before transfer to Siwa and thence by plane to Kabrit. Some of McGonigal's party may have carried out their mission, but most were likely taken as PoWs. However, what was patent was that Squatter left the SAS with less than half its complement – only twenty-one made it back from the raid (including Lewes and Mayne), while Yates and three others were captured (out of total losses of twenty-eight PoWs and six dead).[5]

Stirling and Tait took another day to reach the LRDG, but the SAS CO believed that the strategic raiding concept remained sound, for they had 'wandered about the enemy's . . . flank for . . . days unhindered'. However, he 'was coming to the conclusion that parachuting was not the best way to reach targets' and, during the 250-mile journey to Siwa, he resurrected the idea of the LRDG taking the SAS into battle, discussing it with Easonsmith and Steele. Stirling later reflected that he 'became convinced that this talented band could provide the perfect combination of skills' to assist the SAS. However, another LRDG officer, Captain David Lloyd Owen, whom Easonsmith and Stirling visited en route to Siwa on 24 November, noted that Stirling seemed reticent about the LRDG inserting the SAS behind the lines. This is likely to have been because he realised that the whole premise for his unit was as part of A Force, which required a parachute group. However, over tea, Stirling recounted 'the story of his drop and of all that had gone wrong [and] he was already trying to analyse' how to proceed. Owen 'sensed . . . that he was not really certain that parachuting was the best way', due to its 'limitations . . . inaccuracy [and] its dependency on the weather and availability' of aircraft. Yet, when Owen pushed for LRDG conveyance to battle, Stirling muttered that motor transport was 'a bit slow' and appeared 'sceptical'.

By the time the convoy reached Siwa on 25 November, however, Stirling was 'immensely impressed' by the way that the LRDG worked, and he, Lewes and Mayne agreed that it might be the best option. Indeed, during their first drop, Stirling had confided to Pat Riley and 'Jock' Cheyne (one of its fatalities), 'I think it is the end of parachuting for us', though he later added that, 'Parachuting could not be totally written off.' Whatever the case, he realised that the SAS 'must try again quickly . . . and succeed', if it was to survive, and he told Seekings, 'I don't see the point of parachuting in when [the LRDG] is so much simpler . . . and far more efficient', once more demonstrating that Stirling had no great personal stake in the airborne method. On 2 December, he asked his peers if they were ready to go again, and they all said that they were.[6]

Fortunately, by the time that Stirling was summoned to the Maddalena HQ on 26 November, 'the High Command was fully occupied with Rommel's dash to the Egyptian frontier' and the generally unsatisfactory progress of Crusader, which led to Ritchie's appointment to take command of Eighth Army on 25 November. While the SAS mission had failed, so had the raid on Rommel's HQ and, as Cowles points out, 'Auchinleck and Ritchie were staunch friends' of the SAS. They recognised that Squatter was derailed by 'rotten luck' with the weather and neither was minded to give up on special operations just because two missions had floundered. Hence, after a brief meeting with Ritchie, followed by one with Auchinleck in Cairo, Stirling was given *carte blanche* to continue with raiding as he saw fit.[7]

Meantime, the SAS saw themselves in the Pathé newsreel of Auchinleck's visit on 13 November, before re-equipping at Kabrit. Stirling pressed the case for LRDG co-operation at Eighth Army HQ and, luckily for Stirling, 22nd Guards Brigade's commander, Brigadier John Marriott, arrived shortly after. A 'great friend' of Stirling and Ran Churchill, he had met David at Peter Stirling's flat and 'was amused and impressed by his young friend's activities and listened sympathetically' as he explained that they needed to get into action again as soon as possible. Marriott suggested Stirling visit his erstwhile colleague, Brigadier Denys W. Reid, of E 'Oasis' Force (comprising the 2nd Punjabs and 6th South African Armoured Car Regiment), who was overseeing the activities of the Eighth Army southern flank's motorised units at Jalo – 150 miles south of Benghazi and the Gulf of Sirte airfields, and north-west of the Great Sand Sea – which he had recently captured, along with 600 Italian PoWs.[8] It was the forward base of Major Steele's LRDG A Squadron and ex-Royal Tank Regiment Captain C. A. 'Gus' Holliman's Rhodesian S Patrol. (The LRDG Guards patrols, G1 and G2, operating from Siwa, hit enemy transport on the Agedabia–Benghazi road at the end of November, before returning to their base on 3 December).[9]

Reid had orders to link up on the coast with Marriott by 22 December for a new offensive on Benghazi overseen by Ritchie. This offered the chance for behind the lines raids by the SAS, and Stirling and his colleagues flew out from Kabrit to Bagoush in a Dakota on 3 December, then boarded a Bombay for Jalo on 5 December. Stirling met Reid the next day, and they drew up plans to hit various Axis airfields on 14/15 December.

On 7 December, as Major Steele noted, a 'party of 25 parachute troops under Captain Stirling arrived' at his LRDG base, with the aim of accompanying 'patrols for raids' on Sirte and El Agheila. Stirling addressed his men and informed them that he, Mayne and a party of ten would be dropped by the LRDG about twenty miles from the Sirte aerodrome, while a similar-sized party under Lewes would head for Agheila, with Lieutenant Fraser and three men subsequently making for Agedabia airfield on the Gulf of Sirte, courtesy of Olivey's LRDG patrol.

A convoy of seven 30-cwt Chevrolets armed with Lewis guns and equipped with enough rations for three weeks set off with Stirling, Mayne and ten other ranks on 8 December under Captain Holliman for the Great Sand Sea and Wadi Faregh. On 9 December, 2nd Lieutenant C. S. Morris's five-truck T2 patrol took Lewes's and Fraser's parties towards the Agheila aerodrome. After a couple of days scouting the salt marshes to the south, they grabbed an Italian PoW on the 13th and delivered Lewes and his men ten miles from their target. However, when they got there next day, they found that its aircraft had been removed. Frustrated, they withdrew and, after discussing the situation with Lieutenant Morris, Lewes decided to adopt the guise of an Axis patrol using a captured Lancia truck with a 20-mm Breda gun that they had brought along with them as their lead vehicle. Soon afterwards, they hit twenty-five enemy lorries and numerous ammunition stores, as well as a fortified blockhouse at Mersa Brega port. They made Jalo on 18 December, carrying out demolitions (every other telegraph pole for a mile) and road mining (courtesy of the LRDG's Corporal Garven) en route.

Meantime, on 11 December, sixty miles from Sirte (and 300 miles from Jalo), Stirling and his colleagues were seen by an Italian Ghibli spotter plane as their convoy halted at mid-day when bogged down in rough terrain. The LRDG opened fire and hid beneath camouflage nets in the brush during fifteen minutes of ineffective strafing, before making good their escape. They got within twenty miles of the SAS's target undetected, before being rumbled once more by a Ghibli, though it was too dark for other aircraft to be scrambled to search for them. On 12 December, following a patrol of the area, Stirling, Jimmy Brough and Holliman found an airfield at Tamet not previously detailed by Intelligence. After a quick conference, the SAS decided to split into two parties, Stirling leading one to a point four miles from Sirte, while two of the LRDG trucks peeled off over the salt marshes and low dunefields south of the Via Balbo with Mayne and several companions. Three miles from the landing ground at the north end of Wadi Tamet (thirty miles from Sirte and five from the coast), Mayne and his group alighted and made for the garrison that night (while the LRDG drove south to lay up in the desert).

On approaching Sirte, Stirling's advance was stalled by a minefield, and when he and Brough trod on two sleeping Italians, they were obliged to take flight. By the next afternoon, the Italians had moved thirty or so Caproni aircraft from the airfield and Stirling's opportunity had gone. However, most of the planes were flown the five miles to Tamet and so Mayne's group found plenty of targets on arrival there. They destroyed twenty-four aircraft using twenty-minute time-pencil Lewes bombs, returning unscathed to their rendezvous in the desert, despite having been buzzed by a pair of Me-109s.

On 20 December, Morris and the LRDG left their camp at Ain en Naga and took Fraser and his 'parachute troops up to [the] 16 kilometre post on [the] Agedabia–Haseiat road', twelve miles from Agedabia. Fraser's party struck the airfield on 21 December after a night march and reconnaissance. They returned with Morris to Wadi Faregh and thence Jalo on 23 December (suffering a strafing from two RAF Blenheims en route), having notched up thirty-seven CR-42 fighters out of thirty-nine parked at the air base – a feat deemed by Reid to be 'a wonderful achievement'. Countess Ranfurly was subsequently made aware of what Stirling was up to, noting that he 'and his small unit are doing well in the desert. When the moon is down they are dropped behind enemy lines near landing grounds and dumps.' She continued that they 'sneak past enemy sentries and patrols, fix their bombs on aeroplanes and then make for home [with] the LRDG, which they call "Carter Paterson" [or] the Desert Taxi Company [and] the number of enemy planes they've destroyed is remarkable'.[10]

Once Fraser had returned to Jalo on 23 December, Stirling 'discussed raiding techniques with his officers and the lessons of the previous week'. These included the need to avoid shooting up the target before setting off charges, not being overly cautious on approaching them, and not carrying out advanced patrols that delayed an assault and risked their discovery. Further, they agreed that surprise remained the key to success and, given that the enemy would not expect the same air bases to be hit again so soon, they decided to head out for another series of raids on their now-familiar targets. In addition, Stirling declared that, at least for now, 'parachuting was definitely out'.[11]

On 24 December, Stirling and Mayne set off once more with Holliman's five-truck convoy for Wadi Hamet, and thence Sirte and

Tamet, respectively. Meanwhile, on Boxing Day, Lewes and Fraser's teams made for En Nofilia and Area Philonerum (Marble Arch), respectively, in five trucks under Morris. Arriving at Wadi Tamet on 27 December, Holliman took Stirling's group in three trucks to a spot six miles from their target, while Sergeant Jackson and two LRDG lorries drove Mayne's group to a drop-off point twenty-five miles from their goal. In the early hours, Stirling's party spotted a German armoured unit heading for Agheila thirty miles away, as part of Rommel's retreat from Gazala to Agedabia. After allowing it to pass, they skirted their quarry before dawn, but were stymied by wire obstructions and challenged by a sentry. They retreated and had to content themselves with destroying nine telegraph poles and two lorries. A couple of hours before that, Mayne's group hit Tamet, destroying twenty-seven aircraft (despite the early detonation of some time-pencil charges). Holliman was also in the thick of it, destroying twelve trucks at Tamet, before shooting up Axis units and three camps en route to the rendezvous point to pick up the SAS parties, before making for Jalo. When Morris returned there on 1 January, however, he had less welcome news to report.

On 27 December, Morris had dropped Fraser's group about six miles from Marble Arch, while Lewes's raiders hit the road twenty miles from Nofilia on the next day. After avoiding passing Stukas on 28 December, they counted forty-three German planes on its airfield, but one of the raiders' charges went off prematurely and, before they could launch an attack, the Germans had removed all but two unairworthy machines. The SAS blew them up before being picked up by the LRDG on 30 December. On the following day, the party made for Marble Arch to pick up Fraser's team, but was spotted by an Italian Savoia aircraft, which called in an Me-109 fighter and, later, Stuka dive-bombers that proceeded to keep them pinned down for several hours. By the time that they got to the rendezvous point, Fraser and his group had made for Wadi Faregh – a 200-mile journey that they eventually completed by 11 January. Moreover, during the air attack, Lewes was killed returning fire, and Morris made it back with only one of his trucks intact.[12]

The loss of Lewes was a major blow both to SAS morale and its pool of training and tactical expertise. But while the rest of the SAS made for Kabrit for a short respite, Stirling's immediate concern was to bolster his numbers and re-deploy as soon as possible, in order to keep up the momentum gained by the destruction of some ninety enemy aircraft in a matter of weeks. He made for Cairo and, on 2 January 1942, Countess Ranfurly noted that she had bumped into him at Shepheards, where he told her that his unit had been effectively reduced to four officers and fourteen other ranks. He feared that his small force might be amalgamated with another, such as the SOE or G(R), by Middle East HQ.[13] Indeed, on 25 December, its Deputy Director of Operations, Brigadier Whiteley, sent Lieutenant-General Smith, a memo on the future of the Middle East Commando, the SBS and the SAS. He noted that, 'Stirling want[s] to be absolutely independent and directly under GHQ' command – thereby breaking away from A Force, which Smith regarded as an 'unsatisfactory' arrangement. On the 26th, Smith commented that they needed to guard against nurturing 'a number of little private armies', but he added the caveat that 'Stirling deserves to have charge . . . of the parachute wing'.[14] Tony Kemp notes that there followed on 30–31 December 'a puzzling exchange of correspondence between staff officers at Middle East HQ and Eighth Army HQ' that referred to 'a proposed parachute operation, [yet] there is no evidence that Stirling was planning' one. Nonetheless, Colonel M. B. Jennings of GHQ noted on 30 December that 'Stirling appears to have told someone in RAF Operations' that a drop was in the offing. Jennings continued that no one at GHQ knew about this, but that, 'We all know Stirling's weakness for [being] apt to think out his own operations . . . lay them on without authorisation . . . then offer it to us on a plate.'[15]

Colonel Thirburn at Eighth Army Advanced HQ replied on 31 December that Stirling's 'natural impetuousness and importunity make it difficult for him to stick to any procedure!' While Kemp notes a 'puzzling' lack of evidence that Stirling *was* planning any such operation, it is possible that enquiries had been made in Stirling's absence about the potential for future paratroop drops. Stirling's Ringway training advisor, Peter Warr, who had a parachute course up and running by the new year, would have had a vested interest in such missions, as would Dudley Clarke, and an intervention from either on Stirling's behalf would explain the 'alleged parachute operation' at a point when Stirling himself favoured land-based behind the lines infiltration.[16]

The SAS's ongoing successes in any case convinced the CINC to let Stirling decide which method he thought would pay the biggest dividends in future. Indeed, by this stage, 'Stirling and Mayne . . . were . . . legends in the folklore of the service bars' and Auchinleck was 'satisfied that L Detachment had proved its worth', observing that its raids – as outlined in glowing terms to Middle East HQ by Reid and Marriott – were 'really useful'. Consequently, the Auk asked Stirling 'what he proposed to do next', and the SAS CO suggested a raid on the port of Bouerat, to destroy shipping and fuel supplies, thereby demonstrating the SAS's flexibility in terms of targeting. The CINC agreed, and Stirling's request for a dozen new recruits and an SBS officer was upgraded by his superior to six officers and forty other ranks, while Stirling was promoted to major.[17] Though the SAS had only just begun its illustrious wartime career, the foundations for its expansion had been well and truly laid, and from then on it would go from strength to strength, creating its own legend in the years to come.

Chapter 13

Godfathers of the Regiment

As has been demonstrated, David Stirling was only one of a number of godfathers of the SAS who contributed invaluable ideas, political clout and the timely opportunities that laid the way for the establishment of the regiment. While Stirling played a key role in devising the strategic raiding role and sub-unit size of the SAS, his ideas did not simply stem from inspiration that came to him while he was laid up in a military hospital.

Stirling had a military pedigree and heritage that predisposed him towards special operations, with both the North American wars of the colonies and the South African War being examples with which he was familiar. Stirling's colleagues in Layforce contributed to his ruminations, both from practical actions such as those of Courtney's SBS, and Mather and Jellicoe, as well as from his bedside discussions, notably with his brother Bill, and Jock Lewes, who had experience and knowledge of past and present unorthodox small unit operations, notably those of Robert Rogers.

Furthermore, David discussed his ideas with fellow Shepheards resident Dudley Clarke, who was instrumental in setting up the Commandos, based on his knowledge of previous guerilla wars, not least South Africa (which also featured Boer deception schemes about the size of their forces), First World War Arabia, and inter-war Palestine. Clarke seems likely to have proposed a link-up between Stirling and Wingate and, moreover, to have offered Stirling the chance to parachute as part of A Force's deception scheme, with Wavell's approval. Clarke had already been involved in the development of the parachute Commandos in the UK (dubbing them the 'SAS') and he kept tabs on German airborne operations. Wavell was equally well disposed to paratroops – having witnessed their use before the war – as well as to special forces in general, including the SNS and LRDG (his own father having set up an irregular unit in 1880, while Wavell was also familiar with guerillas from the Napoleonic Wars to Lawrence). Wavell pressed for the development of parachuting after successful dummy drops for the LRDG early in 1941 and he was pressured by Churchill for more raids and paratroopers during that spring. After the German seizure of Crete in May, Churchill once more urged the formation of paratroop units, and Wavell seems to have had the matter in hand by then. Additionally, in June, Stirling was lucky that Wingate was pressing the case for more behind the lines guerilla action, receiving interested attention at Middle East HQ.

Furthermore, Stirling was fortunate that, when Wavell was removed by Churchill – always a staunch supporter of military unorthodoxy – his replacement was Auchinleck. He too had been pursuing his own paratroop plans in India, having been impressed by the 11th SAS in the UK in 1940, as well as facing the German paratroop threat there (not to mention supporting Auxiliary Units for behind the lines operations). Equally, Stirling was blessed that Auchinleck's friend, Ritchie, had been a colleague of Wavell and had family connections with Stirling's cousin Lovat. Ritchie was supportive of David's proposed raiding strategy, authorising him to set up a unit the same size as the Lovat Scouts' 'squadrons' in South Africa (and their nomenclature was even adopted later on).

At that time, Churchill was urging his commanders to do more raids to relieve some of the military pressure on Russia, including the use of paratroops, and so the strategic situation conspired to afford Stirling the opportunity to undertake such operations. More particularly, the new threat posed in the Middle East theatre by the German Me-109 demanded action against German airfields that the RAF was unable to provide, further furnishing Stirling with a chance to act (supported by the RAF).

When devising his own raiding scheme, Stirling was also able to draw on his own experience in the Commandos, his familiarity with the desert war of 1914–18, and information gained soon after his arrival in Cairo in 1941 – through connections at Shepheards and his brother Peter's flat – about the activities of the LRDG (who included

Shepheards residents such as Prendergast) and SOE (who included Bill Stirling's colleague and friend of both Lovat and Waugh, Peter Fleming, as well as Colonel Will Stirling).

David was also aware of the German paratroop operations in Greece and Crete, and most probably of 11th SAS and Ringway too (either through direct contact with 2 Commando or via the likes of his brother and Dudley Clarke). All these considerations fed into Stirling's July paper on the 1st SAS and allowed him to present a compelling case for the continuation of the paratroop experiment first assigned to Lewes, then taken up in his absence by Stirling.

The picture that emerges of the origins of Stirling's SAS is one in which he had far more than 'incredible luck' to present his plans to Ritchie and Auchinleck.[1] The notion that the SAS stemmed simply 'from a germ of an idea in Stirling's fertile' mind and that his 'unrivalled imagination, improvisation and determination' marked him out as 'one of the most ... original military thinkers of all time' overstates the case. He was neither thinking nor acting in isolation and, while he remains the fulcrum of the origins of the SAS Regiment, he was not the only factor in its creation.

While Mike Morgan repeats the received wisdom that in attaining Auchinleck's blessing for his unit, Stirling 'had achieved the near-impossible',[2] the feat was not as preternaturally impressive as the legend might have us believe. Similarly, Jock Lewes's biographer has asserted that, 'There was no tradition of using these techniques prior to the SAS', and that, 'There were certainly no soldiers with experience to guide' Lewes when he undertook the first experimental parachute jumps in the Middle East. He is said, like Stirling, to have devised 'his methods in his imagination', in impressive and splendid isolation.[3]

In fact, neither Lewes nor Stirling acted wholly at their own initiative or in a vacuum cut off from the ideas and example of others. They shared their thoughts and liberally adopted and adapted ideas, their key role being to meld together the many disparate threads of past and recent wisdom to create a unique new unit. They added their own important innovations, with Stirling's strategic raiding role and his force's sub-unit size the most cutting edge of his advances in military thought. But the SAS came about because of a whole panoply of factors, and Stirling was the first to acknowledge that he was but one of its co-founders.

He shares the main credit with a group of godfathers of the regiment far more numerous than has been recognised hitherto, and who, together, created the conditions in which David Stirling was able to forge the world's leading special force.

Notes

Preface – SAS: The Untold Story

1. For UK television coverage of the SAS, for instance: Carlton's *SAS: The Soldier's Story* (1996); BBC2's *SAS: Are You Tough Enough?* (March 2002), *SAS Jungle* (February 2003), *SAS – Embassy Siege* (July 2002), *SAS Desert* (March 2003), *SAS: Survival Secrets* (September 2003), *Hunting Chris Ryan* (October 2003); Channel 4's *Commando* (January 2002); Channel 5's *Gladiators of World War II* (February 2002); UK TV History *Great SAS Missions* (August 2004); and in the press: M. Bowness/R. Blackstock, *The Sun*, 12 January 2002; M. Pitkin, *The Daily Telegraph* (UK/Australia), 18 October 2001. Another blockbuster movie that mentioned the SAS was *Love Actually* (2003), wherein Prime Minister Hugh Grant offers to have the 'awfully nice' SAS eliminate his secretary's ex-boyfriend! As a further example of popular interest in the SAS, there are over a thousand websites dealing with the regiment. Videos made during the 1990s such as those by DD Video, WH Smith and Castle featured former SAS officers, right up to the regiment's former commander, General Sir Peter de la Billière, all, on the face of it, adding authority to the video-makers' portrayal of the SAS's early history.

2. T. L. Jones, *Postwar Counterinsurgency and the SAS, 1945–52: A Special Type of Warfare*, London, 2001; *SAS: The First Secret* Wars, London, 2005; 'The SAS Regiment after World War II' *Book Collector* (255, May 2005).

3. P. Harclerode in R. Holmes (ed.), *The Oxford Companion to Military History*, Oxford, 2001, p. 805. On Stirling's supposed 'unique foresight' and singular 'vision' that was 'his alone', see for instance: M. Morgan, *Daggers Drawn*, Stroud, 2000, p. 2; A. Kemp, *The SAS at War, 1941–45*, London, 1991, p. xii; A. Kemp, *The SAS: The Savage Wars of Peace*, London, 1994, p. 7; A. Kemp, *Teach Yourself Special Forces*, London, 2004, pp. 4–9; R. Bradford & M. Dillon, *Rogue Warrior of the SAS*, London, 1987, p. 26; J. Ladd, *SAS Operations*, London, 1989, p. 1; M. Nicol, *Ultimate Risk*, London, 2004, p. 33.

4. On the origins of the SAS concept: S. Christie, 'As Others See Us – The Golden Road to Samarkand' (*Anarchist Review*) cited in SAS journal, *Mars and Minerva*, 5/3 (winter 1982), p. 5.

5. R. Hunter, *True Stories of the SBS*, London, 1995, p. 20.

6. BBC Radio 4, *Of One Company – The True Story of the Founding of the SAS*, 22 November 2001. For the programme narrator Julian Putkowski's background and an account of the Kinmel Park riot, T. L. Jones, *Rioting In North-East Wales, 1536–1918*, Wrexham, 1997, p. 79.

7. P. Warner, *The Special Air Service*, London, 1971, p. 73.

8. Warner, *Special Air Service*, p. 19.

9. A. Hoe, *David Stirling – The Authorised Biography of the Creator of the SAS*, London, 1994, p. 473. Earl Jellicoe, writing in the Foreword to L. A. Windmill, *Gentleman Jim*, London, 2001, p. ix.

Chapter 1 – The Legend and the Man

1. V. Cowles, *The Phantom Major*, London, 1958, pp. 12–16.

2. Cowles, *Phantom Major*, pp. 12–16; M. James [Pleydell], *Born of the Desert*, London, 1945, reprinted 1991, p. 17.

3. Cowles, *Phantom Major*, pp. 12–16.

4. Cowles, *Phantom Major*, pp. 12–16; Hoe, *Stirling*, pp. 67–8.

5. On Lovat: his autobiography, *March Past*, London, 1978, pp. 98, 101, 160, 167; F. Lindley, *Lord Lovat*, London, 1935, p. 26; on Ritchie: Hoe, *Stirling*, pp. 67–8.

6. A. Swinson, *The Raiders*, London, 1974, p. 43.

7. Cowles, *Phantom Major*, pp. 17, 22.

8. Cowles, *Phantom Major*, pp. 18–20.

9. Cowles, *Phantom Major*, pp. 21–2.

10. Cowles, *Phantom Major*, p. 22.

11. Cowles, *Phantom Major*, pp. 19–21.

12. Cowles, *Phantom Major*, pp. 17–23.

13. Cowles, *Phantom Major*, p. 20.

14. Cowles, *Phantom Major*, pp. 20–1.

15. Cowles, *Phantom Major*, pp. 18–21.

16. Warner, *Special Air Service*, pp. 26–32.

17. Warner, *Special Air Service*, pp. 26–32; Hoe, *Stirling*, p. 55.

18. Warner, *Special Air Service*, pp. 26–32; Colonel D. Stirling, *Memo on The Origins of the SAS Regiment*, Staff College Camberley 1948 Course, 8 November 1948, Brigadier R. W. McLeod Papers, Liddell Hart Centre for Military Archives, London [LHC]; G. Stevens, *The Originals – The Secret History of the SAS in their Own Words*, London, 2005, m/s, p. 14.

19. J. Strawson, *A History of the SAS Regiment*, London, 1984, pp. 12–18.

20. Hoe, *Stirling*, pp. 52–69.

21. Warner, *Special Air Service*, pp. 11, 15; Hoe, *Stirling*, pp. 16–21, 42.

22. Hoe, *Stirling*, pp. 16–23.

23. Hoe, *Stirling*, pp. 23–40.

24. Hoe, *Stirling*, pp. 23–45; A. Kemp, *SAS at War*, p. 2; Bradford & Dillon, *Rogue Warrior*, pp. xiii, 26.

25. Stevens, *Originals* m/s, p. 5.

26. Lovat *March Past*, p. 7.

27. P. R. N. Katcher, *Encyclopedia of British, Provincial and German Units, 1775–83*, Harrisburg, Penn., 1973, pp. 21, 24, 80; Todd W. Braistead (4th Battalion, New Jersey Volunteers), email to author, 19 January 2004.

28. Hoe, *Stirling*, pp. 40–5; Lovat, *March Past*, pp. 141, 160; L. Barlow & R. Smith, *Lovat Scouts, Scottish Horse*, Tunbridge Wells, 1985, p. 1.

Chapter 2 – Stalin's War

1. Hoe, *Stirling*, p. 45.

2. D. Erskine, *The Scots Guards, 1919–55*, London, 1956, p. 21; P. Warner, *Auchinleck*, London, 1982, p. 52.

3. Jones, *Postwar Counterinsurgency*, Ch. 1–2; A. Weale, *Secret Warfare*, London, 1997, p. 50; C. Mather, *When the Grass Stops Growing*, London, 1997, p. 3.

4. J. Parker, *Commandos*, London, 2000, pp. 7, 10; C. Messenger, *The Commandos, 1940–46*, London, 1991, p. 19.

5. P. Wilkinson & J. B. Astley, *Gubbins* and *SOE*, London, 1993, pp. 24, 26–8, 31–8, 70, 77.

6. Wilkinson & Astley, *Gubbins*, pp. 24–38; M. R. D. Foot, *SOE*, London, 1990, pp. 4, 7–11; N. West, *Secret War*, London, 1992, pp. 1, 9, 14–16.

7. On Fleming: B. Hart-Davis, *Peter Fleming*, London, 1974, pp. 214, 216. On Churchill: E. Morris, *Churchill's Private Armies*, London, 1986, pp. 3–4, 7–8.

8. Morris, *Churchill's Private Armies*, p. 28.

9. Erskine, *Scots Guards*, pp. 21–6; Mather, *When the Grass*, pp. 5–8, 10–13, 16–17; J. M. Calvert, *Fighting Mad*, London, 1996, pp. 13, 22, 30–4; J. Cooper, *One of the Originals*, London, 1991, pp. 3, 8. Cooper became the subject of an episode of TV's *This Is Your Life*.

10. S. Hastings, *The Drums of Memory*, London, 1994, p. 17; K. O'Gorman, archivist, Scots Guards HQ, London, interview, 16 July 2001; P. Kemp, *No Colours Or Crest*, London, 1958, pp. 12–18.

11. Weale, *Secret Warfare*, pp. 50–1; Parker, *Commandos*, pp. 8–9, 11; Morris, *Churchill's Private Armies*, pp. 12–16, 59; Lovat, *March Past*, pp. 175–7. Lovat was immortalised in the 1960 movie about the D-Day landings, *The Longest Day*.

12. Hoe, *Stirling*, p. 46.

Chapter 3 – The Independent Companies

1. Morris, *Churchill's Private Armies*, pp. 18–23, 81–2, 84–7; N. Crookenden, *Airborne at War*, London, 1978, pp. 11–12, 15; D. Clarke, Diary 1940, Clarke Papers, 92/2/2, *Wartime Travels, 1939–45* m/s, 19 April 1940, 92/2/10, Imperial War Museum, London [IWM]. On German paratroops: C. MacDonald, *The Lost Battle*, London, 1993, pp. 29–30, 33, 36–8.

2. On the Independent Companies and Norway: Lovat, *March Past*, p. 177; J. Connell, *Wavell – Scholar* and *Soldier*, London, 1964, pp. 132, 158, 175; Morris, *Churchill's Private Armies*, pp. 18–23, 81–7; Wilkinson & Astley, *Gubbins*, pp. 50–2. On Manningham: W. Seymour, *British Special Forces*, London, 1985, p. 6.

3. MoI, *Combined Operations, 1940–42*, London, 1943, p. 10; Parker, *Commandos*, pp. 10–12, 14–17, 19.

4. R. Neillands, *The Raiders*, London, 1990, pp. 3, 5, 9, 11–14, 19–20, 22, 32–3, 35; Wilkinson & Astley, *Gubbins*, pp. 50–2; J. Thompson, *The Imperial War Museum Book of War Behind Enemy Lines*, London, 1998, p. 3.

5. B. Hart-Davis, *Peter Fleming*, London, 1974, pp. 222–3, 225, 228–30; P. Wilkinson, *Foreign Fields*, London, 1997, pp. 100–3.

6. Wilkinson & Astley, *Gubbins*, p. 70; D. Lampe, *The Last Ditch* London, 1968, pp. 2, 82–5.

7. Lovat, *March Past*, p. 177.

8. Hart-Davis, *Peter Fleming*, pp. 233–7; Weale, *Secret Warfare*, pp. 61–2.

9. Calvert, *Fighting Mad*, pp. 47–8.

10. J. Connell, *Auchinleck*, London, 1959, pp. 8, 11–12, 55–9, 66–9.

11. Warner, *Auchinleck*, pp. 14, 17–18, 24, 26, 34–40, 46–8; and on Independent Companies: pp. 54–55, 57, 60, 62–4, 70–2; and on Ritchie: pp. 10–12, 364.

12. Wilkinson & Astley, *Gubbins*, pp. 54–5, 66–7.

13. M. Carver, *Dilemmas of the Desert War*, London, 1986, pp. 147–8; R. Parkinson, *The Auk*, London, 1979, pp. 34–50, 57–8.

14. On Clarke: D. Clarke, *Seven Assignments*, London, 1948, pp. 25, 31, 37, 81, 85, 141, 178, 187, 205–11, 216–17, 241–2.

15. Discussed in more detail in Jones, *Postwar Counterinsurgency*.

16. Field Marshal A. Wavell in Foreword, Clarke, *Seven Assignments*, p. 7; 'Early History – Interview With Colonel Dudley Clarke' (n.d) and Colonel D. Clarke, 'The Start of the Commandos', 30 October 1942, DEFE2/699 (all public records cited are at Kew, unless stated).

17. Messenger, *Commandos*, pp. 26–8.

18. R. A. Beaumont, *Military Elites*, London, 1976, p. 47; T. Holt, *The Deceivers*, London, 2004, p. 10.

19. D. W. Clarke, 'Draft For The Very First Idea of Commandos', 30 May 1940, 'Notes on Commandos', 8 February 1941, which also refers to Pathan/Afghan guerillas, 92/2/8, and *Assignments 4 and 5* m/s, 92/2/9, Clarke Papers, IWM. On Churchill: Connell, *Wavell*, p. 228.

20. Morgan, *Daggers Drawn*, p. 3; N. Nelson, *Shepheards Hotel*, London, 1960, p. xiv; Clarke, *Seven Assignments*, pp. 25, 31, 37, 81–5, 141, 178, 187, 205–17, 241–2.

Chapter 4 – The Kommandos

1. W. S. Churchill, *The Boer War*, London, 1989, *passim*; ; R. S. Churchill, *Young Statesman*, London, 1991, pp. 17, 26, 145; *Youth: 1874–1900*, London, 1966, pp. 454, 461–2, 466, 478, 512, 524, 527–8, 531.

2. Clarke, *Seven Assignments*, pp. 25, 31, 37, 81, 85, 141, 178, 187, 205–11, 216–17, 241–2; MoI, *Combined Operations*, pp. 11–12.

3. M. Chappell, *Army Commandos, 1940–45*, London, 1996, p. 4.

4. P. Young, *Commando*, London, 1974, p. 8; H. St George Saunders, *The Green Beret*, London, 1950, pp. 21–5.

5. Neillands, *Raiders*, p. 17.

6. D. Reitz, *Commando*, London, 1968, pp. 6–7, 11–22, 27, 43–4, 83, 97, 111–13, 115–19, 123, 125, 127, 129–30, 132–4, 140–2, 144–5, 151, 155, 166, 171, 154–75, 178, 183–84, 186, 197, 199–203, 216, 225, 227, 229, 231, 235, 237, 244–6, 248, 251–2, 259, 276–9, 281–2, 285, 290–1, 295–8, 300, 302–3, 309–15, 318.

7. On the Lovat Scouts: Barlow & Smith, *Lovat Scouts*, pp. 1–5; R. Garrett, *The Raiders*, London, 1980, p. 16; Lindley, *Lord Lovat*, pp. 76–85, 88–96, 101–2, 105–7; M. L. Melville, *The Story of the Lovat Scouts*, Edinburgh, 1981, pp. 3, 5–6, 9–19, 56, 60, 65–7; and on Lovat's friends: Lovat, *March Past*, pp. 169–75.

Chapter 5 – The Desert Raiders

1. Brigadier J. Durnford-Slater, *Commando*, London, 1953, p. 14; West, *Secret War*, p. 16; Weale, *Secret Warfare*, pp. 55–7.

2. J. W. Gordon, *The Other Desert War*, London, 1987, pp. 17–18; D. G. C. Sutherland, *He Who Dares*, London, 1998, p. 26. On Libya: R. Jackson, *Desert Commando*, London, 1986, p. 11.

3. Weale, *Secret Warfare*, pp. 15–31; A. Wavell, *The Good Soldier*, London, 1948, pp. 58–60.

4. On fame: R. Ovendale, *The Origins of the Arab-Israeli Wars*, London, 1992, p. 28. A. Calder, Foreword – T. E. Lawrence, *Seven Pillars of Wisdom*, Ware, Herts., 1997, pp. vi, xi, 115; J. Shy & T. Collier, 'Revolutionary War', in P. Paret, *Makers of Modern Strategy*, Oxford, 1986, pp. 830–1.

5. Lawrence, *Seven Pillars*, foreword.

6. Lawrence, *Seven Pillars*, pp. 115, 122, 125–7, 150, 153.

7. Lawrence, *Seven Pillars*, pp. 156, 167–8, 170, 177–9.

8. Lawrence, *Seven Pillars*, pp. 181–6.

9. Lawrence, *Seven Pillars*, pp. 188, 191–4, 200, 206, 214–15, 272, 277, 279, 289–96, 299, 327–34, 363–5, 373, 377–81, 385, 390–2, 410, 414–18, 422, 425, 448, 451, 460, 475, 480, 485–6, 491, 494–6, 499, 506, 514–15, 519, 521, 524–8, 531, 533–9, 565, 568, 577, 586–8, 591–2, 598, 606–8, 618–20, 624, 635–7.

10. J. Wilson, *Lawrence of Arabia*, London, 1989, pp. 529–30, 559, 561; L. James, *The Golden Warrior*, London, 1990, pp. 209, 235; Nelson, *Shepheards*, p. 5.

11. Stirling in B. Sweet-Escott, *Baker Street Irregular*, London, 1965, p. 33.

12. Connell, *Wavell*, pp. 37, 39, 41–2, 122, 132, 134, 146, 158, 175–6, 191.

13. A. W. Lawrence (ed.), *T. E. Lawrence: By His Friends*, London, 1937, *passim*; B. E. Fergusson, *Wavell: Portrait of a Soldier*, London, 1961, pp. 14, 37, 39, 41; R. H. Kiernan, *Wavell*, London, 1945, pp. 56, 105, 109; W. F. Burbridge, *The Military Viceroy*, London, 1943, pp. 5, 9–11; R. J. Collins, *Lord Wavell*, London, 1947, pp. 34–5, 65, 83, 87; H. E. Raugh, *Wavell: A Study In Generalship*, London, 1993, pp. 8, 15, 22; A. P. Wavell, *Soldiers* and *Soldiering*, London, 1953, pp. 94–5, 97, 99; and on Wingate: p. 100.

14. M. Carver, *Wavell and the War in the Middle East, 1940–41*, Austin, Texas, 1993, pp. 5, 8.

15. On Clarke: Morris, *Churchill's Private Armies*, pp. 93–4, 97–8. See contemporary WO reports on Palestine lessons, such as General J. G. Dill, General Staff HQ Palestine, 'Preliminary Notes on the Lessons of the Palestine Rebellion, 1936' (February 1937), WO 191/75, and 'Military Lessons of the Arab Rebellion In Palestine, 1936', General Staff HQ Pal. (1938), WO 191/70.

16. Jones, *Postwar Counterinsurgency*.

17. Y. A. Porath, *The Palestinian Arab National Movement, Volume 2 – 1929–39*, London, 1977, pp. 163, 166–8, 173, 178–86, 191–2, 196–9, 215, 228, 235, 237–41, 249, 254–7; C. J. Townshend, *Britain's Civil Wars*, London, 1986, pp. 103–13; T. Bowden, *The Breakdown of Public Security*, London, 1977, pp. 181, 183, 187, 192–3, 211–13, 238, 243, 301; H. J. Simson, *British Rule* and *Rebellion*, London, 1937, pp. 102–4, 111, 115, 118, 127–331; C. Marlowe, *Rebellion In Palestine*, London, 1946, pp. 145, 150, 152, 155–7, 159–60, 163–4, 190, 193, 195, 197, 200, 202, 204, 216, 224–8, 231; *Seat of Pilate*, London, 1959, pp. 129, 131–2, 134–7, 139, 141, 143–6, 150–1.

18. C. Sykes, *Orde Wingate*, London, 1959, pp. 133, 137–44; Carver, *Wavell*, p. 6; Collins, *Wavell*, pp. 172–3.

19. Sykes, *Wingate*, pp. 146–58, 161, 167–8, 170–2, 174, 176–7, 179–85; Bowden, *Breakdown of Public Security*, pp. 245, 248, 255.

20. Sykes, *Wingate*, p. 192–5; D. Rooney, *Wingate and the Chindits*, London, 1994, pp. 24, 28, 32, 34–44.

21. Sykes, *Wingate*, pp. 197, 224, 228–32; J. Newsinger, *British Counterinsurgency from Palestine to Northern Ireland*, Basingstoke, 2002, p. 4.

Chapter 6 – Striking Back: Europe

1. Seymour, *Special Forces*, pp. 6–7.

2. J. Thompson, *War Behind Enemy Lines*, p. 2; Messenger, *Commandos*, p. 26; Morris, *Churchill's Private Armies*, pp. 75–8; B. E. Fergusson, *The Watery Maze*, London, 1961, pp. 46–7; MoI, *Combined Operations*, pp. 7–9, 12, 15–16, 23–4; Parker, *Commandos*, pp. 25–7. On Clarke: Morris, *Churchill's Private Armies*, pp. 93–4, 97–8.

3. Morris, *Churchill's Private Armies*, pp. 93–4, 97–8.

4. Morris, *Churchill's Private Armies*, pp. 93–8.

5. R. Woollcombe, *The Campaigns of Wavell, 1939–43*, London, 1959, p. 4; Connell, *Wavell*, p. 228; W. S. Churchill, *Their Finest Hour*, London, 1949, pp. 204–5, 207–8; Messenger, *Commandos*, pp. 20–1, 24; Weale, *Secret Warfare*, p. 51; WO Dir. Recruiting and Organisation, 9 June 1940, 'Volunteers For Special Service', 92/2/8, D. Clarke Papers, IWM.

6. MoI, *Combined Operations*, pp. 24–5, 142; Messenger, *Commandos*, p. 33.

7. Weale, *Secret Warfare*, pp. 59–60; Neillands, *Raiders*, p. 36; Young, *Commando*, pp. 12–13.

8. J. Thompson, *War Behind Enemy Lines*, p. 3; Seymour, *Special Forces*, pp. 8–9; Strawson, *SAS*, p. 7; Morris, *Churchill's Private Armies*, pp. 93–4, 97–8; Parker, *Commandos*, pp. 27–30; West, *Secret War*, pp. 16–17.

9. On Laycock: M. Asher, *Get Rommel*, London, 2004, p. 39; Lovat, *March Past*, p. 7; on chemical warfare: T. L. Jones, *The X Site – Britain's Most Mysterious Government Facility*, Rhyl, 2001, *passim*.

10. Gordon, *Desert War*, p. 79; Lovat, *March Past*, p. 7; G. Cook, *Commandos In Action*, London, 1973, pp. 94–5.

11. R. S. Churchill, *Twenty-One Years*, London, 1965, p. 26; and on W. Churchill: A. Kemp, *SAS at War*, p. xiii.

12. M. Anthony (ed.), *The Letters of Evelyn Waugh*, London, 1980, pp. 125–6, 145; M. Davie (ed.), *The Diaries of Evelyn Waugh*, London, 1976, p. 487; Cowles, *Phantom Major*, p. 17; J. Cooper, *Originals*, pp. 2–3, 8–9; P. Young, *Storm from the Sea* London, 1989, p. 24; B. Pitt, *The SBS*, London, 1983, p. 12; Sutherland, *He Who Dares*, p. 34.

Chapter 7 – Target: Fortress Europe

1. Weale, *Secret Warfare*, p. 58; Young, *Commando*, pp. 12–15; Morris, *Churchill's Private Armies*, pp. 98–9; Neillands, *Raiders*, pp. 36–7; Dugan, *Commando*, pp. 15–17, 20; MoI, *Combined Operations*, pp. 25–6; Parker, *Commandos*, pp. 31–3; 3 Cdo. War Diary, 1, 6, 15 July 1940, WO 218/3.

2. P. Kemp, *No Colours*, pp. 18–20; J. Thompson, *War Behind Enemy Lines*, p. 4.

3. Weale, *Secret Warfare*, pp. 60–1; Morris, *Churchill's Private Armies*, p. 59.

4. Lovat, *March Past*, pp. 152, 155, 167–8, 177–80, 182, 186–8.

5. Parker, *Commandos*, pp. 36–7; Sutherland, *He Who Dares*, pp. 27–8.

6. West, *Secret War*, pp. 16–17; D. Rooney, *Mad Mike*, London, 1997, p. 20; Calvert, *Fighting Mad*, pp. 45–7.

7. Morris, *Churchill's Private Armies*, p. 112.

8. Messenger, *Commandos*, p. 36; Saunders, *Green Beret*, pp. 25, 28, 32–3, 42; Garrett, *Raiders*, p. 116.

9. Wilkinson, *Foreign Fields*, p. 101–3; Parkinson, *Auk*, pp. 60–1.

10. Wilkinson & Astley, *Gubbins*, pp. 68–70.

11. A. Taylor (ed.)/N. V. Oxenden, *Auxiliary Units History* and *Achievement, 1940–44*, Parham, Suffolk, 1998, pp. v, 1–4; Lampe, *Last Ditch*, pp. 62–71, 74–5, 80–7, 113, 150.

12. Morris, *Churchill's Private Armies*, pp. 127–31; Parker, *Commandos*, pp. 33–4, 37.

13. Churchill, *Finest Hour*, p. 374.

14. Churchill, *Finest Hour*, pp. 147, 374; Weale, *Secret Warfare*, p. 57; Young, *Commando*, p. 10; Morris, *Churchill's Private Armies*, pp. 89–90; West, *Secret War*, p. 19; Strawson, *SAS*, p. 7.

15. Weale, *Secret Warfare*, pp. 37–40, 58, 61.

16. P. Harclerode, *Para!*, London, 1996, pp. 19–20; Stevens, *Originals* m/s, p. 8.

17. Clarke, *Seven Assignments*, pp. 248–9; 'Wartime Travels, 1939–45' m/s (n.d)., Clarke Papers, 92/2/10, IWM; 'Ringway Remembered' *Mars and Minerva* (8/ 8 December 1992), p. 32; 'Ringway Training' notes (n.d)., Minutes of a Conference at Ringway, 19 July 1940, Sergeant A. Lamley, RASC/2 Commando, 'An account of the experiences of an early parachutist' (n.d)., 'Plane Talk', July 1990, 'Reminiscences of the early days' (n.d)., 1A/1; Squadron Leader L. A. Strange, 'Formation of the Central Landing School', 8 July 1940, CLS memo, 27 July 1940, 1/6, No. 2 Commando Formation and Record, 31 August–25 November 1940, 1/7, Airborne Forces Museum, Aldershot [AFM]; R. Foxall, *The Guinea-Pigs*, London, 1983, pp. 14–15, 19–20, 31–6.

18. G. Ferguson, *The Paras*, London, 1987, pp. 3–4; B. Quarrie, *Airborne Assault*, London, 1991, pp. 37–38; M. Arthur, *Men of the Red Beret*, London, 1990,

pp. xiii–xvi, 6–8; J. Thompson, *Ready For Anything*, London, 1989, pp. 2–4; Beaumont, *Military Elites*, p. 80; B. Gregory & J. Batchelor, *Airborne Warfare*, London, 1979, pp. 16, 41; C. Smith, *The History of the Glider Pilot Regiment*, London, 1992, pp. 7–9; J. Parker, *The Paras*, London, 2000, pp. 4–9; D. Reynolds, *Paras*, London, 1998, pp. 4–10.

19. Durnford-Slater, *Commando*, p. 12; Young, *Commando*, p. 12; Morris, *Churchill's Private Armies*, pp. 108–10, 153–6; Dugan, *Commando*, pp. 225–36, 242, 278; Saunders, *Green Beret*, p. 32; Strawson, *SAS*, p. 8.

20. Ringway papers, AFM, ff. 17.

21. M. Newnham, *Prelude to Glory*, London, 1947, pp. 13–17; K. C. Praval, *India's Paratroopers*, Delhi, India, 1974, pp. 16–19.

22. Seymour, *Special Forces*, pp. 93–94; Strawson, *SAS*, pp. 104, 250; J. Parker, *SBS*, London, 1997, pp. 2, 12–15; A. Kemp, *SAS*, p. 2.

23. Young, *Commando*, p. 17; Morris, *Churchill's Private Armies*, pp. 126–9; Hunter, *SBS*, pp. 21–2; Pitt, *SBS*, p. 12; Major R. J. Courtney 'Special Boat Section' (n.d., 1941), DEFE2/711B.

24. 8 Commando War Diary, September–October 1940, WO 218/8.

25. On Laycock *et al*: Parker, *Commandos*, p. 38; Mather, *When the Grass*, pp. 28–9; No. 8 Commando War Diary, July–October 1940, R. Laycock Training Instructions to Troop Leaders (n.d., 12 August), Ops Instruction 1, 29 August, HQ 46 HLI Inf. Brig, to 8 Commando HQ, 5 October 1940, WO 218/8; R. Laycock, 'The Origin and Work of the Commandos' (n.d)., DEFE2/699; Seymour, *Special Forces*, pp. 9–10; Messenger, *Commandos*, pp. 9–10; Davie, *Diaries*, p. 484; Durnford-Slater *Commando*, pp. 34–9; Weale, *Secret Warfare*, pp. 59, 63; Morris, *Churchill's Private Armies*, pp. 136–8; E. Keyes, *Geoffrey Keyes*, London, 1956, pp. 146; Mather, *When the Grass*, pp. 27–9; Windmill, *Gentleman Jim*, pp. 24–9.

26. 3 Commando War Diary, August–October 1940, WO 218/3. 8 Commando WD, ff. 25; J. Lewes, *Jock Lewes – Co-founder of the SAS*, London, 2000, p. 149.

27. CTC, 'Brief History of CTC, Inverary' (n.d)., DEFE2/699.

28. 3 Commando WD, October–November 1940, WO 218/3; 8 Commando WD, October–November 1940, WO 218/8. On other raids: Seymour, *Special Forces*, p. 13, 66–76. Brigadier J. C. Haydon Instructions, 16 November, Major-General H. C. Stockwell Papers, 3/14, LHC; 18 November 1940, Major-General R. E. Laycock Papers, 7; and Layforce notes, 11, LHC; Parker, *Commandos*, pp. 38–9; SSB Signals WD, October–December, WO 218/2; 8 Commando WD, October–November 1940, WO 218/8.

29. Lewes & Stirling in Lewes, *Jock*, p. 219; Hoe, *Stirling*, pp. 47–8; Bradford & Dillon, *Rogue Warrior*, pp. 18, 21; Sutherland, *He Who Dares*, pp. 28, 30–2, 35–6; Mather, *When the Grass*, pp. 30–34, 37–38; A. Hoe & E. Morris, *Re-enter the SAS*, London, 1994, p. 12.

30. HQ/C Bn. Layforce WD, January–March 1941, WO 218/166; 3 Commando WD January 1941, WO 218/3; J. Cooper, *Originals*, p. 10.

31. Lovat, *March Past*, pp. 234–5; Windmill, *Gentleman Jim*, pp. 5, 31–7, 265; Young, *Commando*, pp. 128, 159; 8 Commando instruction re study, 16 February 1941, Laycock Papers, 11, LHC.

32. Sergeant A. Lamley, 2 Commando, 'An account of the experiences of an early parachutist', (n.d)., Ringway Training 1A/1; Operational Exercise, 2 January 1941, Birth of Airborne Forces, 1940–41, 1/7, AFM; Newnham, *Prelude*, p. 35; Ferguson, *Paras*, pp. 4–6; Reynolds, *Paras*, pp. 12, 19–20; Quarrie, *Airborne*, p. 39; Arthur, *Red Beret*, pp. xv, 3, 8, 15–16.

33. Parkinson, *Auk*, p. 71.

34. Warner, *Auchinleck*, pp. 73–4.

35. Lieutenant-Colonel Jackson, note, 28 November 1940; No. 2 Commando Formation and Record, December 1940–April 1941, Birth of Airborne Forces, 1940–41, 1/7, AFM; Parker, *Paras*, pp. 12–16.

36. No. 2 Commando Formation and Record, December 1940–April 1941, Birth of Airborne Forces, 1940–41, 1/7, AFM; Reynolds, *Paras*, p. 12; Smith, *Glider Pilot*, p. 5; P. Warner, *The Secret Forces of World War 2*, London, 1985, p. 7.

37. 2 Commando Formation and Record, December 1940–April 1941, Birth of Airborne Forces, 1940–41, 1/7, AFM; Foxall, *Guinea Pigs*, pp. 37–60, 183–5.

38. 11 SAS Bn. OOs, 4 March; 26 April 1941, Birth of Airborne Forces, 1940–41, 1/7, AFM; Newnham, *Prelude*, p. 35.

39. Foxall, *Guinea Pigs*, pp. 14–20, 31–60, 183–5; Harclerode, *Para!*, pp. 19–20; Praval, *India's Paratroopers*, pp. 16–19; Reynolds, *Paras*, pp. 12, 19–20; Arthur, *Red Beret*, pp.15–16, MoI, *Combined Operations*, pp. 31–3. On 11 SAS: Strawson, *SAS*, p. 249.

40. Dugan, *Commandos*, p. 280; *Glengyle News*, 12/1 (16 February 1941), WO 218/166. *The War Illustrated* (80, 14 March 1941), referred to German paratroops and added that, 'we also have parachute troops', alluding to Ringway and the Italian SAS raid.

41. Waugh in Davie, *Diaries*, p. 496; A. Cooper, *Cairo in the War, 1939–45*, London, 1995, pp. 87, 89.

Chapter 8 – Striking Back: The Middle East

1. On MEF planning: L. Whittaker, *Some Talk of Private Armies*, Harpenden, Herts, 1984, p. 74.

2. P. Mead, *Orde Wingate and the Historians*, Braunton, Devon, 1987, p. 25; Wavell, *Soldiers*, p. 101; R. Lewin, *The Chief*, London, 1980, pp. 27, 52–4; L. Thompson, *SAS*, Osceola, Florida, 1994, p. 39.

3. Carver, *Wavell*, pp. 5, 7–8, 25, and *Dilemmas*, p. 27; Clarke, *Seven Assignments*, p. 219.

4. D. L. Owen, *The Desert My Dwelling Place*, London, 1986, pp. 44–6, and *Providence Their Guide*, London, 1980, pp. 7–9.

5. Gordon, *Desert War*, pp. 37–9, 57–8.

6. Woollcombe, *Campaigns*, p. 21; MacDonald, *Lost Battle*, pp. 88–9, 92.

7. Collins, *Wavell*, pp. 128–30, 138–41, 145–7, 159–61, 164–5, 458.

8. Gordon, *Desert War*, pp. 37–9, 57–8; Collins, ff. 7.

9. Connell, *Wavell*, pp. 157–8, 176–83, 243, 256, 272, 387, 407; Fergusson, *Wavell*, pp. 23, 25–8, 32–8.

10. Burbridge, *Military Viceroy*, pp. 9–10, 18–19, 21, 31.

11. Connell, *Wavell*, pp. 157–8, 176–83, 243, 256, 272, 387, 407; Fergusson, *Wavell*, pp. 23, 25–8, 32–8; M. Crichton-Stuart, *G Patrol*, London, 1958, p. 7. On Sun Tsu: Lewin, *Chief*, p. 50.

12. Connell, *Wavell*, pp. 157–8, 176–83, 243, 256, 272, 387, 407.

13. Connell, *Wavell*, pp. 222–3, 247–8, 257–8; A. Cooper, *Cairo*, p. 56.

14. On Bagnold and LRPs: LRDG Training Notes, 15 January 1941, Maj-Gen D. Lloyd Owen, Papers, 8211-134-1/2, National Army Museum, London (NAM); Whittaker, *Some Talk*, p. 14; T. J. Constable *Hidden Heroes*, London, 1971, pp. 119–29, 131, 134, 138.

15. Weale, *Secret Warfare*, pp. 84–5; Swinson, *Raiders*, pp. 9, 16, 19–22, 24–37; Cowles, *Phantom Major*, p. 17; Dugan, *Commandos*, pp. 142–51, 169–74; Gordon, *Desert War*, pp. 4, 6, 23–31, 40–5, 48–50, 59.

16. Crichton-Stuart, *G Patrol*, pp. 8–10, 23–4, 28–32, 36–44, 48–55, 60, 64–5; Owen, *Desert*, p. 54, and *Providence*, p. 15; W. B. Kennedy Shaw, *Long Range Desert Group*, London, 1945, pp. 14–16, 35–76; J. Thompson, *War Behind Enemy Lines*, pp. 19–27, 33; Seymour, *Special Forces*, pp. 126–7; Whittaker, *Some Talk*, p. 15; Warner, *Auchinleck*, p. 91.

17. On Benghazi/Fleming: Lewin, *Chief*, pp. 77, 196–7; on SOE: Wilkinson & Astley, *Gubbins*, pp. 70, 72–3, 85–6; on Yak/Thornhill: A. Cooper, *Cairo*, pp. 71, 93–96, 123, 130–1; Sykes, *Wingate*, p. 329; Sweet-Escott, *Baker Street*, pp. 53–4; and on A Force, Hart-Davis *Peter Fleming*, pp. 239–47; Wingate in Sykes, *op cit*, pp. 232–7.

18. On Middle East Commando: Messenger, *Commandos*, pp. 68, 71–2, 74. HLI, 2 Bn., to General O'Connor, 27 September; Colonel J. E. Benson, Coast Raiding Operations note, 1 November 1940, WO 201/333; Brigadier A. Galway, BGS, Operations in W. Desert, note, 15 December 1940, Auchinleck Papers, 121, JRM.

19. Messenger, *Commandos*, pp. 68, 71–2, 74; Whittaker, *Some Talk*, p. 74. W. F. Stirling, *Safety Last*, London, 1953, pp. 199–202.

20. W. E. D. Allen *Guerilla War in Abyssinia*, Harmondsworth, 1943, pp. 36, 41, 45, 69, 74, 78, 87–92, 102, 121; Sykes, *Wingate*, pp. 251–3, 257, 260–90, 296–8, 308–12.

21. Rooney, *Wingate*, pp. 48, 54–69.

22. On Abstention: CREFORCE, to MIDEAST, Operation Blunt note, 19 February; Lieutenant-Colonel F. Symons, CO 50 (ME) Commando, Operation Abstention note, 1 March; Major-General J. F. Evetts/Rear Admiral H. T. Baillie-Grohman/Gp. Captain B. Spackman, Joint Memo by Commanders of Mandible Force on the lessons of Operation Abstention, 9 March; General Evetts, 6 Div. HQ Report on Abstention, 12 March 1941, WO 201/713.

23. Clarke, Morris, *Churchill's Private Armies*, p. 142; Fergusson, *Wavell*, p. 94; Woollcombe, *Campaigns*, p. 4; Messenger, *Commandos*, pp. 74–94.

24. Wavell in Clarke, *Seven Assignments*, Foreword, p. 7; and A Force, GSI, GHQME, to DDMI, 30 December 1940; Colonel D. W. Clarke, Plan Abeam – The Plan Itself, to Colonel F. Thornton, WO MI11, 20 January; *Parade*, January; Colonel Clarke notes, 1 February 1941, WO 169/24904.

25. Colonel Clarke, to Major-General G. Clark, HQ Pal./Transj., 6 March; to Colonel Thornton, WO, 10 April 1941, WO 169/24904; A Force Narrative WD, 13 November 1940–31 December 1941, CAB154/1; Holt, *Deceivers*, p. 10; *Mars and Minerva* (7/2, March 1986), p. 16; Colonel M. Dewar *The Art of Deception In Warfare*, London, 1989, pp. 53–6; C. Cruickshank *Deception In World War 2*, London, 1981, pp. 19–20; D. Owen, *Battle of Wits*, London, 1978, pp. 31–4; D. Mure, *Practise to Deceive*, London, 1977, pp. 20–2, and *Master of Deception*, London, 1980, p. 81; M. Howard, *British Intelligence in the Second World War,* Volume 5 – *Strategic Deception*, London, 1990, pp. xi–xii, 22, 31–5; SIS/SOE, MacDonald, *Lost Battle*, p. 131; Sweet-Escott, *Baker Street*, p. 64.

26. Clarke, *Seven Assignments*, pp. 257–8, 260; Parker, *Commandos*, pp. 43, 51–2, 55–63; Cook, *Commandos*, pp. 70–3.

27. E. Keyes, *Geoffrey*, pp. 142–5, 149, 152–3, 156–7; J. Lodwick, *The Filibusters*, London, 1947, p. 5; Jellicoe in J. Thompson, *War Behind Enemy Lines*, p. 9, and on SBS: pp. 45–6; Saunders, *Green Beret*, pp. 65–7; Bradford & Dillon, *Rogue Warrior*, p. 5; G. B. Courtney, *SBS In World War 2*, London, 1983, pp. 16–17; Hunter, *SBS*, pp. 23–5.

28. Raugh, *Wavell*, pp. 87–91, 198–9; A Force, DCGS, MEF, Maj-Gen A. Smith, to Peter [Fleming?], 14 April 1941, WO 169/24871.

29. HQ/C Bn. Layforce WD, January–March 1941, WO 218/166; 3 Commando WD, December 1940–January 1941, WO 218/3.

30. Seymour, *Special Forces*, pp. 15–16, 78; Parker, *SBS*, p. 18, and *Commandos*, pp. 44–8; Young, *Commando*, pp. 23–4, 34, 40–1; MoI, *Combined Operations*, pp. 33–6, 39–40; Lovat, *March Past*, pp. 193–9, 206–7, 215; Windmill, *Gentleman Jim*, pp. 37–9.

31. R. Crisp, *The Gods Were Neutral*, London, 1960, p. 204.

32. Lieutenant J. T. Tyson, Report of German Parachutist Attack on Corinth Canal, 26 April; Lieutenant-Colonel W. L. Leggatt, GHQME, German Parachute Attack on the Bridge at Corinth, to CGS, 2 May; O.C. 16 Heavy AA Battery, Report on landing of German Parachute Troops near Corinth, n.d. (May 1941), WO 201/2750; G(Ops)ME, Events at Corinth Canal, April; Captain J. F. Phillips, report, 4 May 1941, WO 201/2747.

33. MacDonald, *Lost Battle*, p. 131; Sweet-Escott, *Baker Street*, p. 64; Erskine, *Scots Guards*, p. 78.

34. Crisp, *Gods*, p. 214.

Chapter 9 – Bardia or Bust

1. Lewin, *Chief*, p. 197; Parker, *Paras*, pp. 12–16.

2. HQ/C Bn. Layforce WDs, March–April 1941, WO 218/166.

3. J. Thompson, *Ready for Anything*, p. 18, and *War Behind Enemy Lines*, pp. 20–3; B. Roberts, *Randolph*, London, 1984, pp. 197–203.

4. HQ/C Bn. Layforce WDs, March–April, Operational Order [OO] 1, 15 April, OO2, 19 April, WO 218/166; 8 Cdo./B Bn. WD, January–March, WO 218/170; 3 Commando WD, April; OO1, Major E. C. A. Napier, 16 April 1941, WO 218/171.

5. Weale, *Secret Warfare*, p. 91; Windmill, *Gentleman Jim*, pp. 40, 42.

6. Report of Raid, 20 April, WO 218/166; Commando HQ, GHQME note, 20 April 1941, WO 201/2624; MoI, *Combined Operations*, pp. 32–3.

7. Layforce Stores File, DDSD memo, Formation of Additional LRD Groups, 21 May, WO 201/715; Formation of Additional LRDGs memo (n.d., May 1941), WO 201/716.

8. C. Buckley *Greece and Crete, 1941*, London, 1977, pp. 122–3; Lewin, *Chief*, p. 128; Seymour, *Special Forces*, pp. 78–80, 133–4; Connell, *Wavell*, pp. 447, 457, 471.

9. Brief History of Special Units under Command of A Force (n.d., *c.* 1945); Major-General A. Smith, DCGS, to Peter [Fleming?], 14 April; to GOC Crete, 16 April; Colonel Clarke, Advanced HQ A Force, 'SAS Brigade' note, to CGS, DDMI, 24 April 1941, WO 169/24871. 11 Commando in C Bn. WD, April 1941, WO 218/166.

10. Neillands, *Raiders*, pp. 72–8; Woollcombe, *Campaigns*, p. 110, 128–32; Cook, *Commandos*, pp. 74–6; Sutherland, *He Who Dares*, p. 39. Lewes, *Jock*, p. 161; Morris, *Churchill's Private Armies*, pp. 151, 156; A. Deane-Drummond, *Arrows of Fortune*, London, 1992, pp. 11–14, 30–1.

11. COS memo, Harclerode, *Para!*, p. 23; M. Tugwell, *Airborne to Battle*, London, 1971, p. 123. On India: Linlithgow note, 17 June 1941, Auchinleck Papers, 260/261, John Rylands Museum, Manchester (JRM); Newnham, *Prelude*, pp. 40–2; Connell, *Wavell*, pp. 176–7.

12. Colonel D. Clarke, The Story, 10 April; Instructions for L/Cpl. Smith and Trooper Gurmin, 11 April; note, 12 April; Clarke, to Lieutenant-Colonel G. G. Cox, Staffs. Yeomanry, 20 April; Captain L. R. Palmer, Adjutant, HQ 1 SAS Brigade, to Clarke; MIDEAST, to MILPAL., 6 April; Clarke, to Colonel Thornton, WO , 10 April 1941, WO 169/24904.

13. Major V. H. Jones, Abeam note, 17 May 1941; Brief History of Special Units under Command of A Force (n.d., *c.* 1945); Clarke, to Lieutenant-Colonel de Guingand, JPS, GHQME, 26 May 1941, WO 169/24871; A Force Narrative WD, 13 November 1940–31 December 1941, CAB154/1; RAF Operations Record Book, RAF Helwan, April 1938–March 1945, AIR28/350.

14. HQ Layforce WD, April–June, WO 218/166.

15. P. Wilkinson *Foreign Fields*, p. 113; Wilkinson & Astley, *Gubbins*, pp. 90–91; Hart-Davis *Peter Fleming*, pp. 254, 257; HQ Layforce WD, April–June; Laycock, to Major-General A. Smith, CGS MEFHQ, 6 May; Smith, to Laycock, 6 May; E. Waugh, Layforce HQ, OI10, 13 June, WD, 14 June, WO 218/166; Layforce Diary to Disbandment, 16 September 1941, DEFE2/711B; Brigadier H. W. Wynter, 'The History of Commandos and Special Service Troops in the Middle East and North Africa, January 1941–April 1943' (n.d)., CAB44/152. Lieutenant-Colonel G. A. D. Young, note, 13 May 1941, Laycock Papers, 18, LHC.

16. E. Waugh, Layforce HQ, OI10, 13 June, WD, 14 June, WO 218/166; Davie, *Dairies*, pp. 495–7, 510–11.

17. Layforce Diary to Disbandment, 16 September 1941, DEFE2/711B; Wynter, 'History', CAB44/152; Messenger, *Commandos*, pp. 95–6; Weale, *Secret Warfare*, p. 91; Windmill, *Gentleman Jim*, pp. 40, 42; Collins, *Wavell*, p. 410.

18. E. Waugh, Layforce HQ, OI10, 13 June, WD, 14 June, WO 218/166; Davie, *Dairies*, pp. 495–7, 510–11.

19. Seymour, *Special Forces*, pp. 79–80; Messenger, *Commandos*, pp. 98, 102–3; Young, *Commando*, pp. 42, 47; MacDonald, *Lost Battle*, pp. 159, 169, 175, 187, 211, 253–4, 268, 277, 294, 297.

20. Layforce Diary to Disbandment, 16 September 1941, DEFE2/711B; Davie, *Dairies*, pp. 497, 511.

Chapter 10 – Searching for a Role

1. Hoe & Morris, *Re-enter*, pp. 1, 3, 5; Hoe, *Stirling*, pp. 49–53, 59–60, 194, 279–80.

2. R. Laycock, 'The Origins and Work of the Commandos', (n.d)., DEFE2/699; on LRDG: Colonel J. E. C. McCandlish, DAG, GHQME, Terms of Service, Layforce, 31 May 1941, WO 201/716; Wynter, 'History', CAB44/152.

3. A. Kemp, *SAS at War*, pp. xiii, 1, 4–7.

4. Lewes/Stirling in Lewes, *Jock*, pp. 152–75, 218.

5. Lewes, *Jock*, pp. 162–3; Jellicoe in J. Thompson, *War Behind Enemy Lines*, p. 49; Hoe, *Stirling*, pp. 49–53, 59–60, 194, 279–80; Davie, *Diaries*, pp. 487, 495–6, 511.

6. Seymour, *Special Forces*, p. 96; Major R. J. Courtney, 'Special Boat Section' (n.d., 1941), DEFE2/711B; G. B. Courtney, *SBS*, pp. 9, 17–18.

7. Lewes, *Jock*, pp. 162–3; J. Thompson, *War Behind Enemy Lines*, p. 49; Mather, *When the Grass*, pp. 41, 44–7, 49–50, 303.

8. Group Captain T. B. Laughlin, SBS, to Captain B. P. Schott, n.d.; Captain Schott, Operations Report, July 1942, including 'Brief History of L Detachment SAS Brigade and 1st SAS Regiment', WO 218/173; Parker, *SBS*, pp. 4–8, 21, 25; Weale, *Secret Warfare*, pp. 92, 96; Young, *Commando*, pp. 47–8; Neillands, *Raiders*, pp. 80–90; MoI, *Combined Operations*, pp. 45–6.

9. J. Thompson, *War Behind Enemy Lines*, pp. 36–8; Gordon, *Desert War*, p. 74; Crichton-Stuart, *G Patrol*, pp. 84–6.

10. Davie, *Diaries*, pp. 487, 495–6, 511.

11. Stevens, *Originals* m/s, p. 14.

12. Plan Abeam 'Employment in the field of the dummy "1 SAS Brigade" in Crete and Egypt', A Force Permanent Record, WD Appx. 52, January–August 1941, Lieutenant-Colonel Clarke, to WO DDMI, 15 June 1941, WO 169/24904; BBC Radio 4, *Of One Company – The True Story of the Founding of the SAS*, 22 November 2001, *passim*; Parker, *Commandos*, p. 64; Hoe & Morris, *Re-enter*, pp. 1, 3, 5; Stevens, *Originals* m/s, p. 15.

13. UK TV History, *Great SAS Missions*, Episode 1, 'Birth of the SAS', August 2004 (advisor: Gordon Stevens); D'Arcy 'May 1941' memo (n.d)., WO 218/173; Stevens, *Originals* m/s, pp. 14–15; Hoe, *Stirling*, pp. 49–53, 59–60, 194, 279–80. Intriguingly, when Wavell was CINC India, he complained to Churchill on 14 June 1942 about the lack of equipment for his paratroops there. The Secretary of State for India, Julian Amery, replied that 'a consignment of parachutes for India had found its way to the Middle East', as Wavell would have been aware. Amery continued that it had done so 'due to misadventure or wilful misappropration', hinting at Wavell's involvement while CINCME in Lewes's trial, Praval, *India's Paratroopers*, p. 24.

14. Stevens, *Originals* m/s, pp. 13, 15; Lewes, *Jock*, pp. 162–3; Mather, *When the Grass*, pp. 41, 44–7, 49–50, 303; B. Roberts, *Randolph*, p. 216.

15. D'Arcy 'May 1941' memo (n.d)., WO 218/173.

16. Plan Abeam, ff. 12.

17. D'Arcy, ff. 15; *SAS Regt. Assoc. Newsletter* 26 (November 1954); Cowles, *Phantom Major*, p. 20; J. Thompson, *War Behind Enemy Lines*, pp. 49–50; Warner, *Special Air Service*, p. 28; Strawson, *SAS*, p. 14; T. Geraghty *Who Dares Wins*, London, 1980, p. 10; J. Ramsay, *SAS: The Soldiers' Story*, London, 1996, p. 3; Seymour, *Special Forces*, p. 187.

18. D'Arcy, ff. 17; Lewes, *Jock*, pp. 162–3.

19. Mather, *When the Grass*, pp. 41, 44–7, 49–50, 303.

20. Mather, ff. 19.

21. Seymour, *Special Forces*, pp. 83–4.

22. Lewes, *Jock*, pp. 1–2, 27–32, 47, 50, 82, 88, 131–37, 152–69, 219–21.

23. Lewes, ff. 22; Jellicoe, in Foreword, pp. xiv–xv.

24. Weale, *Secret Warfare*, pp. 6–8; Lewes, ff. 22.

25. For Rogers's 28 Rules: *Regulations For The Rangers Drawn Up By Robert Rogers*, in Maj-Gen H.C. Stockwell Papers, 3/18, LHC; M. Cochrane, *Rogers: A Battle Fought On Snow Shoes*, New Hampshire, 1917, pp. 1–3, 6–8, 32; J. R. Cuneo *Robert Rogers of the Rangers*, New York, 1959, pp. 7–8, 11, 17, 20, 24, 27, 29–33, 35–6, 41, 43–5, 47, 50, 52, 55–57, 59–60, 66, 69–74, 82–3, 90, 97, 100–9, 120; Garrett, *Raiders*, pp. 11–13.

26. Layforce WD, June 1941, WO 218/166; Lewes, *Jock*, 176–8, 194, 219, 246–7; D'Arcy ff. 15; Hoe, *Stirling*, pp. 52–64, 69–72, 347; GHQME, Disbandment Layforce, 2 July 1941, WO 201/731.

27. Connell, *Auk*, pp. 246, 249; Carver, *Wavell*, p. 23.

28. Lieutenant-Colonel R. J. Mansell, GSI note, 28 June 1941, WO 169/24904, 24925; Colonel D. W. Clarke, Advanced HQ A Force, to WO DMI, 4 July 1941, WO 169/24871.

29. Warner, *Auchinleck*, pp. 93, 95, 97, 99, 100–1, 110, 112, 114, 126; Strawson, *SAS*, p. 15.

30. Lewes, *Jock*, 176–8, 194, 219, 246–47; Hoe, *Stirling*, pp. 52, 56–64, 69–72, 347; Messenger, *Commandos*, p. 110.

31. E. Keyes, *Geoffrey*, pp. 182–6; Wilkinson *Foreign Fields*, p. 123.

32. Parker, *Commandos*, p. 64; Lewes, ff. 30.

33. Morgan, *Daggers Drawn*, pp. 23–4, 31, 90; Davie, *Diaries*, pp. 457, 495, 511–12; Countess Ranfurly, *To War With Whitaker*, London, 1994, pp. 93, 98–9; M. T. Wise (ed.), *Joy Street*, London, 1995, pp. 222, 224, 231, 239; Holt, *Deceivers*, pp. 12, 14.

34. Sykes, *Wingate*, pp. 318, 320, 324, 326–7, 332–3.

35. Stevens, *Originals* m/s, p. 5; Lewes, ff. 30.

36. L. Thompson, *SAS*, p. 40; J. V. Byrne, *The General Salutes a Soldier*, London, 1986, p. 97; A. Cooper, *Cairo*, pp. 90–1, 131. On SOE: West, *Secret War*, p. 19; Wilkinson & Astley, *Gubbins*, p. 91; On Stirling: Strawson, *SAS*, p. 16. On LRDG: Crichton-Stuart, *G Patrol*, p. 88; Stevens, *Originals* m/s, p. 5.

37. Lewes, ff. 30; Ranfurly, *Whitaker*, pp. 98–9;

38. Sykes, *Wingate*, pp. 318, 320, 324, 326–7, 332–3; Rooney, *Wingate*, pp. 71–2; Stevens, *Originals* m/s, p. 118.

39. Stevens, *Originals* m/s, pp. 17–18; *Great SAS Missions* 1 (2004).

40. Davie, *Diaries*, pp. 457, 495, 511–12; Fergusson, *Watery Maze*, p. 101.

41. Mather, *When the Grass*, p. 53; Windmill, *Gentleman Jim*, p. 46; Ranfurly, *Whitaker*, pp. 93, 98–9; Wise, *Joy Street*, pp. 222, 224, 231, 239.

42. Stevens, *Originals* m/s, p. 19; M. James, *Born of the Desert*, p. 17; Asher, *Rommel*, pp. 77–8.

43. H. Ross, *Paddy Mayne*, Stroud, Glos., 2003, pp. 62–3; Messenger, *Commandos*, pp. 109–10.

44. Layforce AG note, 'Volunteers for Special Service', 14 July; C Bn. Layforce note, G. Keyes, to Colonel, 14 July 1941, WO 201/716; J. Laffin, *Raiders: Elite Forces Attacks*, London, 2000, p. 23; Stevens, *Originals* m/s, p. 28.

45. Lieutenant A. D. Stirling, 'Case for the retention of a limited number of Special Service troops, for employment as parachutists', 16 July 1941, WO 169/24904; Ross, *Mayne*, pp. 62–3; *Great SAS Missions*, 2004.

46. Stirling, 'Case for' memo, WO 169/24904.

47. Layforce Diary to Disbandment, 16 September 1941, DEFE2/711B.

48. Auchinleck on FE/ME, to WO, 9 July, WO 193/405; On Laycock/Churchill: Messenger, *Commandos*, p. 110; Parker, *Paras*, pp. 20–1, 39, and *Commandos*, p. 64; Windmill, *Gentleman Jim*, p. 54; W. Churchill, to Ismay, 23 July 1941, PREM3/330/9.

49. MIDEAST to TROOPERS, 19 July, WO 201/706; MoI, *Combined Operations*, p. 43; Cowles, *Phantom Major*, p. 23; Asher, *Rommel*, pp. 77–8, plate section caption. Warner notes in *Secret Forces*, p. 19, that the Auk gave permission for SAS training in June, but it was actually July 1941.

50. Lt-Col W. M. Leggatt, G(Trg)., Minutes of Conference, 'Implementation in regard to the build up of the 1st SAS Brigade', 27 July, WO 169/24904; ME Staff Duties, to WO, 18 July, WO 201/731; J. Robertson, K Det. SAS Bgde., to Major V. H. Jones, Adv. HQ A Force, MEHQ, 20 July 1941; Brief History of Special Units under Commando of A Force, (n.d., *c*. 1945), WO 169/24882.

51. A Force Narrative War Diary, 13 November 1940–31 December 1941, CAB154/1; Wynter, 'History', CAB44/152.

52. Wynter, 'History', CAB44/152; Stevens, *Originals* m/s, p. 31.

53. Stirling memo, 8 November 1948, McLeod Papers, LHC; Stevens, *Originals*, p. 38.

54. Other raids: O.C. G Troop, A Bn. Layforce, to Captain E. L. W. Francis, 4 Hussars, 15 July 1941, WO 201/717. S. Bull *SAS*, London, 2000, p. 8; Reynolds, *Paras*, p. 16; Praval, *India's Paratroopers*, p. 19.

55. A Force Narrative War Diary, 13 November 1940–31 December 1941, CAB154/1; Stevens, *Originals* m/s, p. 18; BBC Radio 4, *Of One Company*, 2001; *Great SAS Missions*, 2004; Ross, *Mayne*, pp. 61, 65. Assertions on the naming of

the SAS in, for example: Warner, *Secret Forces*, p. 9; Strawson, *SAS*, pp. 17–18; Morgan, *Daggers Drawn*, p. 5; and re Ritchie connections, p. 25; Lewes, *Jock*, p. 194; Maj-Gen R. E. Laycock, 'Raids in the late war and their lessons', *RUSI Journal* (XCII, November 1947), p. 528; on the Auk: Warner, *Auchinleck*, pp. 99, 114, 126.

Chapter 11 – The Originals

1. On raiding: Neillands, *Raiders*, p. 50; Saunders, *Green Beret*, pp. 52, 54. On SBS: Courtney, *SBS*, pp. 19, 21. On Auchinleck's plans: Parkinson *Auk*, p. 102.

2. On the LRDG: Kennedy Shaw, *LRDG*, pp. 87, 91–2, 108; Owen, *Providence*, p. 46; M. Morgan, *Sting of the Scorpion*, Stroud, Glos., 2000, p. 46; Seymour, *Special Forces*, p. 136.

3. LRIP, R. Leach, *Massacre at Alamein?*, Upton-on-Severn, Worcs., 1996, pp. 51, 55, 59, 63. On Indian airborne forces: Praval, *India's Paratroopers*, p. 19.

4. Lieutenant-General A. Smith, to Commandant IBD, 1 August 1941, WO 201/731; Hoe, *Stirling*, pp. 70–1, 73–83, 86–8.

5. Hoe, ff. 4; Cowles, *Phantom Major*, pp. 23–34; Wynter, 'History', CAB44/152.

6. On Tobruk/Kabrit: Captain P. Dunne (6 Troop), 'The Attack on the Twin Pimples from Tobruk' (n.d., 1941), DEFE2/711B; Lewes, *Jock*, pp. 170–96, 200–7, 215–17, 220–1; Seymour, *Special Forces*, pp. 84–5; Young, *Commando*, p. 48; MoI, *Combined Operations*, pp. 43–4; Sutherland, *He Who Dares*, pp. 15, 41–5; B. Pitt, *The Crucible of War*, London, 1980, pp. 320–4; *The Tiger Kills*, London, 1944, pp. 21–2; Stevens, *Originals* m/s, p. 26; re Pineapples, Laffin, *Raiders*, p. 88.

7. P. Riley, 'The Originals', *Mars and Minerva* (6/3, summer 1984), p. 44; Windmill, *Gentleman Jim*, pp. ix, x, 4–9, 15–17, 44, 55–64, 69; A. Kemp, *SAS at War*, pp. 9–13; Neillands, *Raiders*, pp. 50, 91; Swinson, *Raiders*, p. 47; J. Cooper, *Originals*, pp. 17–20; Stevens, *Originals* m/s, pp. 24, 27.

8. GHQMEF, 'Volunteers for Special Service', to OC C Bn., 8 August; GHQMEF, 'Disbandment of Personnel, C Bn.', 12 August, WO 201/716; C Bn. WD, August 1941, WO 218/171. Auchinleck in Kennedy Shaw, *LRDG*, p. 97.

9. On raids: Saunders, *Green Beret*, p. 52; Bradford & Dillon, *Rogue Warrior*, p. 29; Reynolds, *Paras*, p. 16; Chappell, *Commandos*, p. 12; Ross, *Mayne*, pp. 64–8; Morgan, *Sting*, pp. 24–5; Asher, *Rommel*, pp. 92–3. Ranfurly, *Whitaker*, p. 104; Wise, *Joy Street*, pp. 217, 259, 261–2, 265–6, 271, 276–7.

10. Layforce Diary to Disbandment, 16 September 1941, DEFE2/711B; Ranfurly, *Whitaker*, p. 104; Wise, *Joy Street*, pp. 217, 259, 261–2, 265–6, 271, 276–7.

11. On Mayne: Morgan, *Daggers Drawn*, pp. 37–8; Young, *Commando*, p. 48; Courtney, *SBS*, p. 20. Ranfurly, ff. 10.

12. Lewes, *Jock*, pp. 170–96, 200–7, 215–17, 220–1.

13. Stirling memo, 8 November 1948, McLeod Papers, LHC; Lewes, ff. 12; Stevens, *Originals* m/s, p. 45. On Down and Ringway: Newnham, *Prelude*, pp. 52, 64–5,

77–8, 88; Strawson, *SAS*, p. 18; Airborne Forces at Hardwick Hall Camp, 1941–46, Hardwick Hall Research Correspondence, 165, AFM. On LRDG: Kennedy Shaw, *LRDG*, p. 97.

14. Layforce Diary to Disbandment, 16 September, DEFE2/711B. On SBS/ Commandos: Parker, *SBS*, pp. 22–5; Neillands, *Raiders*, p. 55; MoI, *Combined Operations*, p. 20.

15. Brigadier J. F. M. Whiteley, GHQMEF DDO, to Brigadier A. Galloway, BGS Western Army, 25 September; DDMT, to Whiteley, 2 October, WO 201/731; Auchinleck to Churchill, 16 September 1941, Auchinleck Papers, 337, JRM; Kennedy Shaw, *LRDG*, p. 97.

16. Laycock to Auchinleck, 17 October 1941, DEFE2/711B. On parachutes: GHQ meeting minutes, 28 December 1941, WO 201/731. On Heliopolis: Hoe, *Stirling*, ff. 17.

17. BGS 8 Army, to DDO GHQME, 18 October, WO 201/731. On explosives/ Heliopolis: Hoe, *Stirling*, pp. 86–7; Lewes, *Jock*, pp. 215–23; Cowles, *Phantom Major*, pp. 33–7; J. Cooper, *Originals*, p. 21; Windmill, *Gentleman Jim*, pp. 11–13; Stevens, *Originals* m/s, pp. 50–1, 55.

18. On Ringway: Newnham, *Prelude*, pp. 52, 64–5, 77–8, 88; Airborne Forces at Hardwick Hall Camp, 1941–6, Hardwick Hall Research Correspondence, 165, AFM. On India: Praval, *India's Paratroopers*, pp. 19–22.

19. Lieutenant-General M. B. Jennings, CGS, GHQMEF, 'Training SAS Brigade and Commandos', 24 October 1941, WO 201/731.

Chapter 12 – The First Raids

1. LRDG, Kennedy Shaw, *LRDG*, pp. 111–12; Cook, *Commandos*, pp. 66, 76, 87–8, 96–7; Stevens, *Originals* m/s, p. 61.

2. Lewes, *Jock*, pp. 224–5; Stevens, *Originals* m/s, pp. 58, 61.

3. On Rommel raid: Asher, *Rommel*, *passim*; MoI, *Combined Operations*, pp. 46–51, 67; Messenger, *Commandos*, pp. 112–15; Young, *Commando*, pp. 49, 54–5; Parker, *Commandos*, pp. 65–6; Sutherland, *He Who Dares*, pp. 48–9; J. Thompson, *War Behind Enemy Lines*, pp. 52–5. On SBS: Parker, *SBS*, pp. 27–30.

4. Seekings in *Great SAS Missions*, 2004.

5. A. Kemp, *SAS at War*, pp. 16–19; M. James, *Born of the Desert*, pp. 20–1; Cowles, *Phantom Major*, pp. 38–48; J. Cooper, *Originals*, pp. 23–8; Cook, *Commandos*, p. 107; Ladd, *SAS*, pp. 1–2, 6, 8; Windmill, *Gentleman Jim*, pp. 76, 82; Ross, *Mayne*, pp. 70–3; Stevens, *Originals*, pp. 68, 71.

6. Asher, *Rommel*, pp. 187–95, 245; BBC Radio 4, *Of One Company*, 2001; Hoe, *Stirling*, pp. 99–106; Lewes, *Jock*, pp. 226–30; Kennedy Shaw, *LRDG*, p. 121; Stevens, *Originals*, p. 75.

Notes to pp. 200–9

.ook, *Commandos*, pp. 110–14, 136; Morgan, *Daggers Drawn*, pp. 93–4; J. Thompson, *War Behind Enemy Lines*, pp. 55–6; Cowles, *Phantom Major*, pp. 38–48.

8. Seymour, *Special Forces*, p. 138; Strawson, *SAS*, pp. 30–36; A. Kemp, *SAS at War*, p. 20; Swinson, *Raiders*, pp. 51–3; Dugan, *Commando*, p. 191; Windmill, *Gentleman Jim*, pp. 83–4; Stevens, *Originals* m/s, p. 78.

9. Owen, *Providence*, pp. 60–1, 70–1; Jackson, *Desert Commando*, pp. 16–17.

10. LRDG WD, November 1941, Captain Easonsmith R1 Patrol Recce Report, 26 November, S2 Diary of Events, 20, 22 December 1941, WO 218/89; Major D. G. Steele, LRDG A Squadron WD, December 1941, 2/Lieutenant C. S. Morris, T2 report, 24 December, Captain C. A. Holliman, S1 report, 18 December 1941, WO 218/94; Cowles, *Phantom Major*, pp. 48–69; A. Kemp, *SAS at War*, pp. 20–1; J. Cooper, *Originals* m/s, pp. 30–6; Bradford & Dillon, *Rogue Warrior*, p. 36; Ladd, *SAS*, pp. 9, 11–17; Windmill, *Gentleman Jim*, pp. 84–94; Hoe, *Stirling*, pp. 106–118; Lewes, *Jock*, pp. 233–41; Kennedy Shaw, *LRDG*, pp. 123–24, 126–7; Morgan, *Daggers Drawn*, p. 148; J. Thompson, *War Behind Enemy Lines*, pp. 63–4; Strawson, *SAS*, pp. 35–44; A. Kemp, *SAS at War*, pp. 21–5; Swinson, *Raiders*, pp. 53–64; Ranfurly, *Whitaker*, pp. 50, 110–11; J. Cooper, *Originals*, p. 36; J. V. Byrne, 'The Raid on Agedabia Airfield', *Mars and Minerva* (6/1, summer 1983), p. 34.

11. Cowles, *Phantom Major*, pp. 70–85.

12. LRDG A Squadron WD, December 1941, S1 report, 2 January, T2 report, 2 January 1942, WO 218/94; Ladd, *SAS*, p. 18; Strawson, *SAS*, pp. 44–5; A. Kemp, *SAS at War*, pp. 25–6; Swinson, *Raiders*, pp. 66–7; J. Cooper, *Originals*, p. 37; Windmill, *Gentleman Jim*, pp. 95–102; Kennedy Shaw, *LRDG*, pp. 128–9, 135–6.

13. Ranfurly, *Whitaker*, p. 117.

14. Cook, *Commandos*, pp. 163–64; Swinson, *Raiders*, pp. 67–8; Lewes, *Jock*, pp. 223, 229, 236–40; A. Kemp, *SAS at War*, pp. 27–8.

15. A. Kemp, *SAS at War*, pp. 27–9, 36.

16. Windmill, *Gentleman Jim*, p. 106; Ladd, *SAS*, pp. 19–20; A. Kemp, *SAS at War*, pp. 27–8.

17. Cowles, *Phantom Major*, pp. 85–7; Swinson, *Raiders*, p. 71; Strawson, *SAS*, pp. 47–9; A. Kemp, *SAS at War*, pp. 27–9.

Chapter 13 – Godfathers of the Regiment

1. *Great SAS Missions*, 2004; Morgan, *Daggers Drawn*, pp. 5, 25; Jackson, *Desert Commando*, p. 15.

2. Morgan, *Daggers Drawn*, pp. 19, 21–2, 26.

3. Lewes, *Jock*, pp. 242–3.

Bibliography

Unpublished Primary Sources

Airborne Forces Museum [AFM], Browning Barracks, Aldershot, Hants
Ringway Training 1A/1, 1, 6. Birth of Airborne Forces, 1940–1, 1/7.
Development of Airborne Forces, Summary of Events 1940–3, 1/8. Hardwick
Hall Research Correspondence, 165. Operation Colossus, 2.

Imperial War Museum [IWM], London
Colonel D. Clarke Papers 92/2/2: m/s book Notes 1939, Diary 1940, DWC 8, 9,
10. SAS Regimental Association *Newsletter* 7–11, 21, 26, 33.

Liddell Hart Centre for Military Archives [LHC], King's College, London
Brigadier R. W. McLeod Papers 1, 2. Major-General R. E. Laycock Papers 4, 7,
10–12, 16, 18, 34. Major-General H. Stockwell Papers 3/1, 3/14–24.

National Archives, Kew, Middlesex
Air AIR 28/347, 350, 41/3. Cabinet CAB 44/152, 103/177, 154/1.
Defence DEFE 2/699, 711B. Premier PREM 3/330.9. War Office WO 169/2579,
24870–1, 24882–3, 24904, 24925, 193/405, 201/333, 713, 715–717, 721,
731, 2624, 2747, 2750, 218/1–3, 8, 89, 94, 166, 170–1, 173, 232/10B.

National Army Museum [NAM], London
D. L. Owen, Papers, 8211–134–1/2. SAS Regiment journal, *Mars and Minerva*,
1/7 (June 1962), 3/2 (June 1971), 5/3 (winter 1982), 6/1 (summer 1983), 6/3
(summer 1984), 7/2 (March 1986), 8/4 (May 1989), 8/8 (December 1992), 8/9
(July 1993).

John Rylands Museum [JRM], Manchester
General C. Auchinleck Papers, 15, 92, 121, 260–1, 305, 334, 337, 517, 520,
524, 606, 816.

Correspondence with the author
E. P. Horne, 24 April 2005; Major A. N. B. Ritchie, 9 May 2005; Major-General J.
Thompson, 9 May 2005; M. R. D. Foot, 12, 24 May 2005.

Published Primary Sources

Official Treatise
Anon., *The Tiger Kills*, London, 1944

Anon. (Colonel A. C. Newman) *Combined Operations, 1940–42*, London, 1943

C. Buckley, *Greece and Crete, 1941*, London, 1977

M. R. D. Foot, *SOE*, London, 1990

M. Howard, *British Intelligence in the Second World War, Volume 5 – Strategic Deception*, London, 1990

Personal Treatise

M. Anthony (ed.), *The Letters of Evelyn Waugh*, London, 1980

M. Davie (ed.), *The Diaries of Evelyn Waugh*, London, 1976

B. Pimlott, *The Second World War Diaries of Hugh Dalton* London, 1986

M. T. Wise (ed.), *Joy Street*, London, 1995

Memoirs

Brigadier J. M. Calvert, *Fighting Mad*, London, 1996

R. S. Churchill, *Twenty-One Years*, London, 1965

W. S. Churchill, *Their Finest Hour*, London, 1949

D. Clarke, *Seven Assignments*, London, 1948

J. Cooper, *One of the Originals*, London, 1991

M. Crichton-Stuart, *G Patrol*, London, 1958

M. James [Pleydell], *Born of the Desert*, London, 1945, reprinted 1991

P. Kemp, *No Colours or Crest*, London, 1958

W. B. Kennedy Shaw, *Long Range Desert Group*, London, 1945

Colonel T. E. Lawrence, *Seven Pillars of Wisdom*, Ware, Herts., 1997

Lord Lovat, *March Past*, London, 1978

F. MacLean, *Eastern Approaches*, London, 1965

C. Mather, *When the Grass Stops Growing*, London, 1997

Major-General D. L. Owen, *Providence Their Guide*, London, 1980

_____, *The Desert My Dwelling Place*, London, 1986

Countess of Ranfurly, *To War with Whitaker*, London, 1994

D. Reitz, *Commando*, London, 1968

R. Rogers, *Journals of Major Robert Rogers*, New York, 1961

W. F. Stirling, *Safety Last*, London, 1953

Colonel D. G. C. Sutherland, *He Who Dares*, London, 1998

B. Sweet-Escott, *Baker Street Irregular*, London, 1965

A. D. Wintle, *The Last Englishman*, London, 1968

Secondary Sources

Journal Articles and Chapters

P. Harclerode, 'SAS', in R. Holmes (ed.), *The Oxford Companion to Military History*, Oxford, 2001

T. L. Jones, 'The SAS Regiment after World War II', *Book Collector* (255, May 2005)

Major-General R. E. Laycock, 'Raids in the Late War and Their Lessons', *RUSI Journal* (XCII, November 1947)

C. Rollings, 'WW2 Special Forces', *Book Collector* (93, 1991)

R. A. Scholefield, 'First descent: The parachute pioneers of Tatton and Ringway, 1940–46', (Tatton Park leaflet, 2005)

J. Shy and T. W. Collier, 'Revolutionary War', in P. Paret (ed.), *Makers of Modern Strategy*, Oxford, 1986

Colonel D. Stirling, 'Raids Stratégiques et Missions Spéciales', in *Histoires Mondiale des Parachutistes*, Paris, 1974

Books

W. E. D. Allen, *Guerilla War in Abyssinia*, Harmondsworth, 1943

'JEA', *Geoffrey: Major J. G. Appleyard*, London, 1946

R. Arnold, *The True Book About the Commandos*, London, 1954

M. Arthur, *Men of the Red Beret*, London, 1990

M. Asher, *Get Rommel*, London, 2004

L. Barlow and R. J. Smith, *Lovat Scouts, Scottish Horse*, Tunbridge Wells, 1985

C. Barnett, *The Desert Generals*, London, 1960

R. A. Beaumont, *Military Elites*, London, 1976

T. Bowden, *The Breakdown of Public Security*, London, 1977

R. Bradford and M. Dillon, *Rogue Warrior of the SAS*, London, 1987

S. Bull, *SAS*, London, 2000

W. F. Burbridge, *The Military Viceroy*, London, 1943

J. V. Byrne, *The General Salutes a Soldier*, London, 1986

Lord (Michael) Carver, *Dilemmas of the Desert War*, London, 1986

_____, *Wavell and the War in the Middle East 1940–41*, Austin, Texas, 1993

S. Casson, *Greece against the Axis*, London, 1941

M. Chappell, *Army Commandos, 1940–45*, London, 1996

R. S. Churchill, *Winston Churchill: Youth, 1874–1900*, London, 1966

_____, *Young Statesman*, London, 1991

W. S. Churchill, *The Boer War*, London, 1989

M. Cochrane, *Rogers: A Battle Fought on Snow Shoes*, New Hampshire, 1917

R. J. Collins, *Lord Wavell*, London, 1947

J. Connell, *Auchinleck*, London, 1959

_____, *Wavell – Scholar and Soldier*, London, 1964

T. J. Constable, *Hidden Heroes*, London, 1971

G. Cook, *Commandos in Action*, London, 1973

A. Cooper, *Cairo in the War, 1939–45*, London, 1995

G. B. Courtney, *SBS in World War 2*, London, 1983

V. Cowles, *The Phantom Major*, London, 1958

R. Crisp, *The Gods Were Neutral*, London, 1960

N. Crookenden, *Airborne at War*, London, 1978

C. Cruickshank, *Deception in World War 2*, London, 1987

J. R. Cuneo, *Robert Rogers of the Rangers*, New York, 1959

P. Darman, *A–Z of the SAS*, London, 1992

A. Deane-Drummond, *Arrows of Fortune*, London, 1992

Colonel M. Dewar, *The Art of Deception in Warfare*, London, 1989

S. Dugan, *Commando*, London, 2001

Brigadier J. Durnford-Slater, *Commando*, London, 1953

D. Erskine, *The Scots Guards, 1919–55*, London, 1956

G. Ferguson, *The Paras*, London, 1987

Brigadier B. E. Fergusson, *The Watery Maze*, London, 1961

_____, *Wavell: Portrait of a Soldier*, London, 1961

R. Foxall, *The Guinea Pigs*, London, 1983

R. Garrett, *The Raiders*, London, 1980

T. Geraghty, *This is the SAS*, London, 1982

_____, *Who Dares Wins*, London, 1980

H. Gipson, *The British Empire before the American Revolution, 6: The Years of Defeat*, New York, 1946

A. Goodringe, *The Scots Guards*, London, 1969

J. W. Gordon, *The Other Desert War*, London, 1987

Major A. Greenwood, *Field Marshal Auchinleck*, Witton-le-Wear, Durham, 1992

B. Gregory and J. Batchelor, *Airborne Warfare*, London, 1979

P. Harclerode, *Para!*, London, 1996

B. Hart-Davis, *Peter Fleming*, London, 1974

S. Hastings, *The Drums of Memory*, London, 1994

J. Hetherington, *Airborne Invasion*, London, 1944

R. J. T. Hills, *Phantom Was There*, London, 1951

F. Hilton, *The Paras*, London, 1983

A. Hoe, *David Stirling – The Authorised Biography of the Creator of the SAS*, London, 1994

A. Hoe and E. Morris, *Re-enter the SAS*, London, 1994

T. Holt, *The Deceivers*, London, 2004

R. Hunter, *True Stories of the SAS*, London, 1995

_____, *True Stories of the SBS*, London, 1998

R. Jackson, *Desert Commando*, London, 1986

L. James, *The Golden Warrior*, London, 1990

T. L. Jones, *Postwar Counterinsurgency and the SAS, 1945–52: A Special Type of Warfare*, London, 2001

_____, *Rioting in North-East Wales, 1536–1918*, Wrexham, 1997

_____, *SAS: The First Secret Wars*, London, 2005

_____, *The X Site – Britain's Most Mysterious Government Facility*, Rhyl, 2000

P. R. N. Katcher, *Encyclopedia of British, Provincial and German Units, 1775–83*, Harrisburg, Penn., 1973

A. Kemp, *Teach Yourself Special Forces*, London, 2004

_____, *The SAS at War, 1941–45*, London, 1991

_____, *The SAS: The Savage Wars of Peace, 1947 to the Present*, London, 1994

E. Keyes, *Geoffrey Keyes*, London, 1956

R. H. Kiernan, *Wavell*, London, 1945

J. Ladd, *SAS Operations*, London, 1989

J. Laffin, *Raiders: Elite Forces Attacks*, London, 2000

D. Lampe, *The Last Ditch*, London, 1968

G. Landsborough, *Tobruk Commando*, London, 1956

A. W. Lawrence (ed.), *T. E. Lawrence: By His Friends*, London, 1937

R. Leach, *Massacre at Alamein?*, Upton-upon-Severn, Worcs., 1996

J. Lewes, *Jock Lewes – Co-founder of the SAS*, London, 2000

R. Lewin, *The Chief*, London, 1980

J. E. Lewis (ed.), *The Handbook of the SAS and Elite Forces*, London, 1997

F. Lindley, *Lord Lovat*, London, 1935

J. Lodwick, *The Filibusters*, London, 1947

C. MacDonald, *The Lost Battle*, London, 1993

N. McCrery, *The Complete History of the SAS*, London, 2003

C. Marlowe, *Rebellion In Palestine*, London, 1946

_____, *Seat of Pilate*, London, 1959

P. Mead, *Orde Wingate and the Historians*, Braunton, Devon, 1987

M. L. Melville, *The Story of the Lovat Scouts*, Edinburgh, 1981

C. Messenger, *The Commandos, 1940–46*, London, 1991

M. Morgan, *Daggers Drawn*, Stroud, Glos., 2000

_____, *Sting of the Scorpion*, Stroud, Glos., 2000

E. Morris, *Churchill's Private Armies*, London, 1986

G. Mortimer, *Stirling's Men*, London, 2004

D. Mure, *Master of Deception*, London, 1980

_____, *Practise to Deceive*, London, 1977

R. Neillands, *The Raiders*, London, 1990

N. Nelson, *Shepheards Hotel*, London, 1960

M. Newnham, *Prelude to Glory*, London, 1947

J. Newsinger, *British Counterinsurgency from Palestine to Northern Ireland*, Basingstoke, 2002

M. Nicol, *Ultimate Risk*, London, 2004

R. Ovendale, *The Origins of the Arab-Israeli Wars*, London, 1992

D. Owen, *Battle of Wits*, London, 1978

T. Pakenham, *The Boer War*, London, 1982

J. Parker, *Commandos*, London, 2000

_____, *SBS*, London, 1997

_____, *The Paras*, London, 2000

R. Parkinson, *The Auk*, London, 1979

C. Philip and A. Taylor, *Inside the SAS*, London, 1992

B. Pitt, *The Crucible of War*, London, 1980

_____, *The SBS*, London, 1983

Y. A. Porath, *The Palestinian Arab National Movement, Volume 2 – 1929–39*, London, 1977

K. C. Praval, *India's Paratroopers*, Delhi, 1974

B. Quarrie, *Airborne Assault*, London, 1991

J. Ramsay, *SAS: The Soldiers' Story*, London, 1996

H. E. Raugh, *Wavell: A Study in Generalship*, London, 1993

D. Reynolds, *The Paras*, London, 1998

B. Roberts, *Randolph*, London, 1984

D. Rooney, *Mad Mike*, London, 1997

_____, *Wingate and the Chindits*, London, 1994

H. Ross, *Paddy Mayne*, Stroud, Glos., 2003

M. Ryan, *Secret Operations of the SAS*, London, 2003

H. St George Saunders, *The Green Beret*, London, 1950

W. Seymour, *British Special Forces*, London, 1985

H. J. Simson, *British Rule* and *Rebellion*, London, 1937

C. Smith, *The History of the Glider Pilot Regiment*, London, 1992

G. Stevens, *The Originals – The Secret History of the SAS in their Own Words*, London, 2005

General J. Strawson, *A History of the SAS Regiment*, London, 1984

A. Swinson, *The Raiders*, London, 1974

C. Sykes, *Orde Wingate*, London, 1959

A. Taylor (ed.): N. V. Oxenden, *Auxiliary Units History and Achievement, 1940–44*, Parham, Suffolk, 1998

General J. Thompson, *The Imperial War Museum Book of War Behind Enemy Lines*, London, 1998

J. Thompson, *Ready for Anything*, London, 1989

L. Thompson, *SAS*, Osceola, Florida, 1994

C. J. Townshend, *Britain's Civil Wars*, London, 1986

Brigadier M. Tugwell, *Airborne to Battle*, London, 1971

P. Warner, *Auchinleck*, London, 1981

_____, *Phantom*, London, 1982

_____, *The Secret Forces of World War 2*, London, 1985

_____, *The Special Air Service*, London, 1971

_____, *The Special Boat Squadron*, London, 1983

Field Marshal A. P. Wavell, *Soldiers and Soldiering*, London, 1953

_____, *The Good Soldier*, London, 1948

A. Weale, *Secret Warfare*, London, 1997

_____, *The Real SAS*, London, 1998

N. West, *Secret War*, London, 1992

L. Whittaker, *Some Talk of Private Armies*, Harpenden, Herts., 1984

Who's Who, London, 1969

P. Wilkinson, *Foreign Fields*, London, 1997

P. Wilkinson and J. B. Astley, *Gubbins and SOE*, London, 1993

J. Wilson, *Lawrence of Arabia*, London, 1989

L. A. Windmill, *Gentleman Jim*, London, 2001

R. Woollcombe, *The Campaigns of Wavell, 1939–43*, London, 1959

Brigadier P. Young, *Commando*, London, 1974

_____, *Storm from the Sea*, London, 1989

Index